PELICAN BOOKS

THE ORTHODOX CHURCH

Timothy Ware was born in Bath, Somerset, in 1934 and was educated at Westminster School and Magdalen College, Oxford, where he took a Double First in Classics, as well as reading Theology. After joining the Orthodox Church in 1958, he travelled widely in Greece, staying in particular at the monastery of St John, Patmos, and he is familiar with the life of other Orthodox centres such as Mount Athos and Jerusalem. In 1966 he was ordained priest and became a monk, receiving the new name of Kallistos. Since 1966 he has been back at Oxford as Spalding Lecturer in Eastern Orthodox Studies at the University. He also has pastoral charge of the Greek parish in Oxford. In 1970 he became a Fellow of Pembroke College, Oxford, and since 1973 he has been a member of the international Anglican–Orthodox Joint Doctrinal Commission. In 1982 he was consecrated titular Bishop of Diokleia and appointed assistant bishop in the Orthodox Archdiocese of Thyateira and Great Britain (under the Ecumenical Patriarchate). His other works include *Eustratios Argenti: A Study of the Greek Church under Turkish Rule* (1964) and *The Orthodox Way* (1979). He is also co-translator of two Orthodox service books, *The Festal Menaion* (1969) and *The Lenten Triodion* (1978), and also of *The Philokalia* (in progress: three volumes, 1979, 1981 and 1984).

The
Orthodox Church

TIMOTHY WARE
(*Bishop Kallistos of Diokleia*)

PENGUIN BOOKS

PENGUIN BOOKS

Published by the Penguin Group
27 Wrights Lane, London w8 5TZ, England
Viking Penguin Inc., 40 West 23rd Street, New York, New York 10010, USA
Penguin Books Australia Ltd, Ringwood, Victoria, Australia
Penguin Books Canada Ltd, 2801 John Street, Markham, Ontario, Canada L3R 1B4
Penguin Books (NZ) Ltd, 182–190 Wairau Road, Auckland 10, New Zealand

Penguin Books Ltd, Registered Offices: Harmondsworth, Middlesex, England

First published 1963
Reprinted with revisions 1964
17 19 20 18 16

Printed and bound in Great Britain by
Cox & Wyman Ltd, Reading
Set in Monotype Imprint

Contents

CONTENTS

Introductory Note

THE whole text of the book has been carefully revised for the 1980 reprint and again for the 1983 reprint; in particular, chapters 7, 8, and 9, together with the bibliography, have been brought up to date.

Introduction

'ALL Protestants are Crypto-Papists,' wrote the Russian theologian Alexis Khomiakov to an English friend in the year 1846. '... To use the concise language of algebra, all the West knows but one datum a; whether it be preceded by the positive sign $+$, as with the Romanists, or with the negative $-$, as with the Protestants, the a remains the same. Now a passage to Orthodoxy seems indeed like an apostasy from the past, from its science, creed, and life. It is rushing into a new and unknown world.'[1]

Khomiakov, when he spoke of the datum a, had in mind the fact that western Christians, whether Free Churchmen, Anglicans, or Roman Catholics, have a common background in the past. All alike (although they may not always care to admit it) have been profoundly influenced by the same events: by the Papal centralization and the Scholasticism of the Middle Ages, by the Renaissance, by the Reformation and Counter-Reformation. But behind members of the Orthodox Church – Greeks, Russians, and the rest – there lies a very different background. They have known no Middle Ages (in the western sense) and have undergone no Reformations or Counter-Reformations; they have only been affected in an oblique way by the cultural and religious upheaval which transformed western Europe in the sixteenth and seventeenth centuries. Christians in the west, both Roman and Reformed, generally start by asking the same questions, although they may disagree about the answers. In Orthodoxy, however, it is not merely the answers that are different – the questions themselves are not the same as in the west.

Orthodox see history in another perspective. Consider, for

1. From a letter printed in W. J. Birkbeck, *Russia and the English Church*, p. 67.

example, the Orthodox attitude towards western religious disputes. In the west it is usual to think of Roman Catholicism and Protestantism as opposite extremes; but to an Orthodox they appear as two sides of the same coin. Khomiakov calls the Pope 'the first Protestant', 'the father of German rationalism'; and by the same token he would doubtless have considered the Christian Scientist an eccentric Roman Catholic.[1] 'How are we to arrest the pernicious effects of Protestantism?' he was asked by a High Church Anglican when visiting Oxford in 1847; to which he replied: 'Shake off your Roman Catholicism.' In the eyes of the Russian theologian, the two things went hand in hand; both alike share the same assumptions, for Protestantism was hatched from the egg which Rome had laid.

'A new and unknown world': Khomiakov was right to speak of Orthodoxy in this way. Orthodoxy is not just a kind of Roman Catholicism without the Pope, but something quite distinct from any religious system in the west. Yet those who look more closely at this 'unknown world' will discover much in it which, while different, is yet curiously familiar. 'But that is what I have always believed!' Such has been the reaction of many, on learning more fully about the Orthodox Church and what it teaches; and they are partly right. For more than nine hundred years the Greek East and the Latin West have been growing steadily apart, each following its own way, yet in the early centuries of Christendom both sides can find common ground. Athanasius and Basil lived in the east, but they belong also to the west; and Orthodox who live in France, Britain, or Ireland can in their turn look upon the national saints of these lands – Alban and Patrick, Cuthbert and Bede, Geneviève of Paris and Augustine of Canterbury – not as strangers but as members of their own Church. All Europe was once as much part of Orthodoxy as Greece and Christian Russia are today.

When Khomiakov wrote his letter in 1846, there were in fact few on either side who knew one another by personal contact. Robert Curzon, travelling through the Levant in the

1. Compare P. Hammond, *The Waters of Marah*, p. 10.

1830s in search of manuscripts which he could buy at bargain prices, was disconcerted to find that the Patriarch of Constantinople had never heard of the Archbishop of Canterbury. Matters have certainly changed since then. Travel has become incomparably easier, the physical barriers have been broken down. And travel is no longer necessary: a citizen of western Europe or America need no longer leave his own country in order to observe the Orthodox Church at first hand. Greeks journeying westward from choice or economic necessity, and Slavs driven westward by persecution, have brought their Church with them, establishing across all Europe and America a network of dioceses and parishes, theological colleges and monasteries. Most important of all, in many different communions during the present century there has grown up a compelling and unprecedented desire for the visible unity of all Christians, and this has given rise to a new interest in the Orthodox Church. The Greco-Russian *diaspora* was scattered over the world at the very moment when western Christians, in their concern for reunion, were becoming conscious of the relevance of Orthodoxy, and anxious to learn more about it. In reunion discussions the contribution of the Orthodox Church has often proved unexpectedly illuminating: precisely because the Orthodox have a different background from the west, they have been able to open up fresh lines of thought, and to suggest long-forgotten solutions to old difficulties.

The west has never lacked men whose conception of Christendom was not restricted to Canterbury, Geneva, and Rome; yet in the past such men were voices crying in the wilderness. It is now no longer so. The effects of an alienation which has lasted for more than nine centuries cannot be quickly undone, but at least a beginning has been made.

What is meant by 'the Orthodox Church'? The divisions which have brought about the present fragmentation of Christendom occurred in three main stages, at intervals of roughly five hundred years. The first stage in the separation came in the fifth and sixth centuries, when the 'Lesser' or 'Separated' eastern Churches became divided from the main body of Christians. These Churches fall into two groups, the Nestorian Church of Persia, and the five Monophysite Churches of Armenia, Syria (the so-called 'Jacobite' Church), Egypt (the Coptic Church), Ethiopia, and India. The Nestorians and Monophysites passed out of western consciousness even more completely than the Orthodox Church was later to do. When Rabban Sauma, a Nestorian monk from Peking, visited the west in 1288 (he travelled as far as Bordeaux, where he gave communion to King Edward I of England), he discussed theology with the Pope and Cardinals at Rome, yet they never seem to have realized that from their point of view he was a heretic. As a result of this first division, Orthodoxy became restricted on its eastward side mainly to the Greek-speaking world. Then came the second separation, conventionally dated to the year 1054. The main body of Christians now became divided into two communions: in western Europe, the Roman Catholic Church under the Pope of Rome; in the Byzantine Empire, the Orthodox Church of the East. Orthodoxy was now limited on its westward side as well. The third separation, between Rome and the Reformers in the sixteenth century, is not here our direct concern.

It is interesting to note how cultural and ecclesiastical divisions coincide. Christianity, while universal in its mission, has tended in practice to be associated with three cultures: the Semitic, the Greek, and the Latin. As a result of the first separation the Semitic Christians of Syria, with their flourishing school of theologians and writers, were cut off from the rest of Christendom. Then followed the second separation, which drove a wedge between the Greek and the Latin traditions in Christianity. So it has come about that in Orthodoxy the primary cultural influence has been that of Greece. Yet it must not therefore be thought that the Orthodox Church is exclusively a Greek Church and nothing else, since Syriac and Latin Fathers also have a place in the fullness of Orthodox tradition.

INTRODUCTION

While the Orthodox Church became bounded first on the eastern and then on the western side, it expanded to the north. In 863 Saint Cyril and Saint Methodius, the Apostles of the Slavs, travelled northward to undertake missionary work beyond the frontiers of the Byzantine Empire, and their efforts led eventually to the conversion of Bulgaria, Serbia, and Russia. As the Byzantine power dwindled, these newer Churches of the north increased in importance, and on the fall of Constantinople to the Turks in 1453 the Principality of Moscow was ready to take Byzantium's place as the protectɔ ˙ of the Orthodox world. Within the last 150 years there has been a partial reversal of the situation. Although Constantinople itself still remains in Turkish hands, a pale shadow of its former glory, the Church in Greece is free once more; but Russia and the other Slavonic peoples have passed in their turn under the rule of a non-Christian government.

Such are the main stages which have determined the external development of the Orthodox Church. Geographically its primary area of distribution lies in eastern Europe, in Russia, and along the coasts of the eastern Mediterranean. It is composed at present of the following self-governing or 'autocephalous' Churches:[1]

(1) The four ancient Patriarchates:

Constantinople	(3,000,000)
Alexandria	(250,000)
Antioch	(450,000)
Jerusalem	(60,000)

Though greatly reduced in size, these four Churches for historical reasons occupy a special position in the Orthodox Church, and rank first in honour. The heads of these four Churches bear the title *Patriarch*.

1. After each Church an approximate estimate of size is given. Like all ecclesiastical statistics, these figures are to be treated with caution, and they are in any case intended merely as a rough comparative guide. For many Orthodox Churches, particularly those in communist countries, no up-to-date statistics are available. For the most part the figures indicate nominal rather than active membership.

13

(2) Eleven other autocephalous Churches:

Russia	(100,000,000 before 1917; perhaps 25–50,000,000 today)
Romania	(14,000,000)
Greece	(9,000,000)
Serbia	(in Yugoslavia; 8,000,000)
Bulgaria	(6,000,000)
Georgia	(in the U.S.S.R.: 1,250,000 before 1917)
Cyprus	(450,000)
Poland	(450,000)
Albania	(210,000 in 1944)
Czechoslovakia	(100,000)
Sinai	(less than 100)

All except three of these Churches – Czechoslovakia, Poland, and Albania – are in countries where the Christian population is entirely or predominantly Orthodox. The Churches of Greece, Cyprus, and Sinai are Greek; five of the others – Russia, Serbia, Bulgaria, Czechoslovakia, Poland – are Slavonic. The heads of the Russian, Romanian, Serbian, and Bulgarian Churches are known by the title *Patriarch*; the head of the Georgian Church is called *Catholicos-Patriarch*; the heads of the other churches are called either *Archbishop* or *Metropolitan*.

(3) There are in addition several Churches which, while self-governing in most respects, have not yet attained full independence. These are termed 'autonomous' but not 'autocephalous':

Finland	(66,000)
Japan	(25,000)
China	(perhaps 10,000–20,000)

(4) There are ecclesiastical provinces in western Europe, in North and South America, and in Australia, which depend on the different Patriarchates and autocephalous Churches. In some areas this Orthodox 'diaspora' is slowly achieving self-government. In particular, steps have been taken to form

an autocephalous Orthodox Church in America (about 1,000,000), but this has not yet been officially recognized by the majority of other Orthodox Churches.

The Orthodox Church is thus a family of self-governing Churches. It is held together, not by a centralized organization, not by a single prelate wielding absolute power over the whole body, but by the double bond of unity in the faith and communion in the sacraments. Each Church, while independent, is in full agreement with the rest on all matters of doctrine, and between them all there is full sacramental communion. (Certain divisions exist among the Russian Orthodox, but the situation here is altogether exceptional and, one hopes, temporary in character.) There is in Orthodoxy no one with an equivalent position to the Pope in the Roman Catholic Church. The Patriarch of Constantinople is known as the 'Ecumenical' (or universal) Patriarch, and since the schism between east and west he has enjoyed a position of special honour among all the Orthodox communities; but he does not have the right to interfere in the internal affairs of other Churches. His place resembles that of the Archbishop of Canterbury in the worldwide Anglican communion.

This decentralized system of independent local Churches has the advantage of being highly flexible, and is easily adapted to changing conditions. Local Churches can be created, suppressed, and then restored again, with very little disturbance to the life of the Church as a whole. Many of these local Churches are also national Churches, for during the past in Orthodox countries Church and State have usually been closely linked. But while an independent State often possesses its own autocephalous Church, ecclesiastical divisions do not necessarily coincide with State boundaries. Georgia, for instance, lies within the U.S.S.R., but is not part of the Russian Church, while the territories of the four ancient Patriarchates fall politically in several different countries. The Orthodox Church is a federation of *local*, but not in every case *national*, Churches. It does not have as its basis the political principle of the State Church.

Among the various Churches there is, as can be seen, an enormous variation in size, with Russia at one extreme and Sinai at the other. The different Churches also vary in age, some dating back to Apostolic times, while others are less than a generation old. The Church of Czechoslovakia, for example, only became autocephalous in 1951.

Such are the Churches which make up the Orthodox communion as it is today. They are known collectively by various titles. Sometimes they are called the *Greek* or *Greco-Russian Church*; but this is incorrect, since there are many millions of Orthodox who are neither Greek nor Russian. Orthodox themselves often call their Church the *Eastern Orthodox Church*, the *Orthodox Catholic Church*, the *Orthodox Catholic Church of the East*, or the like. These titles must not be misunderstood, for while Orthodoxy considers itself to be the true Catholic Church, it is not part of the *Roman* Catholic Church; and although Orthodoxy calls itself eastern, it is not something limited to eastern people. Another name often employed is the *Holy Orthodox Church*. Perhaps it is least misleading and most convenient to use the shortest title: the *Orthodox Church*.

Orthodoxy claims to be universal – not something exotic and oriental, but simple Christianity. Because of human failings and the accidents of history, the Orthodox Church has been largely restricted in the past to certain geographical areas. Yet to the Orthodox themselves their Church is something more than a group of local bodies. The word 'Orthodoxy' has the double meaning of 'right belief' and 'right glory' (or 'right worship'). The Orthodox, therefore, make what may seem at first a surprising claim: they regard their Church as the Church which guards and teaches the true belief about God and which glorifies Him with right worship, that is, *as nothing less than the Church of Christ on earth*. How this claim is understood, and what the Orthodox think of other Christians who do not belong to their Church, it is part of the aim of this book to explain.

Part One
HISTORY

CHAPTER I

The Beginnings

In the village there is a chapel dug deep beneath the earth, its entrance carefully camouflaged. When a secret priest visits the village, it is here that he celebrates the Liturgy and the other services. If the villagers for once believe themselves safe from police observation, the whole population gathers in the chapel, except for the guards who remain outside to give warning if strangers appear. At other times services take place in shifts. . . .

The Easter service was held in an apartment of an official State institution. Entrance was possible only with a special pass, which I obtained for myself and for my small daughter. About thirty people were present, among them some of my acquaintances. An old priest celebrated the service, which I shall never forget. 'Christ is risen' we sang softly, but full of joy. . . . The joy that I felt in this service of the Catacomb Church gives me strength to live, even today.

THESE are two accounts[1] of Church life in Russia shortly before the Second World War. But if a few alterations were made, they could easily be taken for descriptions of Christian worship under Nero or Diocletian. They illustrate the way in which during the course of nineteen centuries Christian history has travelled through a full circle. Christians today stand far closer to the early Church than their grandparents did. Christianity began as the religion of a small minority existing in a predominantly non-Christian society, and such it is becoming once more. The Christian Church in its early days was distinct and separate from the State; and now in one country after another the traditional alliance between Church and State is coming to an end. Christianity was at first a *religio*

1. Taken from the periodical *Orthodox Life* (Jordanville, N.Y.), 1959, no. 4, pp. 30-1.

19

illicita, a religion forbidden and persecuted by the government; today persecution is no longer a fact of the past alone, and it is by no means impossible that in the thirty years between 1918 and 1948 more Christians died for their faith than in the three hundred years that followed Christ's Crucifixion.

Members of the Orthodox Church in particular have been made very much aware of these facts, for the vast majority of them live at present in communist countries, under anti-Christian governments. The first period of Christian history, extending from the day of Pentecost to the conversion of Constantine, has a special relevance for contemporary Orthodoxy.

'Suddenly there came from heaven a sound like the rushing of a violent wind, and it filled the whole house where they were sitting. And there appeared to them tongues like flames of fire, divided among them and resting on each one. And they were all filled with the Holy Spirit.' (Acts ii, 2–4.) So the history of the Christian Church begins, with the descent of the Holy Spirit on the Apostles at Jerusalem during the feast of Pentecost, the first Whit Sunday. On that same day through the preaching of Saint Peter three thousand men and women were baptized, and the first Christian community at Jerusalem was formed.

Before long the members of the Jerusalem Church were scattered by the persecution which followed the stoning of Saint Stephen. 'Go forth therefore,' Christ had said, 'and make all nations my disciples' (Matthew xxviii, 19). Obedient to this command they preached wherever they went, at first to Jews, but before long to Gentiles also. Some stories of these Apostolic journeys are recorded by Saint Luke in the book of Acts; others are preserved in the tradition of the Church. The legends about the Apostles may not always be literally true, but it is at any rate certain that within an astonishingly short time small Christian communities had sprung up in all the main centres of the Roman Empire and even in places beyond the Roman frontiers.

The Empire through which these first Christian missionaries travelled was, particularly in its eastern part, an empire of cities. This determined the administrative structure of the primitive Church. The basic unit was the community in each city, governed by its own bishop; to assist the bishop there were presbyters or priests, and deacons. The surrounding countryside depended on the Church of the city. This pattern, with the threefold ministry of bishops, priests, and deacons, was already widely established by the end of the first century. We can see it in the seven short letters which Saint Ignatius, Bishop of Antioch, wrote about the year 107 as he travelled to Rome to be martyred. Ignatius laid emphasis upon two things in particular, the bishop and the Eucharist; he saw the Church as both hierarchical and sacramental. 'The bishop in each Church,' he wrote, 'presides in place of God.' 'Let no one do any of the things which concern the Church without the bishop. . . . Wherever the bishop appears, there let the people be, just as wherever Jesus Christ is, there is the Catholic Church.' And it is the bishop's primary and distinctive task to celebrate the Eucharist, 'the medicine of immortality'.[1]

People today tend to think of the Church as a worldwide organization, in which each local body forms part of a larger and more inclusive whole. Ignatius did not look at the Church in this way. For him the local community *is* the Church. He thought of the Church as a Eucharistic society, which only realizes its true nature when it celebrates the Supper of the Lord, receiving His Body and Blood in the sacrament. But the Eucharist is something that can only happen locally – in each particular community gathered round its bishop; and at every local celebration of the Eucharist it is the *whole* Christ who is present, not just a part of Him. Therefore each local community, as it celebrates the Eucharist Sunday by Sunday, is the Church in its fullness.

The teaching of Ignatius has a permanent place in Orthodox tradition. Orthodoxy still thinks of the Church as a Eucharistic society, whose outward organization, however necessary, is

1. *To the Magnesians,* vi, 1; *To the Smyrnaeans,* viii, 1 and 2; *To the Ephesians,* xx, 2.

secondary to its inner, sacramental life; and Orthodoxy still emphasizes the cardinal importance of the local community in the structure of the Church. To those who attend an Orthodox Pontifical Liturgy,[1] when the bishop stands at the beginning of the service in the middle of the church, surrounded by his flock, Ignatius of Antioch's idea of the bishop as the centre of unity in the local community will occur with particular vividness.

But besides the local community there is also the wider unity of the Church. This second aspect is developed in the writings of another martyr bishop, Saint Cyprian of Carthage (died 258). Cyprian saw all bishops as sharing in the one episcopate, yet sharing it in such a way that each possesses not a part but the whole. 'The episcopate,' he wrote, 'is a single whole, in which each bishop enjoys full possession. So is the Church a single whole, though it spreads far and wide into a multitude of churches as its fertility increases.'[2] There are many churches but only one Church; many *episcopi* but only one episcopate.

There were many others in the first three centuries of the Church who like Cyprian and Ignatius ended their lives as martyrs. The persecutions, it is true, were often local in character and usually limited in duration. Yet although there were long periods when the Roman authorities extended to Christianity a large measure of toleration, the threat of persecution was always there, and Christians knew that at any time this threat could become a reality. The idea of martyrdom had a central place in the spiritual outlook of the early Christians. They saw their Church as founded upon blood – not only the blood of Christ but the blood of those 'other Christs', the martyrs. In later centuries when the Church became 'established' and no longer suffered persecution, the idea of martyrdom did not disappear, but it took other forms: the monastic life, for example, is often regarded by Greek writers as an equivalent to martyrdom. The same approach is found also in the

1. *The Liturgy*: this is the term normally used by Orthodox to refer to the service of Holy Communion, the Mass.
2. *On the Unity of the Church*, 5.

west: take, for instance, a Celtic text – an Irish homily of the seventh century – which likens the ascetic life to the way of the martyr:

Now there are three kinds of martyrdom which are accounted as a Cross to a man, white martyrdom, green martyrdom, and red martyrdom. White martyrdom consists in a man's abandoning everything he loves for God's sake. . . . Green martyrdom consists in this, that by means of fasting and labour he frees himself from his evil desires; or suffers toil in penance and repentance. Red martyrdom consists in the endurance of a Cross or death for Christ's sake.[1]

At many periods in Orthodox history the prospect of red martyrdom has been fairly remote, and the green and white forms prevail. Yet there have also been times, above all in this present century, when Orthodox Christians have once again been called to undergo martyrdom of blood.

It was only natural that the bishops, who, as Cyprian emphasized, share in the one episcopate, should meet together in a council to discuss their common problems. Orthodoxy has always attached great importance to the place of councils in the life of the Church. It believes that the council is the chief organ whereby God has chosen to guide His people, and it regards the Catholic Church as essentially a *conciliar* Church. (Indeed, in Russian the same adjective *soborny* has the double sense of 'catholic' and 'conciliar', while the corresponding noun, *sobor*, means both 'church' and 'council'.) In the Church there is neither dictatorship nor individualism, but harmony and unanimity; men remain free but not isolated, for they are united in love, in faith, and in sacramental communion. In a council, this idea of harmony and free unanimity can be seen worked out in practice. In a true council no single member arbitrarily imposes his will upon the rest, but each consults with the others, and in this way they all freely achieve a 'common mind'. A council is a living embodiment of the essential nature of the Church.

1. Quoted in J. Ryan, *Irish Monasticism*, London, 1931, p. 197.

The first council in the Church's history is described in Acts xv. Attended by the Apostles, it met at Jerusalem to decide how far Gentile converts should be subject to the Law of Moses. The Apostles, when they finally reached their decision, spoke in terms which in other circumstances might appear presumptuous: 'It seemed right to the Holy Spirit and to us . . .' (Acts xv, 28). Later councils have ventured to speak with the same confidence. An isolated individual may well hesitate to say: 'It seemed right to the Holy Spirit and to *me*'; but when gathered in council, the members of the Church can together claim an authority which individually none of them possesses.

The Council of Jerusalem, assembling as it did the leaders of the entire Church, was an exceptional gathering, for which there is no parallel until the Council of Nicaea in 325. But by Cyprian's time it had already become usual to hold local councils, attended by all the bishops in a particular civil province of the Roman Empire. A local council of this type normally met in the provincial capital, under the presidency of the bishop of the capital, who was given the title *Metropolitan*. As the third century proceeded, councils widened in scope and began to include bishops not from one but from several civil provinces. These larger gatherings tended to assemble in the chief cities of the Empire, such as Alexandria or Antioch; and so it came about that the bishops of certain great cities began to acquire an importance above the provincial Metropolitans. But for the time being nothing was decided about the precise status of these great sees. Nor during the third century itself did this continual expansion of councils reach its logical conclusion: as yet (apart from the Apostolic Council) there had only been local councils, of lesser or greater extent, but no 'general' council, formed of bishops from the whole Christian world, and claiming to speak in the name of the whole Church.

In 312 an event occurred which utterly transformed the outward situation of the Church. As he was riding through France with his army, the Emperor Constantine looked up into the sky and saw a cross of light in front of the sun. With the cross there was an inscription: *In this sign conquer.* As a result of this vision, Constantine became the first Roman Emperor to embrace the Christian faith. On that day in France a train of events was set in motion which brought the first main period of Church history to an end, and which led to the creation of the Christian Empire of Byzantium.

CHAPTER 2

Byzantium, I:
The Church of the Seven Councils

All profess that there are seven holy and Ecumenical Councils, and these are the seven pillars of
the faith of the Divine Word on which He erected His
holy mansion, the Catholic and Ecumenical Church.
John II, Metropolitan of Russia (1080-89)

THE ESTABLISHMENT OF AN IMPERIAL CHURCH

CONSTANTINE stands at a watershed in the history of the
Church. With his conversion, the age of the martyrs and the
persecutions drew to an end, and the Church of the Catacombs
became the Church of the Empire. The first great effect of
Constantine's vision was the so-called 'Edict' of Milan, which
he and his fellow Emperor Licinius issued in 313, proclaiming
the official toleration of the Christian faith. And though at first
Constantine granted no more than toleration, he soon made it
clear that he intended to favour Christianity above all the other
tolerated religions in the Roman Empire. Theodosius, within
fifty years of Constantine's death, had carried this policy
through to its conclusion: by his legislation he made Christianity not merely the most highly favoured but the only recognized
religion of the Empire. The Church was now established. 'You
are not allowed to exist,' the Roman authorities had once said
to the Christians. Now it was the turn of paganism to be
suppressed.

Constantine's vision of the Cross led also, in his lifetime, to
two further consequences, equally momentous for the later development of Christendom. First, in 324 he decided to move
the capital of the Roman Empire eastward from Italy to the
shores of the Bosphorus. Here, on the site of the Greek city of

Byzantium, he built a new capital, which he named after himself, 'Constantinoupolis'. The motives for this move were in part economic and political, but they were also religious: the Old Rome was too deeply stained with pagan associations to form the centre of the Christian Empire which he had in mind. In the New Rome things were to be different: after the solemn inauguration of the city in 330, he laid down that at Constantinople no pagan rites should ever be performed. Constantine's new capital has exercised a decisive influence upon the development of Orthodox history.

Secondly, Constantine summoned the first General or Ecumenical Council of the Christian Church at Nicaea in 325. If the Roman Empire was to be a Christian Empire, then Constantine wished to see it firmly based upon the one orthodox faith. It was the duty of the Nicene Council to elaborate the content of that faith. Nothing could have symbolized more clearly the new relation between Church and State than the outward circumstances of the gathering at Nicaea. The Emperor himself presided, 'like some heavenly messenger of God' as one of those present, Eusebius, Bishop of Caesarea, expressed it. At the conclusion of the Council the bishops dined with the Emperor. 'The circumstances of the banquet,' wrote Eusebius (who was inclined to be impressed by such things), 'were splendid beyond description. Detachments of the bodyguard and other troops surrounded the entrance of the palace with drawn swords, and through the midst of these the men of God proceeded without fear into the innermost of the imperial apartments. Some were the Emperor's own companions at table, others reclined on couches ranged on either side. One might have thought it was a picture of Christ's kingdom, and a dream rather than reality.'[1] Matters had certainly changed since the time when Nero employed Christians as living torches to illuminate his gardens at night. Nicaea was the first of seven General Councils; and these, like the city of Constantine, occupy a central position in the history of Orthodoxy.

The three events – the Edict of Milan, the foundation of

1. *The Life of Constantine*, iii, 10 and 15.

Constantinople, and the Council of Nicaea – mark the Church's coming of age.

THE FIRST SIX COUNCILS (325–681)

The life of the Church in the earlier Byzantine period is dominated by the seven General Councils. These Councils fulfilled a double task. First, they clarified and articulated the visible organization of the Church, crystallizing the position of the five great sees or *Patriarchates*, as they came to be known. Secondly, and more important, the Councils defined once and for all the Church's teaching upon the fundamental doctrines of the Christian faith – the Trinity and the Incarnation. All Christians agree in regarding these things as 'mysteries' which lie beyond human understanding and language. The bishops, when they drew up definitions at the Councils, did not imagine that they had explained the mystery; they merely sought to exclude certain false ways of speaking and thinking about it. To prevent men from deviating into error and heresy, they drew a fence around the mystery; that was all.

The discussions at the Councils at times sound abstract and remote, yet they were inspired by a very practical purpose: the salvation of man. Man, so the New Testament teaches, is separated from God by sin, and cannot through his own efforts break down the wall of separation which his sinfulness has created. God has therefore taken the initiative: He became man, was crucified, and rose from the dead, thereby delivering humanity from the bondage of sin and death. This is the central message of the Christian faith, and it is this message of redemption that the Councils were concerned to safeguard. Heresies were dangerous and required condemnation, because they impaired the teaching of the New Testament, setting up a barrier between man and God, and so making it impossible for man to attain full salvation.

Saint Paul expressed this message of redemption in terms of *sharing*. Christ shared our poverty that we might share the riches of His divinity: 'Our Lord Jesus Christ, though he was rich, yet for your sake became poor, that you through his poverty might become rich' (2 Corinthians viii, 9). In Saint John's Gospel the same idea is found in a slightly different form. Christ states that He has given His disciples a share in the divine glory, and He prays that they may achieve union with God: 'The glory which Thou, Father, gavest me I have given to them, that they may be one, just as we are one; I in them, and Thou in me, that they may be perfectly one' (John xvii, 22–3). The Greek Fathers took these and similar texts in their literal sense, and dared to speak of man's 'deification' (in Greek, *theosis*). If man is to share in God's glory, they argued, if he is to be 'perfectly one' with God, this means in effect that man must be 'deified': he is called to become by grace what God is by nature. Accordingly Saint Athanasius summed up the purpose of the Incarnation by saying: 'God became man that we might be made god.'[1]

Now if this 'being made god', this *theosis*, is to be possible, Christ the Saviour must be both fully man and fully God. No one less than God can save man; therefore if Christ is to save, He must be God. But only if He is also truly a man, as we are, can we men participate in what He has done for us. A bridge is formed between God and man by the Incarnate Christ who is both. 'Hereafter you shall see heaven open,' Our Lord promised, 'and the angels of God ascending and descending upon the Son of Man' (John i, 51). Not only angels use that ladder, but the human race.

Christ must be fully God and fully man. Each heresy in turn undermined some part of this vital affirmation. Either Christ was made less than God (Arianism); or His manhood was so divided from His Godhead that He became two persons instead of one (Nestorianism); or He was not presented as truly man (Monophysitism, Monothelitism). Each Council defended this affirmation. The first two, held in the fourth century, concentrated upon the earlier part (that Christ must be fully God) and formulated the doctrine of the Trinity. The next four, during the fifth, sixth, and seventh centuries, turned to the

1. *On the Incarnation*, 54.

second part (the fullness of Christ's manhood) and also sought to explain how manhood and Godhead could be united in a single person. The seventh Council, in defence of the Holy Icons, seems at first to stand somewhat apart, but like the first six it was ultimately concerned with the Incarnation and with man's salvation.

The main work of the Council of Nicaea in 325 was the condemnation of Arianism. Arius, a priest in Alexandria, maintained that the Son was inferior to the Father, and, in drawing a dividing line between God and creation, he placed the Son among created things: a superior creature, it is true, but a creature none the less. His motive, no doubt, was to protect the uniqueness and the transcendence of God, but the effect of his teaching, in making Christ less than God, was to render man's deification impossible. Only if Christ is truly God, the Council answered, can He unite us to God, for none but God Himself can open to man the way of union. Christ is 'one in essence' (*homoousios*) with the Father. He is no demigod or superior creature, but God in the same sense that the Father is God: 'true God from true God,' the Council proclaimed in the Creed which it drew up, 'begotten not made, *one in essence* with the Father'.

The Council of Nicaea dealt also with the visible organization of the Church. It singled out for mention three great centres: Rome, Alexandria, and Antioch (Canon VI). It also laid down that the see of Jerusalem, while remaining subject to the Metropolitan of Caesarea, should be given the next place in honour after these three (Canon VII). Constantinople naturally was not mentioned, since it was not officially inaugurated as the new capital until five years later; it continued to be subject, as before, to the Metropolitan of Heraclea.

The work of Nicaea was taken up by the second Ecumenical Council, held at Constantinople in 381. This Council expanded and adapted the Nicene Creed, developing in particular the teaching upon the Holy Spirit, whom it affirmed to be God even as the Father and Son are God: 'who proceeds from the Father, who with the Father and the Son together is worshipped and together glorified'. The Council also altered the provisions of the Sixth Canon of Nicaea. The position of Constantinople, now the capital of the Empire, could no longer be ignored, and it was assigned the second place, after Rome and above Alexandria. 'The Bishop of Constantinople shall have the prerogatives of honour after the Bishop of Rome, because Constantinople is New Rome' (Canon III).

Behind the definitions of the Councils lay the work of theologians, who gave precision to the words which the Councils employed. It was the supreme achievement of Saint Athanasius of Alexandria to draw out the full implications of the key word in the Nicene Creed: *homoousios*, one in essence or substance, consubstantial. Complementary to his work was that of the three Cappadocian Fathers, Saints Gregory of Nazianzus, known in the Orthodox Church as Gregory the Theologian (?329–?90), Basil the Great (?330–79), and his younger brother Gregory of Nyssa (died 394). While Athanasius emphasized the unity of God – Father and Son are one in essence (*ousia*) – the Cappadocians stressed God's three-ness – Father, Son, and Holy Spirit are three persons (*hypostaseis*). Preserving a delicate balance between the threeness and the oneness in God, they gave full meaning to the classic summary of Trinitarian doctrine, *three persons in one essence*. Never before or since has the Church possessed four theologians of such stature within a single generation.

After 381 Arianism quickly ceased to be a living issue, except in certain parts of western Europe. The controversial aspect of the Council's work lay in its third Canon, which was resented alike by Rome and by Alexandria. Old Rome wondered where the claims of New Rome would end: might not Constantinople before long claim first place? Rome chose therefore to ignore the offending Canon, and not until the Lateran Council (1215) did the Pope formally recognize Constantinople's claim to second place. (Constantinople was at that time in the hands of the Crusaders and under the rule of a Latin Patriarch.) But the Canon was equally a challenge to Alexandria, which hitherto had occupied the first place in the east. The next seventy years witnessed a sharp conflict between Constantinople and Alexandria, in which for a time the victory went to the latter. The first major Alexandrian success was at the Synod of the Oak, when Theophilus of Alexandria secured the deposition and exile of the Bishop of Constantinople, Saint John Chrysostom, 'John of the Golden Mouth' (?344–407). A fluent and eloquent preacher – his sermons must often have lasted for an hour or more – John expressed in popular form the theological ideas put forward by Athanasius and the Cappadocians. A man of strict and austere life, he was inspired by a deep compassion for the poor and by a burning zeal for social righteousness. Of all the Fathers he is perhaps the best loved in the Orthodox Church, and the one whose works are most widely read.

Alexandria's second major success was won by the nephew and successor of Theophilus, Saint Cyril of Alexandria (died 444), who brought about the fall of another Bishop of Constantinople, Nestorius, at the third General Council, held in Ephesus (431). But at Ephesus there was more at stake than the rivalry of two great sees. Doctrinal issues, quiescent since 381, once more emerged, centring now not on the Trinity but on the Person of Christ. Cyril and Nestorius agreed that Christ was fully God, one of the Trinity, but they diverged in their descriptions of His manhood and in their method of explaining the union of God and man in a single person. They represented different traditions or schools of theology. Nestorius, brought up in the school of Antioch, upheld the integrity of Christ's manhood, but distinguished so emphatically between the manhood and the Godhead that he seemed in danger of ending, not with one person, but with two persons coexisting in the same body. Cyril, the protagonist of the opposite tradition of Alexandria, started from the unity of Christ's person rather than the diversity of His manhood and Godhead, but spoke about Christ's humanity less vividly than the Antiochenes. Either approach, if pressed too far, could lead to heresy, but the Church had need of both in order to form a balanced picture of the whole Christ. It was a tragedy for Christendom that the two schools, instead of balancing one another, entered into conflict.

Nestorius precipitated the controversy by declining to call the Virgin Mary 'Mother of God' (*Theotokos*). This title was already accepted in popular devotion, but it seemed to Nestorius to imply a confusion of Christ's manhood and His Godhead. Mary, he argued – and here his Antiochene 'separatism' is evident – is only to be called 'Mother of Man' or at the most 'Mother of Christ', since she is mother only of Christ's humanity, not of His divinity. Cyril, supported by the Council, answered with the text 'The Word was made flesh' (John i, 14): Mary is God's mother, for 'she bore the Word of God made flesh'.[1] What Mary bore was not a man loosely united to God, but a single and undivided person, who is God and man at once. The name *Theotokos* safeguards the unity of Christ's person: to deny her this title is to separate the Incarnate Christ into two, breaking down the bridge between God and man and erecting within Christ's person a middle wall of partition. Thus we can see that not only titles of devotion were involved at Ephesus, but the very message of salvation. The same primacy that the word *homoousios* occupies in the doctrine of the Trinity, the word *Theotokos* holds in the doctrine of the Incarnation.

Alexandria won another victory at a second Council held in Ephesus in 449, but this gathering, unlike its predecessor of 431, was not accepted by the Church at large. It was felt that the Alexandrian party had this time gone too far. Dioscorus and Eutyches, pressing Cyril's teaching to extremes, maintained that in Christ there was not only a unity of personality but a single nature – Monophysitism. It seemed to their opponents – although the Monophysites themselves denied that this was a just interpretation of their views – that such a way of speaking endangered the fullness of Christ's manhood, which in Monophysitism became so fused with His divinity as to be swallowed up in it like a drop of water in the ocean.

Only two years later, in 451, the Emperor summoned to Chalcedon a fresh gathering of bishops, which the Church of Byzantium and the west regarded as the fourth General Council. The pendulum now swung back in an Antiochene direction.

1. See the first of Cyril's *Twelve Anathemas*.

The Council reacted strongly against Monophysite terminology, and stated that while Christ is one person, there is in Him not one nature but two. The bishops acclaimed the *Tome* of Saint Leo the Great, Pope of Rome (died 461), in which the two natures are clearly distinguished. In their proclamation of faith they stated their belief in 'one and the same Son, perfect in Godhead and perfect in manhood, truly God and truly man ... acknowledged *in two natures* unconfusedly, unchangeably, indivisibly, inseparably; the difference between the natures is in no way removed because of the union, but rather the peculiar property of each nature is preserved, and both combine in one person and in one *hypostasis*'. The Definition of Chalcedon, we may note, is aimed not only at the Monophysites ('in two natures, unconfusedly, unchangeably'), but also at the followers of Nestorius ('one and the same Son ... indivisibly, inseparably').

But Chalcedon was more than a defeat for Alexandrian theology: it was a defeat for Alexandrian claims to rule supreme in the east. Canon xxviii of Chalcedon confirmed Canon iii of Constantinople, assigning to New Rome the place next in honour after Old Rome. Leo repudiated this Canon, but the east has ever since recognized its validity. The Council also freed Jerusalem from the jurisdiction of Caesarea and gave it the fifth place among the great sees. The system later known among Orthodox as the Pentarchy was now complete, whereby five great sees in the Church were held in particular honour, and a settled order of precedence was established among them: in order of rank, Rome, Constantinople, Alexandria, Antioch, Jerusalem. All five claimed Apostolic foundation. The first four were the most important cities in the Roman Empire; the fifth was added because it was the place where Christ had suffered on the Cross and risen from the dead. The bishop in each of these cities received the title *Patriarch*. The five Patriarchates between them divided into spheres of jurisdiction the whole of the known world, apart from Cyprus, which was granted independence by the Council of Ephesus and has remained self-governing ever since.

When speaking of the Orthodox conception of the Pentarchy there are two possible misunderstandings which must be avoided. First, the system of Patriarchs and Metropolitans is a matter of *ecclesiastical organization*. But if we look at the Church from the viewpoint not of ecclesiastical order but of *divine right*, then we must say that all bishops are essentially equal, however humble or exalted the city over which each presides. All bishops share equally in the apostolic succession, all have the same sacramental powers, all are divinely appointed teachers of the faith. If a dispute about doctrine arises, it is not enough for the Patriarchs to express their opinion: *every* diocesan bishop has the right to attend a General Council, to speak, and to cast his vote. The system of the Pentarchy does not impair the essential equality of all bishops, nor does it deprive each local community of the importance which Ignatius assigned to it.

In the second place, Orthodox believe that among the five Patriarchs a special place belongs to the Pope. The Orthodox Church does not accept the doctrine of Papal authority set forth in the decrees of the Vatican Council of 1870, and taught today in the Roman Catholic Church; but at the same time Orthodoxy does not deny to the Holy and Apostolic See of Rome a *primacy of honour*, together with the right (under certain conditions) to hear appeals from all parts of Christendom. Note that we have used the word 'primacy', not 'supremacy'. Orthodox regard the Pope as the bishop 'who presides in love', to adapt a phrase of Saint Ignatius: Rome's mistake – so Orthodox believe – has been to turn this primacy or 'presidency of love' into a supremacy of external power and jurisdiction.

This primacy which Rome enjoys takes its origin from three factors. First, Rome was the city where Saint Peter and Saint Paul were martyred, and where Peter was bishop. The Orthodox Church acknowledges Peter as the first among the Apostles: it does not forget the celebrated 'Petrine texts' in the Gospels (Matthew xvi, 18–19; Luke xxii, 32; John xxi, 15–17) – although Orthodox theologians do not understand these texts in quite the same way as modern Roman Catholic commentators.

And while many Orthodox theologians would say that not only the Bishop of Rome but all bishops are successors of Peter, yet most of them at the same time admit that the Bishop of Rome is Peter's successor in a special sense. Secondly, the see of Rome also owed its primacy to the position occupied by the city of Rome in the Empire: she was the capital, the chief city of the ancient world, and such in some measure she continued to be even after the foundation of Constantinople. Thirdly, although there were occasions when Popes fell into heresy, on the whole during the first eight centuries of the Church's history the Roman see was noted for the purity of its faith: other Patriarchates wavered during the great doctrinal disputes, but Rome for the most part stood firm. When hard pressed in the struggle against heretics, men felt that they could turn with confidence to the Pope. Not only the Bishop of Rome, but *every* bishop, is appointed by God to be a teacher of the faith; yet because the see of Rome had in practice taught the faith with an outstanding loyalty to the truth, it was above all to Rome that men appealed for guidance in the early centuries of the Church.

But as with Patriarchs, so with the Pope: the primacy assigned to Rome does not overthrow the essential equality of all bishops. The Pope is the first bishop in the Church – but he is the *first among equals*.

Ephesus and Chalcedon were a rock of Orthodoxy, but they were also a terrible rock of offence. The Arians had been gradually reconciled and formed no lasting schism. But to this day there exist Nestorian Christians who cannot accept the decisions of Ephesus, and Monophysites who cannot accept those of Chalcedon. The Nestorians lay for the most part outside the Empire, and little more is heard of them in Byzantine history. But large numbers of Monophysites, particularly in Egypt and Syria, were subjects of the Emperor, and repeated though unsuccessful efforts were made to bring them back into communion with the Byzantine Church. As so often, theological differences were made more bitter by cultural and national tension. Egypt and Syria, both predominantly non-Greek in language and background, resented the power of Greek Constantinople, alike in religious and in political matters. Thus ecclesiastical schism was reinforced by political separatism. Had it not been for these non-theological factors, the two sides might perhaps have reached a theological understanding after Chalcedon. Many modern scholars are inclined to think that the difference between Monophysites and 'Chalcedonians' was basically one of terminology, not of theology: the two parties used different language, but ultimately both were concerned to uphold the same truths.

The Definition of Chalcedon was supplemented by two later Councils, both held at Constantinople. The fifth Ecumenical Council (553) reinterpreted the decrees of Chalcedon from an Alexandrian point of view, and sought to explain, in more constructive terms than Chalcedon had used, how the two natures of Christ unite to form a single person. The sixth Ecumenical Council (680–1) condemned the Monothelite heresy, a new form of Monophysitism. The Monothelites argued that although Christ has two natures, yet since He is a single person, He has only one will. The Council replied that if He has two natures, then He must also have two wills. The Monothelites, like the Monophysites, impaired the fullness of Christ's humanity, since manhood without a human will would be incomplete, a mere abstraction. Since Christ is true man as well as true God, He must have a human will as well as a divine.

During the fifty years before the meeting of the sixth Council, Byzantium was faced with a sudden and alarming development: the rise of Islam. The most striking fact about Mohammedan expansion is its speed. When the Prophet died in 632, his authority scarcely extended beyond the Hejaz. But within fifteen years his Arab followers had taken Syria, Palestine, and Egypt; within fifty years they were at the walls of Constantinople and almost captured the city; within a hundred they had swept across North Africa, advanced through Spain, and forced western Europe to fight for its life at the Battle of Poitiers. The Arab invasions have been called 'a centrifugal explosion, driving in every direction small bodies of mounted raiders in quest of food, plunder, and conquest. The old empires were in no state to resist them.'[1] Christendom survived, but only with difficulty. The Byzantines lost their eastern possessions, and the three Patriarchates of Alexandria, Antioch, and Jerusalem passed under infidel control; within the Christian Empire of the East, the Patriarchate of Constantinople was now without rival. Henceforward Byzantium was never free for very long from Mohammedan attacks, and although it held out for eight centuries more, yet in the end it succumbed.

THE HOLY ICONS

Disputes concerning the Person of Christ did not cease with the Council of 681, but were extended in a different form into the eighth and ninth centuries. The struggle centred on the Holy Icons, the pictures of Christ, the Mother of God, and the Saints, which were kept and venerated both in churches and in private homes. The Iconoclasts or icon-smashers, suspicious of any religious art which represented human beings or God, demanded the destruction of icons; the opposite party, the Iconodules or venerators of icons, vigorously defended the place of icons in the life of the Church. The struggle was not merely a conflict between two conceptions of Christian art. Deeper issues were involved: the character of Christ's human nature, the Christian attitude towards matter, the true meaning of Christian redemption.

The Iconoclasts may have been influenced from the outside by Jewish and Moslem ideas, and it is significant that three years before the first outbreak of Iconoclasm in the Byzantine Empire, the Mohammedan Caliph Yezid ordered the removal of all icons within his dominions. But Iconoclasm was not simply imported from outside; within Christianity itself there had always existed a 'puritan' outlook, which condemned icons because it saw in all images a latent idolatry. When the Isaurian Emperors attacked icons, they found plenty of sup-

1. H. St L. B. Moss, in Baynes and Moss, *Byzantium: an Introduction*, Oxford, 1948, pp. 11–12.

port inside the Church. Typical of this puritan outlook is the action of Saint Epiphanius of Salamis (?315–403), who, on finding in a Palestinian village church a curtain woven with the figure of Christ, tore it down with indignation. This attitude was always strong in Asia Minor, and some hold that the Iconoclast movement was an Asiatic protest against Greek tradition. But there are difficulties in such a view; the controversy was really a split *within* the Greek tradition.

The Iconoclast controversy, which lasted some 120 years, falls into two phases. The first period opened in 726 when Leo III began his attack on icons, and ended in 780 when the Empress Irene suspended the persecution. The Iconodule position was upheld by the seventh and last Ecumenical Council (787), which met (as the first had done) at Nicaea. Icons, the Council proclaimed, are to be kept in churches and honoured with the same relative veneration as is shown to other material symbols, such as 'the precious and life-giving Cross' and the Book of the Gospels. A new attack on icons, started by Leo V the Armenian in 815, continued until 843 when the icons were again reinstated, this time permanently, by another Empress, Theodora. The final victory of the Holy Images in 843 is known as 'the Triumph of Orthodoxy', and is commemorated in a special service celebrated on 'Orthodoxy Sunday', the first Sunday in Lent. During this service the true faith – Orthodoxy – is proclaimed, its defenders are honoured, and anathemas pronounced on all who attack the Holy Icons or the Seven General Councils:

To those who reject the Councils of the Holy Fathers, and their traditions which are agreeable to divine revelation, and which the Orthodox Catholic Church piously maintains, ANATHEMA! ANATHEMA! ANATHEMA!

The chief champion of the icons in the first period was Saint John of Damascus (?675–749), in the second Saint Theodore of Studium (759–826). John was able to work the more freely because he dwelt in Moslem territory, out of reach of the Byzantine government. It was not the last time that Islam acted unintentionally as the protector of Orthodoxy.

One of the distinctive features of Orthodoxy is the place which it assigns to icons. An Orthodox church today is filled with them: dividing the sanctuary from the body of the building there is a solid screen, the iconostasis, entirely covered with icons, while other icons are placed in special shrines around the church; and perhaps the walls are covered with icons in fresco or mosaic. An Orthodox prostrates himself before these icons, he kisses them and burns candles in front of them; they are censed by the priest and carried in procession. What do these gestures and actions mean? What do icons signify, and why did John of Damascus and others regard them as important?

We shall consider first the charge of idolatry, which the Iconoclasts brought against the Iconodules; then the positive value of icons as a means of instruction; and finally their doctrinal importance.

(1) *The question of idolatry.* When an Orthodox kisses an icon or prostrates himself before it, he is not guilty of idolatry. The icon is not an idol but a symbol; the veneration shown to images is directed, not towards stone, wood, and paint, but towards the person depicted. This had been pointed out some time before the Iconoclast controversy by Leontius of Neapolis (died about 650):

> We do not make obeisance to the nature of wood, but we revere and do obeisance to Him who was crucified on the Cross. . . . When the two beams of the Cross are joined together I adore the figure because of Christ who on the Cross was crucified, but if the beams are separated, I throw them away and burn them.[1]

Because icons are only symbols, Orthodox do not *worship* them, but *reverence* or *venerate* them. John of Damascus carefully distinguished between the relative honour or veneration shown to material symbols, and the worship due to God alone.

(2) *Icons as part of the Church's teaching.* Icons, said Leontius, are 'opened books to remind us of God';[2] they are

1. Migne, *Patrologia Graeca* (*P.G.*), xciv, 1384D.
2. *P.G.* xciv, 1276A.

one of the means which the Church employs in order to teach the faith. He who lacks learning or leisure to study works of theology has only to enter a church to see unfolded before him on the walls all the mysteries of the Christian religion. If a pagan asks you to show him your faith, said the Iconodules, take him into church and place him before the icons.[1]

(3) *The doctrinal significance of icons.* Here we come to the real heart of the Iconoclast dispute. Granted that icons are not idolatrous; granted that they are useful for instruction; but are they not only permissible but necessary? Is it *essential* to have icons? The Iconodules held that it is, because icons safeguard a full and proper doctrine of the Incarnation. Iconoclasts and Iconodules agreed that God cannot be represented in His eternal nature: 'no man has seen God at any time' (John i, 18). But, the Iconodules continued, the Incarnation has made a representational religious art possible: God can be depicted because He became man and took flesh. Material images, argued John of Damascus, can be made of Him who took a material body:

Of old God the incorporeal and uncircumscribed was not depicted at all. But now that God has appeared in the flesh and lived among men, I make an image of the God who can be seen. I do not worship matter but I worship the Creator of matter, who for my sake became material and deigned to dwell in matter, who through matter effected my salvation. I will not cease from worshipping the matter through which my salvation has been effected.[2]

The Iconoclasts, by repudiating all representations of God, failed to take full account of the Incarnation. They fell, as so many puritans have done, into a kind of dualism. Regarding matter as a defilement, they wanted a religion freed from all contact with what is material; for they thought that what is spiritual must be non-material. But this is to betray the Incarnation, by allowing no place to Christ's humanity, to His body;

1. *Ad Constantinum Cabalinum, P.G.* xcv, 325C. Icons are a part of Holy Tradition (see p. 214).
2. *On Icons,* I, 16 (*P.G.* xciv, 1245A).

it is to forget that man's body as well as his soul must be saved and transfigured. The Iconoclast controversy is thus closely linked to the earlier disputes about Christ's person. It was not merely a controversy about religious art, but about the Incarnation and the salvation of man.

God took a material body, thereby proving that matter can be redeemed: 'The Word made flesh has deified the flesh,' said John of Damascus.[1] God has 'deified' matter, making it 'spirit-bearing'; and if flesh became a vehicle of the Spirit, then so – though in a different way – can wood and paint. The Orthodox doctrine of icons is bound up with the Orthodox belief that the whole of God's creation, material as well as spiritual, is to be redeemed and glorified. In the words of Nicholas Zernov (1898–1980) – what he says of Russians is true of all Orthodox:

[Icons] were for the Russians not merely paintings. They were dynamic manifestations of man's spiritual power to redeem creation through beauty and art. The colours and lines of the [icons] were not meant to imitate nature; the artists aimed at demonstrating that men, animals, and plants, and the whole cosmos, could be rescued from their present state of degradation and restored to their proper 'Image'. The [icons] were pledges of the coming victory of a redeemed creation over the fallen one. . . . The artistic perfection of an icon was not only a reflection of the celestial glory – it was a concrete example of matter restored to its original harmony and beauty, and serving as a vehicle of the Spirit. The icons were part of the transfigured cosmos.[2]

As John of Damascus put it:

The icon is a song of triumph, and a revelation, and an enduring monument to the victory of the saints and the disgrace of the demons.[3]

The conclusion of the Iconoclast dispute, the meeting of the seventh Ecumenical Council, the Triumph of Orthodoxy in 843 – these mark the end of the second period in Orthodox

1. *On Icons*, I, 21 (*P.G.* xciv, 1253B).
2. *The Russians and their Church*, pp. 107–8.
3. *On Icons*, II, 11 (*P.G.* xciv, 1296B).

history, the period of the Seven Councils. These Seven Councils are of immense importance to Orthodoxy. For members of the Orthodox Church, their interest is not merely historical but contemporary; they are the concern not only of scholars and clergy, but of all the faithful. 'Even illiterate peasants,' said Dean Stanley, 'to whom, in the corresponding class of life in Spain or Italy, the names of Constance and Trent would probably be quite unknown, are well aware that their Church reposes on the basis of the Seven Councils, and retain a hope that they may yet live to see an eighth General Council, in which the evils of the time will be set straight.'[1] Orthodox often call themselves 'the Church of the Seven Councils'. By this they do not mean that the Orthodox Church has ceased to think creatively since 787. But they see in the period of the Councils the great age of theology; and, next to the Bible, it is the Seven Councils which the Orthodox Church takes as its standard and guide in seeking solutions to the new problems which arise in every generation.

SAINTS, MONKS, AND EMPERORS

Not without reason has Byzantium been called 'the icon of the heavenly Jerusalem'. Religion entered into every aspect of Byzantine life. The Byzantine's holidays were religious festivals; the races which he attended in the Circus began with the singing of hymns; his trade contracts invoked the Trinity and were marked with the sign of the Cross. Today, in an untheological age, it is all but impossible to realize how burning an interest was felt in religious questions by every part of society, by laity as well as clergy, by the poor and uneducated as well as the Court and the scholars. Gregory of Nyssa describes the unending theological arguments in Constantinople at the time of the second General Council:

The whole city is full of it, the squares, the market places, the cross-roads, the alleyways; old-clothes men, money changers, food sellers: they are all busy arguing. If you ask someone to

1. *Lectures on the History of the Eastern Church* (Everyman Edition), p. 99.

43

give you change, he philosophizes about the Begotten and the Unbegotten; if you inquire about the price of a loaf, you are told by way of reply that the Father is greater and the Son inferior; if you ask 'Is my bath ready?' the attendant answers that the Son was made out of nothing.[1]

This curious complaint indicates the atmosphere in which the Councils met. So violent were the passions aroused that sessions were not always restrained or dignified. 'Synods and councils I salute from a distance,' Gregory of Nazianzus dryly remarked, 'for I know how troublesome they are.' 'Never again will I sit in those gatherings of cranes and geese.'[2] The Fathers at times supported their cause by questionable means: Cyril of Alexandria, for example, in his struggle against Nestorius, bribed the Court heavily and terrorized the city of Ephesus with a private army of monks. Yet if Cyril was intemperate in his methods, it was because of his consuming desire that the right cause should triumph; and if Christians were at times acrimonious, it was because they cared about the Christian faith. Perhaps disorder is better than apathy. Orthodoxy recognizes that the Councils were attended by imperfect men, but it believes that these imperfect men were guided by the Holy Spirit.

The Byzantine bishop was not only a distant figure who attended Councils; he was also in many cases a true father to his people, a friend and protector to whom men confidently turned when in trouble. The concern for the poor and oppressed which John Chrysostom displayed is found in many others. Saint John the Almsgiver, Patriarch of Alexandria (died 619), for example, devoted all the wealth of his see to helping those whom he called 'my brethren, the poor'. When his own resources failed, he appealed to others: 'He used to say,' a contemporary recorded, 'that if, without ill-will, a man were to strip the rich right down to their shirts in order to give to the poor, he would do no wrong.'[3] 'Those whom you call

1. *On the Deity of the Son* (*P.G.* xlvi, 557B).
2. *Letter* 124; *Poems about Himself*, xvii, 91.
3. Leontius of Neapolis, *A Supplement to the Life of John the Almsgiver*, 21.

poor and beggars,' John said, 'these I proclaim my masters and helpers. For they, and they alone, can really help us and bestow upon us the kingdom of heaven.'[1] The Church in the Byzantine Empire did not overlook its social obligations, and one of its principal functions was charitable work.

Monasticism played a decisive part in the religious life of Byzantium, as it has done in that of all Orthodox countries. It has been rightly said that 'the best way to penetrate Orthodox spirituality is to enter it through monasticism'.[2] 'There is a great richness of forms of the spiritual life to be found within the bounds of Orthodoxy, but monasticism remains the most classical of all.'[3] The monastic life first emerged as a definite institution in Egypt at the start of the fourth century, and from there it spread rapidly across Christendom. It is no coincidence that monasticism should have developed immediately after Constantine's conversion, at the very time when the persecutions ceased and Christianity became fashionable. The monks with their austerities were martyrs in an age when martyrdom of blood no longer existed; they formed the counterbalance to an established Christendom. Men in Byzantine society were in danger of forgetting that Byzantium was an icon and symbol, not the reality; they ran the risk of identifying the kingdom of God with an earthly kingdom. The monks by their withdrawal from society into the desert fulfilled a prophetic and eschatological ministry in the life of the Church. They reminded Christians that the kingdom of God is not of this world.

Monasticism has taken three chief forms, all of which had appeared in Egypt by the year 350, and all of which are still to be found in the Orthodox Church today. There are first the *hermits*, men leading the solitary life in huts or caves, and even in tombs, among the branches of trees, or on the tops of pillars. The great model of the eremitic life is the father of monasticism himself, Saint Antony of Egypt (251–356). Secondly there is the *community life*, where monks dwell together under a

1. Leontius, *Supplement*, 2.
2. P. Evdokimov, *L'Orthodoxie*, p. 20.
3. V. Lossky, *The Mystical Theology of the Eastern Church*, p. 17.

common rule and in a regularly constituted monastery. Here the great pioneer was Saint Pachomius of Egypt (286–346), author of a rule later used by Saint Benedict in the west. Basil the Great, whose ascetic writings have exercised a formative influence on eastern monasticism, was a strong advocate of the community life. Giving a social emphasis to monasticism, he urged that religious houses should care for the sick and poor, maintaining hospitals and orphanages, and working directly for the benefit of society at large. But in general eastern monasticism has been far less concerned than western with active work; in Orthodoxy a monk's primary task is the life of prayer, and it is through this that he serves others. It is not so much what a monk *does* that matters, as what he *is*. Finally there is a form of the monastic life intermediate between the first two, the *semi-eremitic life*, a 'middle way' where instead of a single highly organized community there is a loosely knit group of small settlements, each settlement containing perhaps between two and six brethren living together under the guidance of an elder. The great centres of the semi-eremitic life in Egypt were Nitria and Scetis, which by the end of the fourth century had produced many outstanding monks – Ammon the founder of Nitria, Macarius of Egypt and Macarius of Alexandria, Evagrius of Pontus, and Arsenius the Great. (This semi-eremitic system is found not only in the east but in the far west, in Celtic monasticism.)

Because of its monasteries, fourth-century Egypt was regarded as a second Holy Land, and travellers to Jerusalem felt their pilgrimage to be incomplete unless it included the ascetic houses of the Nile. In the fifth and sixth centuries leadership in the monastic movement shifted to Palestine, with Saint Euthymius the Great (died 473) and his disciple Saint Sabbas (died 532). The monastery founded by Saint Sabbas in the Jordan valley can claim an unbroken history to the present day; it was to this community that John of Damascus belonged. Almost as old is another important house with an unbroken history to the present, the monastery of Saint Catherine at Mount Sinai, founded by the Emperor Justinian (reigned 527–65). With

Palestine and Sinai in Arab hands, monastic pre-eminence in the Byzantine Empire passed to the huge monastery of the Studium at Constantinople, originally founded in 463; Saint Theodore was Abbot here and revised the rule of the community.

Since the tenth century the chief centre of Orthodox monasticism has been Athos, a rocky peninsula in North Greece jutting out into the Aegean and culminating at its tip in a peak 6,670 feet high. Known as 'the Holy Mountain', Athos contains twenty 'ruling' monasteries and a large number of smaller houses, as well as hermits' cells; the whole peninsula is given up entirely to monastic settlements, and in the days of its greatest expansion it is said to have contained nearly forty thousand monks. One out of the twenty ruling monasteries has by itself produced 26 Patriarchs and 144 bishops: this gives some idea of the importance of Athos in Orthodox history.

There are no 'Orders' in Orthodox monasticism. In the west a monk belongs to the Carthusian, the Cistercian, or some other Order; in the east he is simply a member of the one great brotherhood which includes all monks and nuns, although of course he is attached to a particular monastic house. Western writers sometimes refer to Orthodox monks as 'Basilian monks' or 'monks of the Basilian Order', but this is not correct. Saint Basil is an important figure in Orthodox monasticism, but he founded no Order, and although two of his works are known as the *Longer Rules* and the *Shorter Rules*, these are in no sense comparable to the *Rule* of Saint Benedict.

A characteristic figure in Orthodox monasticism is the 'elder' or 'old man' (Greek *gerōn*; Russian *starets*, plural *startsi*). The elder is a monk of spiritual discernment and wisdom, whom others – either monks or people in the world – adopt as their guide and spiritual director. He is sometimes a priest, but often a lay monk; he receives no special ordination or appointment to the work of eldership, but is guided to it by the direct inspiration of the Spirit. The elder sees in a concrete and practical way what the will of God is in relation to each person who comes to consult him: this is the elder's special gift or *charisma*. The earliest and most celebrated of the monastic *startsi* was Saint Antony himself. The first part of his life, from eighteen to fifty-five, he spent in withdrawal and solitude; then, though still living in the desert, he abandoned this life of strict enclosure, and began to receive visitors. A group of disciples gathered round him, and besides these disciples there was a far larger circle of people who came, often from a long distance, to ask his advice; so great was the stream of visitors that, as Antony's biographer Athanasius put it, he became a physician to all Egypt. Antony has had many successors, and in most of them the same outward pattern of events is found – *a withdrawal in order to return.* A monk must first withdraw, and in silence must learn the truth about himself and God. Then, after this long and rigorous preparation in solitude, having gained the gifts of discernment which are required of an elder, he can open the door of his cell and admit the world from which formerly he fled.

At the heart of the Christian polity of Byzantium was the Emperor, who was no ordinary ruler, but God's representative on earth. If Byzantium was an icon of the heavenly Jerusalem, then the earthly monarchy of the Emperor was an image or icon of the monarchy of God in heaven; in church men prostrated themselves before the icon of Christ, and in the palace before God's living icon – the Emperor. The labyrinthine palace, the Court with its elaborate ceremonial, the throne room where mechanical lions roared and musical birds sang: these things were designed to make clear the Emperor's status as vicegerent of God. 'By such means,' wrote the Emperor Constantine VII Porphyrogenitus, 'we figure forth the harmonious movement of God the Creator around this universe, while the imperial power is preserved in proportion and order.'[1] The Emperor had a special place in the Church's worship: he could not of course celebrate the Eucharist, but he received communion 'as priests do', he preached sermons, on certain feasts he censed the altar. The vestments which Ortho-

1. *Book of Ceremonies*, Prologue.

dox bishops now wear are the vestments once worn by the Emperor in church.

The life of Byzantium formed a unified whole, and there was no rigid line of separation between the religious and the secular, between Church and State: the two were seen as parts of a single organism. Hence it was inevitable that the Emperor played an active part in the affairs of the Church. Yet at the same time it is not just to accuse Byzantium of Caesaro-Papism, of subordinating the Church to the State. Although Church and State formed a single organism, yet within this one organism there were two distinct elements, the priesthood (*sacerdotium*) and the imperial power (*imperium*); and while working in close cooperation, each of these elements had its own proper sphere in which it was autonomous. Between the two there was a 'symphony' or 'harmony', but neither element exercised absolute control over the other.

This is the doctrine expounded in the great code of Byzantine law drawn up under Justinian (see the sixth *Novel*) and repeated in many other Byzantine texts. Take for example the words of Emperor John Tzimisces: 'I recognize two authorities, priesthood and empire; the Creator of the world entrusted to the first the care of souls and to the second the control of men's bodies. Let neither authority be attacked, that the world may enjoy prosperity.'[1] Thus it was the Emperor's task to summon councils and to carry their decrees into effect, but it lay beyond his powers to dictate the content of those decrees: it was for the bishops gathered in council to decide what the true faith was. Bishops were appointed by God to teach the faith, whereas the Emperor was the protector of Orthodoxy, but not its exponent. Such was the theory, and such in great part was the practice also. Admittedly there were many occasions on which the Emperor interfered unwarrantably in ecclesiastical matters; but when a serious question of principle arose, the authorities of the Church quickly showed that they had a will of their own. Iconoclasm, for example, was vigorously championed by a whole series of Emperors, yet for all

1. Quoted in N. H. Baynes, *Byzantine Studies*, London, 1955, p. 52.

that it was successfully rejected by the Church. In Byzantine history Church and State were closely interdependent, but neither was subordinate to the other.

There are many today, not only outside but within the Orthodox Church, who sharply criticize the Byzantine Empire and the idea of a Christian society for which it stands. Yet were the Byzantines entirely wrong? They believed that Christ, who lived on earth as a man, has redeemed every aspect of human existence, and they held that it was therefore possible to baptize not human individuals only but the whole spirit and organization of society. So they strove to create a polity entirely Christian in its principles of government and in its daily life. Byzantium in fact was nothing less than an attempt to accept and to apply the full implications of the Incarnation. Certainly the attempt had its dangers: in particular the Byzantines often fell into the error of identifying the earthly kingdom of Byzantium with the Kingdom of God, the Greek people with God's people. Certainly Byzantium fell far short of the high ideal which it set itself, and its failure was often lamentable and disastrous. The tales of Byzantine duplicity, violence, and cruelty are too well known to call for repetition here. They are true – but they are only a part of the truth. For behind all the shortcomings of Byzantium can always be discerned the great vision by which the Byzantines were inspired: to establish here on earth a living icon of God's government in heaven.

CHAPTER 3

Byzantium, II:
The Great Schism

We are unchanged; we are still the same as we were
in the eighth century. ... Oh that you could only
consent to be again what you were once, when we
were both united in faith and communion!

Alexis Khomiakov

THE ESTRANGEMENT OF EASTERN AND WESTERN
CHRISTENDOM

ONE summer afternoon in the year 1054, as a service was about
to begin in the Church of the Holy Wisdom[1] at Constantinople,
Cardinal Humbert and two other legates of the Pope entered
the building and made their way up to the sanctuary. They had
not come to pray. They placed a Bull of Excommunication
upon the altar and marched out once more. As he passed
through the western door, the Cardinal shook the dust from
his feet with the words: 'Let God look and judge.' A deacon
ran out after him in great distress and begged him to take back
the Bull. Humbert refused; and it was dropped in the street.

It is this incident which has conventionally been taken to
mark the beginning of the great schism between the Orthodox
east and the Latin west. But the schism, as historians now
generally recognize, is not really an event whose beginning can
be exactly dated. It was something that came about gradually,
as the result of a long and complicated process, starting well
before the eleventh century and not completed until some time
after.

In this long and complicated process, many different

1. In Greek, 'Hagia Sophia'; often called 'Saint Sophia' or 'Sancta
Sophia' by English writers.

influences were at work. The schism was conditioned by cultural, political, and economic factors; yet its fundamental cause was not secular but theological. In the last resort it was over matters of doctrine that east and west quarrelled – two matters in particular: the Papal claims and the *filioque*. But before we look more closely at these two major differences, and before we consider the actual course of the schism, something must be said about the wider background. Long before there was an open and formal schism between east and west, the two sides had become *strangers* to one another; and in attempting to understand how and why the communion of Christendom was broken, we must start with this fact of increasing estrangement.

When Paul and the other Apostles travelled around the Mediterranean world, they moved within a closely knit political and cultural unity: the Roman Empire. This Empire embraced many different national groups, often with languages and dialects of their own. But all these groups were governed by the same Emperor; there was a broad Greco–Roman civilization in which educated people throughout the Empire shared; either Greek or Latin was understood almost everywhere in the Empire, and many could speak both languages. These facts greatly assisted the early Church in its missionary work.

But in the centuries that followed, the unity of the Mediterranean world gradually disappeared. The political unity was the first to go. From the end of the third century the Empire, while still theoretically one, was usually divided into two parts, an eastern and a western, each under its own Emperor. Constantine furthered this process of separation by founding a second imperial capital in the east, alongside Old Rome in Italy. Then came the barbarian invasions at the start of the fifth century: apart from Italy, much of which remained within the Empire for some time longer, the west was carved up among barbarian chiefs. The Byzantines never forgot the ideals of Rome under Augustus and Trajan, and still regarded their Empire as in theory universal; but Justinian was the last Emperor who seriously attempted to bridge the gulf between theory and fact, and his conquests in the west were soon abandoned. The political unity of the Greek east and the Latin west was destroyed by the barbarian invasions, and never permanently restored.

The severance was carried a stage further by the rise of Islam: the Mediterranean, which the Romans once called *mare nostrum*, 'our sea', now passed largely into Arab control. Cultural and economic contacts between the eastern and western Mediterranean never entirely ceased, but they became far more difficult.

Cut off from Byzantium, the west proceeded to set up a 'Roman' Empire of its own. On Christmas Day in the year 800 the Pope crowned Charles the Great, King of the Franks, as Emperor. Charlemagne sought recognition from the ruler at Byzantium, but without success; for the Byzantines, still adhering to the principle of imperial unity, regarded Charlemagne as an intruder and the Papal coronation as an act of schism within the Empire. The creation of a Holy Roman Empire in the west, instead of drawing Europe closer together, only served to alienate east and west more than before.

The cultural unity lingered on, but in a greatly attenuated form. Both in east and west, men of learning still lived within the classical tradition which the Church had taken over and made its own; but as time went on they began to interpret this tradition in increasingly divergent ways. Matters were made more difficult by problems of language. The days when educated men were bilingual were over. By the year 450 there were very few in western Europe who could read Greek, and after 600, although Byzantium still called itself the *Roman* Empire, it was rare for a Byzantine to speak Latin, the language of the Romans. Photius, the greatest scholar in ninth century Constantinople, could not read Latin; and in 864 a 'Roman' Emperor at Byzantium, Michael III, even called the language in which Virgil once wrote 'a barbarian and Scythic tongue'. If Greeks wished to read Latin works or vice versa, they could do so only in translation, and usually they did not trouble to do even that: Psellus, an eminent Greek savant of the eleventh century, had so sketchy a knowledge of Latin literature that he confused Caesar with Cicero. Because they no longer drew upon the same sources nor read the same books, Greek east and Latin west drifted more and more apart.

It was an ominous but significant precedent that the cultural renaissance in Charlemagne's Court should have been marked at its outset by a strong anti-Greek prejudice. The hostility and defiance which the new Roman Empire of the west felt towards Constantinople extended beyond the political field to the cultural. Men of letters in Charlemagne's entourage were not prepared to copy Byzantium, but sought to create a new Christian civilization of their own. In fourth-century Europe there had been one Christian civilization, in thirteenth-century Europe there were two; perhaps it is in the reign of Charlemagne that the schism of civilizations first becomes clearly apparent.

The Byzantines for their part remained enclosed in their own world of ideas, and did little to meet the west half way. Alike in the ninth and in later centuries they usually failed to take western learning as seriously as it deserved. They dismissed all 'Franks' as barbarians and nothing more.

These political and cultural factors could not but affect the life of the Church, and make it harder to maintain religious unity. Cultural and political estrangement can lead only too easily to ecclesiastical disputes, as may be seen from the case of Charlemagne. Refused recognition in the political sphere by the Byzantine Emperor, he was quick to retaliate with a charge of heresy against the Byzantine Church: he denounced the Greeks for not using the *filioque* in the Creed (of this we shall say more in a moment) and he declined to accept the decisions of the seventh Ecumenical Council. It is true that Charlemagne only knew of these decisions through a faulty translation which seriously distorted their true meaning; but he seems in any case to have been semi-Iconoclast in his views.

The different political situations in east and west made the Church assume different outward forms, so that men came gradually to think of Church order in conflicting ways. From the start there had been a certain difference of emphasis here between east and west. In the east there were many Churches whose foundation went back to the Apostles; there was a strong sense of the equality of all bishops, of the collegial and conciliar nature of the Church. The east acknowledged the Pope as the first bishop in the Church, but saw him as the first among equals. In the west, on the other hand, there was only one great see claiming Apostolic foundation – Rome – so that Rome came to be regarded as *the* Apostolic see. The west, while it accepted the decisions of the Ecumenical Councils, did not play a very active part in the Councils themselves; the Church was seen less as a college and more as a monarchy – the monarchy of the Pope.

This initial divergence in outlook was made more acute by political developments. As was only natural, the barbarian invasions and the consequent breakdown of the Empire in the west served greatly to strengthen the autocratic structure of the western Church. In the east there was a strong secular head, the Emperor, to uphold the civilized order and to enforce law. In the west, after the advent of the barbarians, there was only a plurality of warring chiefs, all more or less usurpers. For the most part it was the Papacy alone which could act as a centre of unity, as an element of continuity and stability in the spiritual and political life of western Europe. By force of circumstances, the Pope assumed a part which the Greek Patriarchs were not called to play: he became an autocrat, an absolute monarch set up over the Church, issuing commands – in a way that few if any eastern bishops have ever done – not only to his ecclesiastical subordinates but to secular rulers as well. The western Church became centralized to a degree unknown anywhere in the four Patriarchates of the east (except possibly in Egypt). Monarchy in the west; in the east collegiality.

Nor was this the only effect which the barbarian invasions had upon the life of the Church. In Byzantium there were many educated laymen who took an active interest in theology. The

55

'lay theologian' has always been an accepted figure in Ortho-doxy: some of the most learned Byzantine Patriarchs – Pho-tius, for example – were laymen before their appointment to the Patriarchate. But in the west the only effective education which survived through the Dark Ages was provided by the Church for its clergy. Theology became the preserve of the priests, since most of the laity could not even read, much less comprehend the technicalities of theological discussion. Ortho-doxy, while assigning to the episcopate a special teaching office, has never known this sharp division between clergy and laity which arose in the western Middle Ages.

Relations between eastern and western Christendom were also made more difficult by the lack of a common language. Be-cause the two sides could no longer communicate easily with one another, and each could no longer read what the other wrote, theological misunderstandings arose more easily; and these were often made worse by mistranslation – at times, one fears, deliberate and malicious mistranslation.

East and west were becoming strangers to one another, and this was something from which both were likely to suffer. In the early Church there had been unity in the faith, but a di-versity of theological schools. From the start Greeks and Latins had each approached the Christian Mystery in their own way. The Latin approach was more practical, the Greek more specu-lative; Latin thought was influenced by juridical ideas, by the concepts of Roman law, while the Greeks understood theology in the context of worship and in the light of the Holy Liturgy. When thinking about the Trinity, Latins started with the unity of the Godhead, Greeks with the threeness of the persons; when reflecting on the Crucifixion, Latins thought primarily of Christ the Victim, Greeks of Christ the Victor; Latins talked more of redemption, Greeks of deification; and so on. Like the schools of Antioch and Alexandria within the east, these two distinctive approaches were not in themselves contradictory; each served to supplement the other, and each had its place in the fullness of Catholic tradition. But now that the two sides were becoming strangers to one another – with no political and little cultural unity, with no common language – there was a danger that each side would follow its own approach in isolation and push it to extremes, forgetting the value in the opposite point of view.

We have spoken of the different doctrinal approaches in east and west; but there were two points of doctrine where the two sides no longer supplemented one another, but entered into direct conflict – the Papal claims and the *filioque*. The factors which we have mentioned in previous paragraphs were sufficient in themselves to place a serious strain upon the unity of Christendom. Yet for all that, unity might still have been maintained, had there not been these two further points of difficulty. To them we must now turn. It was not until the middle of the ninth century that the full extent of the disagreement first came properly into the open, but the two differences themselves date back considerably earlier.

We have already had occasion to mention the Papacy when speaking of the different political situations in east and west; and we have seen how the centralized and monarchical structure of the western Church was reinforced by the barbarian invasions. Now so long as the Pope claimed an absolute power only in the west, Byzantium raised no objections. The Byzantines did not mind if the western Church was centralized, so long as the Papacy did not interfere in the east. The Pope, however, believed his immediate power of jurisdiction to extend to the east as well as to the west; and as soon as he tried to enforce this claim within the eastern Patriarchates, trouble was bound to arise. The Greeks assigned to the Pope a primacy of honour, but not the universal supremacy which he regarded as his due. The Pope viewed infallibility as his own prerogative, the Greeks held that in matters of the faith the final decision rested not with the Pope alone, but with a Council representing *all* the bishops of the Church. Here we have two different conceptions of the visible organization of the Church.

The Orthodox attitude to the Papacy is admirably expressed by a twelfth-century writer, Nicetas, Archbishop of Nicomedia:

My dearest brother, we do not deny to the Roman Church the primacy amongst the five sister Patriarchates; and we recognize her right to the most honourable seat at an Ecumenical Council. But she has separated herself from us by her own deeds, when through pride she assumed a monarchy which does not belong to her office. . . . How shall we accept decrees from her that have been issued without consulting us and even without our knowledge? If the Roman Pontiff, seated on the lofty throne of his glory, wishes to thunder at us and, so to speak, hurl his mandates at us from on high, and if he wishes to judge us and even to rule us and our Churches, not by taking counsel with us but at his own arbitrary pleasure, what kind of brotherhood, or even what kind of parenthood can this be? We should be the slaves, not the sons, of such a Church, and the Roman See would not be the pious mother of sons but a hard and imperious mistress of slaves.[1]

That was how an Orthodox felt in the twelfth century, when the whole question had come out into the open. In earlier centuries the Greek attitude to the Papacy was basically the same, although not yet sharpened by controversy. Up to 850, Rome and the east avoided an open conflict over the Papal claims, but the divergence of views was not the less serious for being partially concealed.

The second great difficulty was the *filioque*. The dispute involved the words about the Holy Spirit in the Nicene-Constantinopolitan Creed. Originally the Creed ran: 'I believe . . . in the Holy Spirit, the Lord, the Giver of Life, *who proceeds from the Father*, who with the Father and the Son together is worshipped and together glorified.' This, the original form, is recited unchanged by the east to this day. But the west inserted an extra phrase 'and from the Son' (in Latin, *filioque*), so that the Creed now reads 'who proceeds from the Father *and the Son*'. It is not certain when and where this addition was first made, but it seems to have originated in Spain, as a safeguard against Arianism. At any rate the Spanish Church interpolated the *filioque* at the third Council of Toledo (589), if not before.

1. Quoted in S. Runciman, *The Eastern Schism*, p. 116.

From Spain the addition spread to France and thence to Germany, where it was welcomed by Charlemagne and adopted at the semi-Iconoclast Council of Frankfort (794). It was writers at Charlemagne's Court who first made the *filioque* into an issue of controversy, accusing the Greeks of heresy because they recited the Creed in its original form. But Rome, with typical conservatism, continued to use the Creed without the *filioque* until the start of the eleventh century. In 808 Pope Leo III wrote in a letter to Charlemagne that, although he himself believed the *filioque* to be doctrinally sound, yet he considered it a mistake to tamper with the wording of the Creed. Leo deliberately had the Creed, without the *filioque*, inscribed on silver plaques and set up in Saint Peter's. For the time being Rome acted as mediator between Germany and Byzantium.

It was not until after 850 that the Greeks paid much attention to the *filioque*, but once they did so, their reaction was sharply critical. Orthodoxy objected (and still objects) to this addition in the Creed, for two reasons. First, the Ecumenical Councils specifically forbade any changes to be introduced into the Creed; and if an addition has to be made, certainly nothing short of another Ecumenical Council is competent to make it. The Creed is the common possession of the whole Church, and a part of the Church has no right to tamper with it. The west, in arbitrarily altering the Creed without consulting the east, is guilty (as Khomiakov put it) of moral fratricide, of a sin against the unity of the Church. In the second place, Orthodox believe the *filioque* to be theologically untrue. They hold that the Spirit proceeds from the Father alone, and consider it a heresy to say that He proceeds from the Son as well. It may seem to many that the point at issue is so abstruse as to be unimportant. But Orthodox would say that since the doctrine of the Trinity stands at the heart of the Christian faith, a small change of emphasis in Trinitarian theology has far-reaching consequences in many other fields. Not only does the *filioque* destroy the balance between the three persons of the Holy Trinity: it leads also to a false understanding of the work of the Spirit in the world, and so encourages a false doctrine of the Church.[1]

Besides these two major issues, the Papacy and the *filioque*, there were certain lesser matters of Church worship and discipline which caused trouble between east and west: the Greeks allowed married clergy, the Latins insisted on priestly celibacy; the two sides had different rules of fasting; the Greeks used leavened bread in the Eucharist, the Latins unleavened bread or 'azymes'.

Around 850 east and west were still in full communion with one another and still formed one Church. Cultural and political divisions had combined to bring about an increasing estrangement, but there was no open schism. The two sides had different conceptions of Papal authority and recited the Creed in different forms, but these questions had not yet been brought fully into the open.

But in 1190 Theodore Balsamon, Patriarch of Antioch and a great authority on Canon Law, looked at matters very differently:

For many years [he does not say how many] the western Church has been divided in spiritual communion from the other four Patriarchates and has become alien to the Orthodox. . . . So no Latin should be given communion unless he first declares that he will abstain from the doctrines and customs that separate him from us, and that he will be subject to the Canons of the Church, in union with the Orthodox.[2]

In Balsamon's eyes, communion had been broken; there was a definite schism between east and west. The two no longer formed one visible Church.

In this transition from estrangement to schism, four incidents are of particular importance: the quarrel between

1. I have given here the standard Orthodox view of the *filioque*; it should be noted, however, that certain Orthodox theologians consider the *filioque* merely an unauthorized addition to the Creed, not necessarily heretical in itself.
2. Quoted in Runciman, *The Eastern Schism*, p. 139.

Photius and Pope Nicholas I (usually known as the 'Photian schism': the east would prefer to call it the schism of Nicholas); the incident of the Diptychs in 1009; the attempt at reconciliation in 1053–4 and its disastrous sequel; and the Crusades.

FROM ESTRANGEMENT TO SCHISM: 858–1204

In 858, fifteen years after the triumph of icons under Theodora, a new Patriarch of Constantinople was appointed – Photius, known to the Orthodox Church as Saint Photius the Great. He has been termed 'the most distinguished thinker, the most outstanding politician, and the most skilful diplomat ever to hold office as Patriarch of Constantinople'.[1] Soon after his accession he became involved in a dispute with Pope Nicholas I (858–67). The previous Patriarch, Saint Ignatius, had been exiled by the Emperor and while in exile had resigned under pressure. The supporters of Ignatius, declining to regard this resignation as valid, considered Photius a usurper. When Photius sent a letter to the Pope announcing his accession, Nicholas decided that before recognizing Photius he would look further into the quarrel between the new Patriarch and the Ignatian party. Accordingly in 861 he sent legates to Constantinople.

Photius had no desire to start a dispute with the Papacy. He treated the legates with great deference, inviting them to preside at a council in Constantinople, which was to settle the issue between Ignatius and himself. The legates agreed, and together with the rest of the council they decided that Photius was the legitimate Patriarch. But when his legates returned to Rome, Nicholas declared that they had exceeded their powers, and he disowned their decision. He then proceeded to retry the case himself at Rome: a council held under his presidency in 863 recognized Ignatius as Patriarch, and proclaimed Photius to be deposed from all priestly dignity. The Byzantines took no notice of this condemnation, and sent no answers to the Pope's letters. Thus an open breach existed between the Churches of Rome and Constantinople.

1. G. Ostrogorsky, *History of the Byzantine State*, p. 199.

The dispute clearly involved the Papal claims. Nicholas was a great reforming Pope, with an exalted idea of the prerogatives of his see, and he had already done much to establish an absolute power over all bishops in the west. But he believed this absolute power to extend to the east also: as he put it in a letter of 865, the Pope is endowed with authority 'over all the earth, that is, over *every* Church'. This was precisely what the Byzantines were not prepared to grant. Confronted with the dispute between Photius and Ignatius, Nicholas thought that he saw a golden opportunity to enforce his claim to universal jurisdiction: he would make both parties submit to his arbitration. But he realized that Photius had submitted *voluntarily* to the inquiry by the Papal legates, and that his action could not be taken as a recognition of Papal supremacy. This (among other reasons) was why Nicholas had cancelled his legates' decisions. The Byzantines for their part were willing to allow appeals to Rome, but only under the specific conditions laid down in Canon III of the Council of Sardica (343). This Canon states that a bishop, if under sentence of condemnation, can appeal to Rome, and the Pope, if he sees cause, can order a retrial; this retrial, however, is not to be conducted by the Pope himself at Rome, but by the bishops of the provinces adjacent to that of the condemned bishop. Nicholas, so the Byzantines felt, in reversing the decisions of his legates and demanding a retrial at Rome itself, was going far beyond the terms of this Canon. They regarded his behaviour as an unwarrantable and uncanonical interference in the affairs of another Patriarchate.

Soon not only the Papal claims but the *filioque* became involved in the dispute. Byzantium and the west (chiefly the Germans) were both launching great missionary offensives among the Slavs.[1] The two lines of missionary advance, from the east and from the west, soon converged; and when Greek and German missionaries found themselves at work in the same land, it was difficult to avoid a conflict, since the two missions were run on widely different principles. The clash naturally brought to

1. See pages 82–4.

the fore the question of the *filioque*, used by the Germans in the Creed, but not used by the Greeks. The chief point of trouble was Bulgaria, a country which Rome and Constantinople alike were anxious to add to their sphere of jurisdiction. The Khan Boris was at first inclined to ask the German missionaries for baptism: threatened, however, with a Byzantine invasion, he changed his policy and around 865 accepted baptism from Greek clergy. But Boris wanted the Church in Bulgaria to be independent, and when Constantinople refused to grant autonomy, he turned to the west in hope of better terms. Given a free hand in Bulgaria, the Latin missionaries promptly launched a violent attack on the Greeks, singling out the points where Byzantine practice differed from their own: married clergy, rules of fasting, and above all the *filioque*. At Rome itself the *filioque* was still not in use, but Nicholas gave full support to the Germans when they insisted upon its insertion in Bulgaria. The Papacy, which in 808 had mediated between the Germans and the Greeks, was now neutral no longer.

Photius was naturally alarmed by the extension of German influence in the Balkans, on the very borders of the Byzantine Empire; but he was much more alarmed by the question of the *filioque*, now brought forcibly to his attention. In 867 he took action. He wrote an Encyclical Letter to the other Patriarchs of the east, denouncing the *filioque* at length and charging those who used it with heresy. Photius has often been blamed for writing this letter: even the great Roman Catholic historian Francis Dvornik, who is in general highly sympathetic to Photius, calls his action on this occasion a 'futile attack', and says 'the lapse was inconsiderate, hasty, and big with fatal consequences'.[1] But if Photius really considered the *filioque* heretical, what else could he do except speak his mind? It must also be remembered that it was not Photius who first made the *filioque* a matter of controversy, but Charlemagne and his scholars seventy years before: the west was the original aggressor, not the east. Photius followed up his letter by summoning a council to Constantinople, which declared Pope Nicholas

1. F. Dvornik, *The Photian Schism*, p. 433.

excommunicate, terming him 'a heretic who ravages the vineyard of the Lord'.

At this critical point in the dispute, the whole situation suddenly changed. In this same year (867) Photius was deposed from the Patriarchate by the Emperor. Ignatius became Patriarch once more, and communion with Rome was restored. In 869–70 another Council was held at Constantinople, known as the 'Anti-Photian Council', which condemned and anathematized Photius, reversing the decisions of 867. This Council, later reckoned in the west as the eighth Ecumenical Council, opened with the unimpressive total of 12 bishops, although numbers at subsequent sessions rose to 103.

But there were further changes to come. The 869–70 Council requested the Emperor to resolve the status of the Bulgarian Church, and not surprisingly he decided that it should be assigned to the Patriarchate of Constantinople. Realizing that Rome would allow him less independence than Byzantium, Boris accepted this decision. From 870, then, the German missionaries were expelled and the *filioque* was heard no more in the confines of Bulgaria. Nor was this all. At Constantinople, Ignatius and Photius were reconciled to one another, and when Ignatius died in 877, Photius once more succeeded him as Patriarch. In 879 yet another council was held in Constantinople, attended by 383 bishops – a notable contrast with the meagre total at the anti-Photian gathering ten years previously. The Council of 869 was anathematized and all condemnations of Photius were withdrawn; these decisions were accepted without protest at Rome. So Photius ended victorious, recognized by Rome and ecclesiastically master of Bulgaria. Until recently it was thought that there was a second 'Photian schism', but Dr Dvornik has proved with devastating conclusiveness that this second schism is a myth: in Photius' later period of office (877–86) communion between Constantinople and the Papacy remained unbroken. The Pope at this time, John VIII (872–82), was no friend to the Germans and did not press the question of the *filioque*, nor did he attempt to enforce the Papal claims in the east. Perhaps he recognized how seriously the policy of Nicholas had endangered the unity of Christendom.

Thus the schism was outwardly healed, but no real solution had been reached concerning the two great points of difference which the dispute between Nicholas and Photius had forced into the open. Matters had been patched up, and that was all.

Photius, always honoured in the east as a saint, a leader of the Church, and a theologian, has in the past been regarded by the west with less enthusiasm, as the author of a schism and little else. His good qualities are now more widely appreciated. 'If I am right in my conclusions,' so Dr Dvornik ends his monumental study, 'we shall be free once more to recognize in Photius a great Churchman, a learned humanist, and a genuine Christian, generous enough to forgive his enemies, and to take the first step towards reconciliation.'[1] In the general historical reappraisal of the schism by recent writers, nowhere has the change been so startling as in the verdict on Saint Photius.

At the beginning of the eleventh century there was fresh trouble over the *filioque*. The Papacy at last adopted the addition: at the coronation of Emperor Henry II at Rome in 1014, the Creed was sung in its interpolated form. Five years earlier, in 1009, the newly-elected Pope Sergius IV sent a letter to Constantinople which may have contained the *filioque*, although this is not certain. Whatever the reason, the Patriarch of Constantinople, also called Sergius, did not include the new Pope's name in the Diptychs: these are lists, kept by each Patriarch, which contain the names of the other Patriarchs, living and departed, whom he recognizes as orthodox. The Diptychs are a visible sign of the unity of the Church, and deliberately to omit a man's name from them is tantamount to a declaration that one is not in communion with him. After 1009 the Pope's name did not appear again in the Diptychs of Constantinople; technically, therefore, the Churches of Rome and Constantinople were out of communion from that date.

1. *The Photian Schism*, p. 432.

But it would be unwise to press this technicality too far. Diptychs were frequently incomplete, and so do not form an infallible guide to Church relations. The Constantinopolitan lists before 1009 often lacked the Pope's name, simply because new Popes at their accession failed to notify the east. The omission in 1009 aroused no comment at Rome, and even at Constantinople men quickly forgot why and when the Pope's name had first been dropped from the Diptychs.

As the eleventh century proceeded, new factors brought relations between the Papacy and the eastern Patriarchates to a further crisis. The previous century had been a period of grave instability and confusion for the see of Rome, a century which Cardinal Baronius justly termed an age of iron and lead in the history of the Papacy. But Rome now reformed itself, and under the rule of men such as Hildebrand (Pope Gregory VII) it gained a position of power in the west such as it had never before achieved. The reformed Papacy naturally revived the claims to universal jurisdiction which Nicholas had made. The Byzantines on their side had grown accustomed to dealing with a Papacy that was for the most part weak and disorganized, and so they found it difficult to adapt themselves to the new situation. Matters were made worse by political factors, such as the military aggression of the Normans in Byzantine Italy, and the commercial aggression of the Italian maritime cities in the eastern Mediterranean during the eleventh and twelfth centuries.

In 1054 there was a severe quarrel. The Normans had been forcing the Greeks in Byzantine Italy to conform to Latin usages; the Patriarch of Constantinople, Michael Cerularius, in return demanded that the Latin churches at Constantinople should adopt Greek practices, and in 1052, when they refused, he closed them. This was perhaps harsh, but as Patriarch he was fully entitled to act in this manner. Among the practices to which Michael and his supporters particularly objected was the Latin use of 'azymes' or unleavened bread in the Eucharist, an issue which had not figured in the dispute of the ninth century. In 1053, however, Cerularius took up a more conciliatory attitude and wrote to Pope Leo IX, offering to restore the Pope's name to the Diptychs. In response to this offer, and to settle the disputed questions of Greek and Latin usages, Leo in 1054 sent three legates to Constantinople, the chief of them being Humbert, Bishop of Silva Candida. The choice of Cardinal Humbert was unfortunate, for both he and Cerularius were men of stiff and intransigent temper, whose mutual encounter was not likely to promote good will among Christians. The legates, when they called on Cerularius, did not create a favourable impression. Thrusting a letter from the Pope at him, they retired without giving the usual salutations; the letter itself, although signed by Leo, had in fact been drafted by Humbert, and was distinctly unfriendly in tone. After this the Patriarch refused to have further dealings with the legates. Eventually Humbert lost patience, and laid a Bull of Excommunication against Cerularius on the altar of the Church of the Holy Wisdom: among other ill-founded charges in this document, Humbert accused the Greeks of *omitting* the *filioque* from the Creed! Humbert promptly left Constantinople without offering any further explanation of his act, and on returning to Italy he represented the whole incident as a great victory for the see of Rome. Cerularius and his synod retaliated by anathematizing Humbert (but not the Roman Church as such). The attempt at reconciliation left matters worse than before.

But even after 1054 friendly relations between east and west continued. The two parts of Christendom were not yet conscious of a great gulf of separation between them, and men on both sides still hoped that the misunderstandings could be cleared up without too much difficulty. The dispute remained something of which ordinary Christians in east and west were largely unaware. It was the Crusades which made the schism definitive: they introduced a new spirit of hatred and bitterness, and they brought the whole issue down to the popular level.

From the military point of view, however, the Crusades began with great éclat. Antioch was captured from the Turks in 1098, Jerusalem in 1099: the first Crusade was a brilliant, if bloody,[1] success. Both at Antioch and Jerusalem the Crusaders proceeded to set up Latin Patriarchs. At Jerusalem this was reasonable, since the see was vacant at the time; and although in the years that followed there existed a succession of Greek Patriarchs of Jerusalem, living exiled in Cyprus, yet within Palestine itself the whole population, Greek as well as Latin, at first accepted the Latin Patriarch as their head. A Russian pilgrim at Jerusalem in 1106-7, Abbot Daniel of Tchernigov, found Greeks and Latins worshipping together in harmony at the Holy Places, though he noted with satisfaction that at the ceremony of the Holy Fire the Greek lamps were lit miraculously while the Latin had to be lit from the Greek. But at Antioch the Crusaders found a Greek Patriarch actually in residence: shortly afterwards, it is true, he withdrew to Constantinople, but the local Greek population was unwilling to recognize the Latin Patriarch whom the Crusaders set up in his place. Thus from 1100 there existed in effect a local schism at Antioch. After 1187, when Saladin captured Jerusalem, the situation in the Holy Land deteriorated: two rivals, resident within Palestine itself, now divided the Christian population between them – a Latin Patriarch at Acre, a Greek at Jerusalem. These local schisms at Antioch and Jerusalem were a sinister development. Rome was very far away, and if Rome and Constantinople quarrelled, what practical difference did it make to the average Christian in Syria or Palestine? But when two rival bishops claimed the same throne and two hostile congregations existed in the same city, the schism became an immediate reality in which simple believers were directly involved.

But worse was to follow in 1204, with the taking of Constantinople during the Fourth Crusade. The Crusaders were originally bound for Egypt, but were persuaded by Alexius, son of Isaac Angelus, the dispossessed Emperor of Byzantium, to

1. 'In the Temple and the porch of Solomon,' wrote Raymond of Argiles, 'men rode in blood up to their knees and bridle reins. . . . The city was filled with corpses and blood.' (Quoted in A. C. Krey, *The First Crusade*, Princeton, 1921, p. 261.)

turn aside to Constantinople in order to restore him and his father to the throne. This western intervention in Byzantine politics did not go happily, and eventually the Crusaders, disgusted by what they regarded as Greek duplicity, lost patience and sacked the city. Eastern Christendom has never forgotten those three appalling days of pillage. 'Even the Saracens are merciful and kind,' protested Nicetas Choniates, 'compared with these men who bear the Cross of Christ on their shoulders.' What shocked the Greeks more than anything was the wanton and systematic sacrilege of the Crusaders. How could men who had specially dedicated themselves to God's service treat the things of God in such a way? As the Byzantines watched the Crusaders tear to pieces the altar and icon screen in the Church of the Holy Wisdom, and set prostitutes on the Patriarch's throne, they must have felt that those who did such things were not Christians in the same sense as themselves.

Constantinopolitana
civitas diu profana

'City of Constantinople, so long ungodly': so sang the French Crusaders of Angers, as they carried home the relics which they had stolen. Can we wonder if the Greeks after 1204 also looked on the Latins as *profani*? Christians in the west still do not realize how deep is the disgust and how lasting the horror with which Orthodox regard actions such as the sack of Constantinople by the Crusaders.

'The Crusaders brought not peace but a sword; and the sword was to sever Christendom.'[1] The long-standing doctrinal disagreements were now reinforced on the Greek side by an intense national hatred, by a feeling of resentment and indignation against western aggression and sacrilege. After 1204 there can be no doubt that Christian east and Christian west were divided into two.

In recounting the history of the schism recent writers have rightly emphasized the importance of 'non-theological factors'.

1. S. Runciman, *The Eastern Schism*, p. 101.

But vital dogmatic issues were also involved. When full allowance has been made for all the cultural and political difficulties, it still remains true that in the end it was differences of doctrine – the *filioque* and the Papal claims – which brought about the separation between Rome and the Orthodox Church, just as it is differences of doctrine which still prevent their reconciliation. The schism was for both parties 'a spiritual commitment, a conscious taking of sides in a matter of faith'.[1]

Orthodoxy and Rome each believes itself to have been right and its opponent wrong upon these points of doctrine; and so Rome and Orthodoxy since the schism have each claimed to be the true Church. Yet each, while believing in the rightness of its own cause, must look back at the past with sorrow and repentance. Both sides must in honesty acknowledge that they could and should have done more to prevent the schism. Both sides were guilty of mistakes on the human level. Orthodox, for example, must blame themselves for the pride and contempt with which during the Byzantine period they regarded the west; they must blame themselves for incidents such as the riot of 1182, when many Latin residents at Constantinople were massacred by the Byzantine populace. (None the less there is no action on the Byzantine side which can be compared to the sack of 1204.) And each side, while claiming to be the one true Church, must admit that on the human level it has been grievously impoverished by the separation. The Greek east and the Latin west needed and still need one another. For both parties the great schism has proved a great tragedy.

TWO ATTEMPTS AT REUNION; THE HESYCHAST CONTROVERSY

In 1204 the Crusaders set up a shortlived Latin kingdom at Constantinople, which came to an end in 1261 when the Greeks recovered their capital. Byzantium survived for two centuries

1. V. Lossky, *The Mystical Theology of the Eastern Church*, p. 13.

more, and these years proved a time of great cultural, artistic, and religious revival. But politically and economically the restored Byzantine Empire was in a precarious state, and found itself more and more helpless in the face of the Turkish armies which pressed upon it from the east.

Two important attempts were made to secure reunion between the Christian east and west, the first in the thirteenth and the second in the fifteenth century. The moving spirit behind the first attempt was Michael VIII (reigned 1259-82), the Emperor who recovered Constantinople. While doubtless sincerely desiring Christian unity on religious grounds, his motive was also political: threatened by attacks from Charles of Anjou, sovereign of Sicily, he desperately needed the support and protection of the Papacy, which could best be secured through a union of the Churches. A reunion Council was held at Lyons in 1274. The Orthodox delegates who attended agreed to recognize the Papal claims and to recite the Creed with the *filioque*. But the union proved no more than an agreement on paper, since it was fiercely rejected by the overwhelming majority of clergy and laity in the Byzantine Church, as well as by Bulgarian and the other Orthodox countries. The general reaction to the Council of Lyons was summed up in words attributed to the Emperor's sister: 'Better that my brother's Empire should perish, than the purity of the Orthodox faith.' The union of Lyons was formally repudiated by Michael's successor, and Michael himself, for his 'apostasy', was deprived of Christian burial.

Meanwhile east and west continued to grow further apart in their theology and in their whole manner of understanding the Christian life. Byzantium continued to live in a Patristic atmosphere, using the ideas and language of the Greek Fathers of the fourth century. But in western Europe the tradition of the Fathers was replaced by Scholasticism – that great synthesis of philosophy and theology worked out in the twelfth and thirteenth centuries. Western theologians now came to employ new categories of thought, a new theological method, and a new terminology which the east did not understand. To an ever-increasing extent the two sides were losing a common 'universe of discourse'.

Byzantium on its side also contributed to this process: here too there were theological developments in which the west had neither part nor share, although there was nothing so radical as the Scholastic revolution. These theological developments were connected chiefly with the *Hesychast Controversy*, a dispute which arose at Byzantium in the middle of the fourteenth century, and which involved the doctrine of God's nature and the methods of prayer used in the Orthodox Church.

To understand the Hesychast Controversy, we must turn back for the moment to the earlier history of eastern mystical theology. The main features of this mystical theology were worked out by Clement (died 215) and by Origen of Alexandria (died 253–4), whose ideas were developed in the fourth century by the Cappadocians, especially Gregory of Nyssa, and by their disciple Evagrius of Pontus (died 399), a monk in the Egyptian desert. There are two trends in this mystical theology, not exactly opposed, but certainly at first sight inconsistent: the 'way of negation' and the 'way of union'. The way of negation – *apophatic theology*, as it is often called – speaks of God in negative terms. God cannot be properly apprehended by man's mind; human language, when applied to Him, is always inexact. It is therefore less misleading to use negative language about God rather than positive – to refuse to say what God is, and to state simply what He is not. As Gregory of Nyssa put it: 'The true knowledge and vision of God consist in this – in seeing that He is invisible, because what we seek lies beyond all knowledge, being wholly separated by the darkness of incomprehensibility.'[1]

Negative theology reaches its classic expression in the so-called 'Dionysian' writings. For many centuries these books were thought to be the work of Saint Dionysius the Areopagite, Paul's convert at Athens (Acts xvii, 34); but they are in fact by an unknown author, who probably lived towards the end of

1. *The Life of Moses*, II, 163 (377A).

the fifth century and belonged to circles sympathetic to the Monophysites. Saint Maximus the Confessor (died 662) composed commentaries on the Dionysian writings, and so ensured for them a permanent place in Orthodox theology. Dionysius has also had a great influence on the west: it has been reckoned that he is quoted 1,760 times by Thomas Aquinas in the *Summa*, while a fourteenth-century English chronicler records that the *Mystical Theology* of Dionysius 'ran through England like the wild deer'. The apophatic language of Dionysius was repeated by many others. 'God is infinite and incomprehensible,' wrote John of Damascus, 'and all that is comprehensible about Him is His infinity and incomprehensibility. . . . God does not belong to the class of existing things: not that He has no existence, but that He is above all existing things, nay even above existence itself.'[1]

This emphasis on God's transcendence would seem at first sight to exclude any direct experience of God. But in fact many of those who made greatest use of negative theology – Gregory of Nyssa, for example, or Dionysius, or Maximus – also believed in the possibility of a true mystical union with God; they combined the 'way of negation' with the 'way of union', with the tradition of the mystics or *hesychasts*. (The name hesychast is derived from the Greek word *hesychia*, meaning 'quiet'. A hesychast is one who in silence devotes himself to inner recollection and secret prayer.) While using the apophatic language of negative theology, these writers claimed an immediate experience of the unknowable God, a personal union with Him who is unapproachable. How were the two 'ways' to be reconciled? How can God be both knowable and unknowable at once?

This was one of the questions which was posed in an acute form in the fourteenth century. Connected with it was another, the question of the body and its place in prayer. Evagrius, like Origen, sometimes borrowed too heavily from Platonism: he wrote of prayer in intellectual terms, as an activity of the mind rather than of the whole man, and he seemed to allow no

1. *On the Orthodox Faith* I, 4 (*P.G.* xciv, 800B).

positive role to man's body in the process of redemption and deification. But the balance between mind and body is redressed in another ascetic writing, the Macarian Homilies. (These were traditionally attributed to Saint Macarius of Egypt (?300–90), but it is now thought that they were written in Syria during the late fourth or the beginning of the fifth century.) The Macarian Homilies revert to a more Biblical idea of man – not a soul imprisoned in a body (as in Greek thought), but a single and united whole, soul and body together. Where Evagrius speaks of the *mind*, Macarius uses the Hebraic idea of the *heart*. The change of emphasis is significant, for the heart includes the *whole* man – not only intellect, but will, emotions, and even body.

Using 'heart' in this Macarian sense, Orthodox often talk about 'Prayer of the Heart'. What does the phrase mean? When a man begins to pray, at first he prays with the lips, and has to make a conscious intellectual effort in order to realize the the meaning of what he says. But if he perseveres, praying continually with recollection, his intellect and his heart become united: he 'finds the place of the heart', his spirit acquires the power of 'dwelling in the heart', and so his prayer becomes 'prayer of the heart'. It becomes something not merely said by the lips, not merely thought by the intellect, but offered spontaneously by the whole being of man – lips, intellect, emotions, will, and body. The prayer fills the entire consciousness, and no longer has to be forced out, but says itself. This Prayer of the Heart cannot be attained simply through our own efforts, but is a gift conferred by the grace of God.

When Orthodox writers use the term 'Prayer of the Heart', they usually have in mind one particular prayer, the Jesus Prayer. Among Greek spiritual writers, first Diadochus of Photice (mid fifth century) and later Saint John Climacus of Mount Sinai (?579–?649) recommended, as a specially valuable form of prayer, the constant repetition or remembrance of the name 'Jesus'. In course of time the Invocation of the Name became crystallized into a short sentence, known as the Jesus

Prayer: *Lord Jesus Christ, Son of God, have mercy on me.*[1] By the thirteenth century (if not before), the recitation of the Jesus Prayer had become linked to certain physical exercises, designed to assist concentration. Breathing was carefully regulated in time with the Prayer, and a particular bodily posture was recommended: head bowed, chin resting on the chest, eyes fixed on the place of the heart.[2] This is often called 'the Hesychast method of prayer', but it should not be thought that for the Hesychasts these exercises constituted the essence of prayer. They were regarded, not as an end in themselves, but as a help to concentration – as an accessory useful to some, but not obligatory upon all. The Hesychasts knew that there can be no mechanical means of acquiring God's grace, and no techniques leading automatically to the mystical state.

For the Hesychasts of Byzantium, the culmination of mystical experience was the vision of Divine and Uncreated Light. The works of Saint Symeon the New Theologian (949–1022), the greatest of the Byzantine mystics, are full of this 'Light mysticism'. When he writes of his own experiences, he speaks again and again of the Divine Light: 'fire truly divine,' he calls it, 'fire uncreated and invisible, without beginning and immaterial'. The Hesychasts believed that this light which they experienced was identical with the Uncreated Light which the three disciples saw surrounding Jesus at His Transfiguration on Mount Thabor. But how was this vision of Divine Light to be reconciled with the apophatic doctrine of God the transcendent and unapproachable?

All these questions concerning the transcendence of God, the role of the body in prayer, and the Divine Light came to a head in the middle of the fourteenth century. The Hesychasts were violently attacked by a learned Greek from Italy, Barlaam the Calabrian, who stated the doctrine of God's 'otherness'

1. In modern Orthodox practice the Prayer sometimes ends, '…have mercy on me *a sinner*'. (Compare the Publican's Prayer, Luke xviii, 13.)
2. There are interesting parallels between the Hesychast 'method' and Hindu *Yoga* or Mohammedan *Dhikr*; but the points of similarity must not be pressed too far.

and unknowability in an extreme form. It is sometimes suggested that Barlaam was influenced here by the Nominalist philosophy that was current in the west at this date; but more probably he derived his teaching from Greek sources. Starting from a one-sided exegesis of Dionysius, he argued that God can only be known *indirectly*; Hesychasm (so he maintained) was wrong to speak of an immediate experience of God, for any such experience is impossible. Seizing on the bodily exercises which the Hesychasts employed, Barlaam accused them of holding a grossly materialistic conception of prayer. He was also scandalized by their claim to attain a vision of the Divine and Uncreated Light: here again he charged them with falling into a gross materialism. How can a man see God's essence with his bodily eyes? The light which the Hesychasts beheld, in his view, was not the eternal light of the Divinity, but a temporary and created light.

The defence of the Hesychasts was taken up by Saint Gregory Palamas (1296–1359), Archbishop of Thessalonica. He upheld a doctrine of man which allowed for the use of bodily exercises in prayer, and he argued, against Barlaam, that the Hesychasts did indeed experience the Divine and Uncreated Light of Thabor. To explain how this was possible, Gregory developed the distinction between the essence and the energies of God. It was Gregory's achievement to set Hesychasm on a firm dogmatic basis, by integrating it into Orthodox theology as a whole, and by showing how the Hesychast vision of Divine Light in no way undermined the apophatic doctrine of God. His teaching was confirmed by two councils held at Constantinople in 1341 and 1351, which, although local and not Ecumenical, yet possess a doctrinal authority in Orthodox theology scarcely inferior to the Seven General Councils themselves. But western Christendom has never officially recognized these two councils, although many western Christians personally accept the theology of Palamas.

Gregory began by reaffirming the Biblical doctrine of man and of the Incarnation. Man is a single, united whole: not only man's mind but the *whole* man was created in the image of God.[1] Man's body is not an enemy, but partner and collaborator with his soul. Christ, by taking a human body at the Incarnation, has 'made the *flesh* an inexhaustible source of sanctification'.[2] Here Gregory took up and developed the ideas implicit in earlier writings, such as the Macarian Homilies; the same emphasis on man's body, as we have seen, lies behind the Orthodox doctrine of icons. Gregory went on to apply this doctrine of man to the Hesychast methods of prayer: the Hesychasts, so he argued, in placing such emphasis on the part of the body in prayer, are not guilty of a gross materialism but are simply remaining faithful to the Biblical doctrine of man as a unity. Christ took human flesh and saved the whole man; therefore it is the *whole* man – body and soul together – that prays to God.

From this Gregory turned to the main problem: how to combine the two affirmations, that man knows God and that God is by nature unknowable. Gregory answered: we know the *energies* of God, but not His *essence*. This distinction between God's essence (*ousia*) and His energies goes back to the Cappadocian Fathers. 'We know our God from His energies,' wrote Saint Basil, 'but we do not claim that we can draw near to His essence. For His energies come down to us, but His essence remains unapproachable.'[3] Gregory accepted this distinction. He affirmed, as emphatically as any exponent of negative theology, that God is in essence absolutely unknowable. 'God is not a nature,' he wrote, 'for He is above all nature; He is not a being, for He is above all beings. ... No single thing of all that is created has or ever will have even the slightest communion with the supreme nature, or nearness to it.'[4] But however remote from us in His essence, yet in His energies God has revealed Himself to men. These energies are not something that exists apart from God, not a gift which God confers upon men: they are God Himself in His action and revelation to the world. God exists complete and entire in each of His divine energies. The world, as Gerard Manley

1. *P.G.* cl, 1361C.   2. *Homily* 16 (*P.G.* cli, 193B).
3. *Letter* 234, 1.   4. *P.G.* cl, 1176C.

Hopkins said, is charged with the grandeur of God; all creation is a gigantic Burning Bush, permeated but not consumed by the ineffable and wondrous fire of God's energies.[1]

It is through these energies that God enters into a direct and immediate relationship with mankind. In relation to man, the divine energy is in fact nothing else than the *grace of God*; grace is not just a 'gift' of God, not just an object which God bestows on men, but a direct manifestation of the living God Himself, a personal confrontation between creature and Creator. 'Grace signifies all the abundance of the divine nature, in so far as it is communicated to men.'[2] When we say that the saints have been transformed or 'deified' by the grace of God, what we mean is that they have a direct experience of God Himself. They *know* God – that is to say, God in His energies, not in His essence.

God is Light, and therefore the experience of God's energies takes the form of Light. The vision which the Hesychasts receive is (so Palamas argued) not a vision of some created light, but of the Light of the Godhead Itself – the same Light of the Godhead which surrounded Christ on Mount Thabor. This Light is not a sensible or material light, but it can be seen with physical eyes (as by the disciples at the Transfiguration), since when a man is deified, his bodily faculties as well as his soul are transformed. The Hesychasts' vision of Light is therefore a true vision of God in His divine energies; and they are quite correct in identifying it with the Uncreated Light of Thabor.

Palamas, therefore, preserved God's transcendence and avoided the pantheism to which an unguarded mysticism easily leads; yet he allowed for God's immanence, for His continual presence in the world. God remains 'the Wholly Other', and yet through His energies (which are God Himself) He enters into an immediate relationship with the world. God is a living God, the God of history, the God of the Bible, who became Incarnate in Christ. Barlaam, in excluding all direct knowledge of God and in asserting that the Divine Light is something

1. Compare Maximus, *Ambigua*, P.G. xci, 1148D.
2. V. Lossky, *The Mystical Theology of the Eastern Church*, p. 162.

created, set too wide a gulf between God and man. Gregory's fundamental concern in opposing Barlaam was therefore the same as that of Athanasius and the General Councils: to safeguard man's direct approach to God, to uphold man's full deification and entire redemption. That same doctrine of salvation which underlay the disputes about the Trinity, the Person of Christ, and the Holy Icons, lies also at the heart of the Hesychast controversy.

'Into the closed world of Byzantium,' wrote Dom Gregory Dix, 'no really fresh impulse ever came after the sixth century ... Sleep began ... in the ninth century, perhaps even earlier, in the sixth.'[1] The Byzantine controversies of the fourteenth century amply demonstrate the falsity of such an assertion. Certainly Gregory Palamas was no revolutionary innovator, but firmly rooted in the tradition of the past; yet he was a creative theologian of the first rank, and his work shows that Orthodox theology did not cease to be active after the eighth century and the seventh Ecumenical Council.

Among the contemporaries of Gregory Palamas was the lay theologian Nicholas Cabasilas, who was sympathetic to the Hesychasts, although not closely involved in the controversy. Cabasilas is the author of a *Commentary on the Divine Liturgy*, which has become the classic Orthodox work on this subject; he also wrote a treatise on the sacraments entitled *The Life in Jesus Christ*. The writings of Cabasilas are marked by two things in particular: a vivid sense of the person of Christ 'the Saviour', who, as he puts it, 'is closer to us than our own soul';[2] and a constant emphasis upon the sacraments. For him the mystical life is essentially a life in Christ and a life in the sacraments. There is a danger that mysticism may become speculative and individualist – divorced from the historical revelation in Christ and from the corporate life of the Church with its sacraments; but the mysticism of Cabasilas is always Christocentric, sacramental, ecclesial. His work shows how closely mysticism and the sacramental life were linked together

1. *The Shape of the Liturgy*, London, 1945, p. 548.
2. *P.G.* cl, 712A.

in Byzantine theology. Palamas and his circle did not regard mystical prayer as a means of bypassing the normal institutional life of the Church.

A second reunion Council was held at Florence in 1438-9. The Emperor John VIII (reigned 1425-48) attended in person, together with the Patriarch of Constantinople and a large delegation from the Byzantine Church, as well as representatives from the other Orthodox Churches. There were prolonged discussions, and a genuine attempt was made by both sides to reach a true agreement on the great points of dispute. At the same time it was difficult for the Greeks to discuss theology dispassionately, for they knew that the political situation had now become desperate: the only hope of defeating the Turks lay in help from the west. Eventually a formula of union was drawn up, covering the *filioque*, Purgatory, azymes, and the Papal claims; and this was signed by all the Orthodox present at the Council except one – Mark, Archbishop of Ephesus, later canonized by the Orthodox Church. The Florentine Union was based on a twofold principle: unanimity in matters of doctrine; respect for the legitimate rites and traditions peculiar to each Church. Thus in matters of doctrine, the Orthodox accepted the Papal claims (although here the wording of the formula of union was vague and ambiguous); they accepted the *filioque*; they accepted the Roman teaching on Purgatory (as a point of dispute between east and west, this only came into the open in the thirteenth century). But so far as 'azymes' were concerned, no uniformity was demanded: Greeks were allowed to use leavened bread, while Latins were to continue to employ unleavened.

But the Union of Florence, though celebrated throughout western Europe – bells were rung in all the parish churches of England – proved no more of a reality in the east than its predecessor at Lyons. John VIII and his successor Constantine XI, the last Emperor of Byzantium and the eightieth in succession since Constantine the Great, both remained loyal to the union; but they were powerless to enforce it on their subjects, and did not even dare to proclaim it publicly at Constantinople until 1452. Many of those who signed at Florence revoked their signatures when they reached home. The decrees of the Council were never accepted by more than a minute fraction of the Byzantine clergy and people. The Grand Duke Lucas Notaras, echoing the words of the Emperor's sister after Lyons, remarked: 'I would rather see the Moslem turban in the midst of the city than the Latin mitre.'

John and Constantine had hoped that the Union of Florence would secure them military help from the west, but small indeed was the help which they actually received. On 7 April 1453 the Turks began to attack Constantinople by land and sea. Outnumbered by more than twenty to one, the Byzantines maintained a brilliant but hopeless defence for seven long weeks. In the early hours of 29 May the last Christian service was held in the great Church of the Holy Wisdom. It was a united service of Orthodox and Roman Catholics, for at this moment of crisis the supporters and opponents of the Florentine Union forgot their differences. The Emperor went out after receiving communion, and died fighting on the walls. Later the same day the city fell to the Turks, and the most glorious church in Christendom became a mosque.

It was the end of the Byzantine Empire. But it was not the end of the Patriarchate of Constantinople, far less the end of Orthodoxy.

CHAPTER 4

The Conversion of the Slavs

The religion of grace spread over the earth and
finally reached the Russian people. . . . The gracious
God who cared for all other countries now no longer
neglects us. It is his desire to save us and lead us
to reason.

Hilarion, Metropolitan of Russia (1051–?1054)

CYRIL AND METHODIUS

FOR Constantinople the middle of the ninth century was a
period of intensive missionary activity. The Byzantine Church,
freed at last from the long struggle against the Iconoclasts,
turned its energies to the conversion of the pagan Slavs who lay
beyond the frontiers of the Empire, to the north and the north-
west – Moravians, Bulgarians, Serbs, and Russians. Photius
was the first Patriarch of Constantinople to initiate missionary
work on a large scale among these Slavs. He selected for the
task two brothers, Greeks from Thessalonica, Constantine
(826–69) and Methodius (?815–85). In the Orthodox Church
Constantine is usually called by the name Cyril which he took
on becoming a monk. Known in earlier life as 'Constantine
the Philosopher', he was the ablest among the pupils of
Photius, and was familiar with a wide range of languages, including Hebrew, Arabic, and even the Samaritan dialect. But
the special qualification which he and his brother enjoyed was
their knowledge of Slavonic: in childhood they had learnt the
dialect of the Slavs around Thessalonica, and they could speak
it fluently.

The first missionary journey of Cyril and Methodius was a
short visit around 860 to the Khazars, who lived north of the
Caucasus region. This expedition had no permanent results,
and some years later the Khazars adopted Judaism. The

brothers' real work began in 863 when they set out for Moravia (roughly equivalent to the modern Czechoslovakia). They went in answer to an appeal from the Prince of the land, Rostislav, who asked that Christian missionaries be sent, capable of preaching to the people in their own tongue and of taking services in Slavonic. Slavonic services required a Slavonic Bible and Slavonic service books. Before they set out for Moravia the brothers had already set to work on this enormous task of translation. They had first to invent a suitable Slavonic alphabet. In their translation the brothers used the form of Slavonic familiar to them from childhood, the Macedonian dialect spoken by the Slavs around Thessalonica. In this way the dialect of the Macedonian Slavs became *Church Slavonic*, which remains to the present day the liturgical language of the Russian and certain other Slavonic Orthodox Churches.

One cannot overestimate the significance, for the future of Orthodoxy, of the Slavonic translations which Cyril and Methodius carried with them as they left Byzantium for the unknown north. Few events have been so important in the missionary history of the Church. From the start the Slav Christians enjoyed a precious privilege, such as none of the peoples of western Europe shared at this time: they heard the Gospel and the services of the Church in a tongue which they could understand. Unlike the Church of Rome in the west with its insistence on Latin, the Orthodox Church has never been rigid in the matter of languages; its normal policy is to hold services in the language of the people.

In Moravia, as in Bulgaria, the Greek mission soon clashed with German missionaries at work in the same area. The two missions not only depended on different Patriarchates, but worked on different principles. Cyril and Methodius used Slavonic in their services, the Germans Latin; Cyril and Methodius recited the Creed in its original form, the Germans inserted the *filioque*. To free his mission from German interference, Cyril decided to place it under the immediate protection of the Pope. Cyril's action in appealing to Rome shows that he did not take the quarrel between Photius and Nicholas too seriously; for him east and west were still united as one Church, and it was not a matter of primary importance whether he depended on Constantinople or Rome, so long as he could continue to use Slavonic in Church services. The brothers travelled to Rome in person in 868 and were entirely successful in the appeal. Hadrian II, Nicholas I's successor at Rome, received them favourably and gave full support to the Greek mission, confirming the use of Slavonic as the liturgical language of Moravia. He approved the brothers' translations, and laid copies of their Slavonic service books on the altars of the principal churches in the city.

Cyril died at Rome (869), but Methodius returned to Moravia. Sad to say, the Germans ignored the Pope's decision and obstructed Methodius in every possible way, even putting him in prison for more than a year. When Methodius died in 885, the Germans expelled his followers from the country, selling a number of them into slavery. Traces of the Slavonic mission lingered on in Moravia for two centuries more, but were eventually eradicated; and Christianity in its western form, with Latin culture and the Latin language (and of course the *filioque*), became universal. The attempt to found a Slavonic national Church in Moravia came to nothing. The work of Cyril and Methodius, so it seemed, had ended in failure.

Yet in fact this was not so. Other countries, where the brothers had not themselves preached, benefited from their work, most notably Bulgaria, Serbia, and Russia. Boris, Khan of Bulgaria, as we have seen, wavered for a time between east and west, but finally accepted the jurisdiction of Constantinople. The Byzantine missionaries in Bulgaria, however, lacking the vision of Cyril and Methodius, at first used Greek in Church services, a language as unintelligible as Latin to the ordinary Bulgar. But after their expulsion from Moravia, the disciples of Methodius turned naturally to Bulgaria, and here introduced the principles employed in the Moravian mission. Greek was replaced by Slavonic, and the Christian culture of Byzantium was presented to the Bulgars in a Slavonic form which they could assimilate. The Bulgarian Church grew rapidly. Around 926, during the reign of Tsar Symeon the Great (reigned 893–927), an independent Bulgarian Patriarchate was created, and this was recognized by the Patriarchate of Constantinople in 927. The dream of Boris – an autocephalous Church of his own – became a reality within half a century of his death. Bulgaria was the first national Church of the Slavs.

Byzantine missionaries went likewise to Serbia, which accepted Christianity in the second half of the ninth century, around 867–74. Serbia also lay on the dividing line between eastern and western Christendom, but after a period of uncertainty it followed the example of Bulgaria, not of Moravia, and came under Constantinople. Here too the Slavonic service books were introduced and a Slavonic–Byzantine culture grew up. The Serbian Church gained a partial independence under Saint Sava (1176–1235), the greatest of Serbian national saints, who in 1219 was consecrated at Nicaea as Archbishop of Serbia. In 1346 a Serbian Patriarchate was created, which was recognized by the Church of Constantinople in 1375.

The conversion of Russia was also due indirectly to the work of Cyril and Methodius; but of this we shall speak further in the next section. With Bulgars, Serbs, and Russians as their 'spiritual children', the two Greeks from Thessalonica abundantly deserve their title, 'Apostles of the Slavs'.

Another Orthodox nation in the Balkans, Romania, has a more complex history. The Romanians, though influenced by their Slav neighbours, are primarily Latin in language and ethnic character. Dacia, corresponding to part of modern Romania, was a Roman province during 106–271; but the Christian communities founded there in this period seem to have disappeared after the Romans withdrew. Part of the Romanian people was apparently converted to Christianity by the Bulgarians in the late ninth or early tenth century, but the full conversion of the two Romanian principalities of Wallachia and Moldavia did not occur until the fourteenth century. Those who think of Orthodoxy as being exclusively 'eastern', as Greek and Slav in character, should not overlook the fact that the Church of Romania, the second largest Orthodox Church today, is predominantly Latin.

Byzantium conferred two gifts upon the Slavs: a fully articulated system of Christian doctrine and a fully developed Christian civilization. When the conversion of the Slavs began in the ninth century, the great period of doctrinal controversies, the age of the Seven Councils, was at an end; the main outlines of the faith – the doctrines of the Trinity and the Incarnation – had already been worked out, and were delivered to the Slavs in their definitive form. Perhaps this is why the Slavonic Churches have produced few original theologians, while the religious disputes which have arisen in Slavonic lands have usually not been dogmatic in character. But this faith in the Trinity and the Incarnation did not exist in a vacuum; with it went a whole Christian culture and civilization, and this too the Greek missionaries brought with them from Byzantium. The Slavs were Christianized and civilized at the same time.

The Greeks communicated this faith and civilization not in an alien but in a Slavonic garb (here the translations of Cyril and Methodius were of capital importance); what the Slavs borrowed from Byzantium they were able to make their own. Byzantine culture and the Orthodox faith, if at first limited mainly to the ruling classes, became in time an integral part of the daily life of the Slavonic peoples as a whole. The link between Church and people was made even firmer by the system of creating independent national Churches.

Certainly this close identification of Orthodoxy with the life of the people, and in particular the system of national Churches, have had unfortunate consequences. Because Church and nation were so closely associated, the Orthodox Slavs have often confused the two and have made the Church serve the ends of national politics; they have sometimes tended to think of their faith as primarily Serb, Russian, or Bulgar, and to forget that it is primarily Orthodox and Catholic. Nationalism has been the bane of Orthodoxy for the last ten centuries. Yet the integration of Church and people has in the end proved immensely beneficial. Christianity among the Slavs became in very truth the religion of the *whole* people, a *popular* religion in the best sense. In 1949 the Communists of Bulgaria published a law stating: 'The Bulgarian Orthodox Church is in form, substance, and spirit a People's Democratic Church.' Strip the words of their political associations, and behind them there lies an important truth.

THE BAPTISM OF RUSSIA: THE KIEV PERIOD (988–1237)

Photius also made plans to convert the Slavs of Russia. Around 864 he sent a bishop to Russia, but this first Christian foundation was exterminated by Oleg, who assumed power at Kiev (the chief Russian city at this time) in 878. Russia, however, continued to undergo a steady Christian infiltration from Byzantium, Bulgaria, and Scandinavia, and there was certainly a church at Kiev in 945. The Russian Princess Olga became Christian in 955, but her son Svyatoslav refused to follow her example, saying that his retinue would laugh at him if he received Christian baptism. But around 988 Olga's grandson Vladimir (reigned 980–1015) was converted to Christianity and married Anna, the sister of the Byzantine Emperor. Orthodoxy became the State religion of Russia, and such it remained until 1917. Vladimir set to in earnest to Christianize his realm: priests, relics, sacred vessels, and icons were imported; mass baptisms were held in the rivers; Church courts were set up, and ecclesiastical tithes instituted. The great idol of the god Perun, with its silver head and gold moustaches, was rolled ignominiously down from the hill-top above Kiev. 'Angel's trumpet and Gospel's thunder sounded through all the towns. The air was sanctified by the incense that ascended towards God. Monasteries stood on the mountains. Men and women, small and great, all people filled the holy churches.'[1] So the Metropolitan Hilarion described the event sixty years afterwards, doubtless idealizing a little; for Kievan Russia was not at

1. Quoted in G. P. Fedotov, *The Russian Religious Mind*, p. 410.

once completely converted to Christianity, and the Church was at first restricted mainly to the cities, while much of the countryside remained pagan until the fourteenth and fifteenth centuries.

Vladimir placed the same emphasis upon the social implications of Christianity as John the Almsgiver had done. Whenever he feasted with his Court, he distributed food to the poor and sick; nowhere else in medieval Europe were there such highly organized 'social services' as in tenth-century Kiev. Other rulers in Kievan Russia followed Vladimir's example. Prince Vladimir Monomachos (reigned 1113-25) wrote in his *Testament* to his sons: 'Above all things forget not the poor, and support them to the extent of your means. Give to the orphan, protect the widow, and permit the mighty to destroy no man.'[1] Vladimir was also deeply conscious of the Christian law of mercy, and when he introduced the Byzantine law code at Kiev, he insisted on mitigating its more savage and brutal features. There was no death penalty in Kievan Russia, no mutilation, no torture; corporal punishment was very little used.[2]

The same gentleness can be seen in the story of Vladimir's two sons, Boris and Gleb. On Vladimir's death in 1015, their elder brother Svyatopolk attempted to seize their principalities. Taking literally the commands of the Gospel, they offered no resistance, although they could easily have done so; and each in turn was murdered by Svyatopolk's emissaries. If any blood were to be shed, Boris and Gleb preferred that it should be their own. Although they were not martyrs for the faith, but victims in a political quarrel, they were both canonized, being given the special title of 'Passion Bearers': it was felt that by their innocent and voluntary suffering they had shared in the Passion of Christ. Russians have always laid great emphasis on the place of suffering in the Christian life.

In Kievan Russia, as in Byzantium and the medieval west,

1. Quoted in G. Vernadsky, *Kievan Russia*, New Haven, 1948, p. 195.
2. In Byzantium the death penalty existed, but was hardly ever applied; the punishment of mutilation, however, was employed with distressing frequency.

monasteries played an important part. The most influential of them all was the *Petchersky Lavra*, the Monastery of the Caves at Kiev. Founded around 1051 by Saint Antony, a Russian who had lived on Mount Athos, it was reorganized by his successor Saint Theodosius (died 1074), who introduced there the rule of the monastery of the Studium at Constantinople. Like Vladimir, Theodosius was conscious of the social consequences of Christianity, and applied them in a radical fashion, identifying himself closely with the poor, much as Saint Francis of Assisi did in the west. Boris and Gleb followed Christ in his sacrificial death; Theodosius followed Christ in his life of poverty and voluntary 'self-emptying'. Of noble birth, he chose in childhood to wear coarse and patched garments and to work in the fields with the slaves. 'Our Lord Jesus Christ,' he said, 'became poor and humbled Himself, offering Himself as an example, so that we should humble ourselves in His name. He suffered insults, was spat upon, and beaten, for our salvation; how just it is, then, that we should suffer in order to gain Christ.'[1] Even when Abbot he wore the meanest kind of clothing and rejected all outward signs of authority. Yet at the same time he was the honoured friend and adviser of nobles and princes. The same ideal of humility is seen in others, for example Bishop Luke of Vladimir (died 1185) who, in the words of the *Vladimir Chronicle*, 'bore upon himself the humiliation of Christ, not having a city here but seeking a future one'. It is an ideal found often in Russian folklore, and in writers such as Tolstoy and Dostoyevsky.

Vladimir, Boris and Gleb, and Theodosius were all intensely concerned with the practical implications of the Gospel: Vladimir in his concern for social justice and his desire to treat criminals with mercy; Boris and Gleb in their resolution to follow Christ in His voluntary suffering and death; Theodosius in his self-identification with the humble. These four saints embody some of the most attractive features in Kievan Christianity.

1. Nestor, 'Life of Saint Theodosius', in G. P. Fedotov, *A Treasury of Russian Spirituality*, p. 27.

The Russian Church during the Kievan period was subject to Constantinople, and until 1237 the Metropolitans of Russia were usually Greek. In memory of the days when the Metropolitan came from Byzantium, the Russian Church continues to sing in Greek the solemn greeting to a bishop, *eis polla eti, despota* ('unto many years, O master'). But of the rest of the bishops, about half were native Russians in the Kievan period; one was even a converted Jew, and another a Syrian.

Kiev enjoyed relations not only with Byzantium but with western Europe, and certain features in the organization of the early Russian Church, such as ecclesiastical tithes, were not Byzantine but western. Many western saints who do not appear in the Byzantine calendar were venerated at Kiev; a prayer to the Holy Trinity composed in Russia during the eleventh century lists English saints such as Alban and Botolph, and a French saint, Martin of Tours. Some writers have even argued that until 1054 Russian Christianity was as much Latin as Greek, but this is a great exaggeration. Russia was closer to the west in the Kiev period than at any other time until the reign of Peter the Great, but she owed immeasurably more to Byzantine than to Latin culture. Napoleon was correct historically when he called Emperor Alexander I of Russia 'a Greek of the Lower Empire'.

It has been said that it was Russia's greatest misfortune that she was allowed too little time to assimilate the full spiritual inheritance of Byzantium. In 1237 Kievan Russia was brought to a sudden and violent end by the Mongol invasions; Kiev was sacked, and the whole Russian land was overrun, except the far north around Novgorod. A visitor to the Mongol Court in 1246 recorded that he saw in Russian territory neither town nor village, but only ruins and countless human skulls. But if Kiev was destroyed, the Christianity of Kiev remained a living memory:

Kievan Russia, like the golden days of childhood, was never dimmed in the memory of the Russian nation. In the pure fountain of her literary works anyone who wills can quench his religious thirst; in her venerable authors he can find his guide through the complexities of the modern world. Kievan Christianity has the same value for the Russian religious mind as Pushkin for the Russian artistic sense: that of a standard, a golden measure, a royal way.[1]

THE RUSSIAN CHURCH UNDER THE MONGOLS
(1237–1448)

The suzerainty of the Mongol Tartars over Russia lasted from 1237 until 1480. But after the great battle of Kulikovo (1380), when the Russians dared at last to face their oppressors in an open fight and actually defeated them, Mongol overlordship was considerably weakened; by 1450 it had become largely nominal. More than anything else, it was the Church which kept alive Russian national consciousness in the thirteenth and fourteenth centuries, as the Church was later to preserve a sense of unity among the Greeks under Turkish rule. The Russia which emerged from the Mongol period was a Russia greatly changed in outward appearance. Kiev never recovered from the sack of 1237, and its place was taken in the fourteenth century by the Principality of Moscow. It was the Grand Dukes of Moscow who inspired the resistance to the Mongols and who led Russia at Kulikovo. The rise of Moscow was closely bound up with the Church. When the town was still small and comparatively unimportant, Peter, Metropolitan of Russia from 1308 to 1326, decided to settle there; and henceforward it remained the city of the chief hierarch of Russia.

Three figures in the history of the Russian Church during the Mongol period call for particular mention, all of them saints: Alexander Nevsky, Stephen of Perm, and Sergius of Radonezh.

Alexander Nevsky (died 1263), one of the great warrior saints of Russia, has been compared with his western contemporary, Saint Louis, King of France. He was Prince of Novgorod, the one major principality in Russia to escape unharmed in 1237. But soon after the coming of the Tartars, Alexander found himself threatened by other enemies from the

1. G. P. Fedotov, *The Russian Religious Mind*, p. 412.

west: Swedes, Germans, and Lithuanians. It was impossible to fight on two fronts at once. Alexander decided to submit to Tartar overlordship and to pay tribute; but against his western opponents he put up a vigorous resistance, inflicting two decisive defeats upon them – over the Swedes in 1240 and over the Teutonic Knights in 1242. His reason for treating with the Tartars rather than the west was primarily religious: the Tartars took tribute but refrained from interfering in the life of the Church, whereas the Teutonic Knights had as their avowed aim the reduction of the Russian 'schismatics' to the jurisdiction of the Pope. This was the very period when a Latin Patriarch reigned in Constantinople, and the German Crusaders in the north aimed to break Orthodox Novgorod, just as their fellow Crusaders in the south had broken Orthodox Constantinople in 1204. But Alexander, despite the Mongol menace, refused any religious compromise. 'Our doctrines are those preached by the Apostles,' he is reported to have replied to messengers from the Pope. ' . . . The tradition of the Holy Fathers of the Seven Councils we scrupulously keep. As for your words, we do not listen to them and we do not want your doctrine.'[1] Two centuries later the Greeks after the Council of Florence made the same choice: political submission to the infidel rather than what they felt would be spiritual capitulation to the Church of Rome.

Stephen of Perm brings us to another aspect of Church life under the Mongols: missionary work. From its early days the Russian Church was a missionary Church, and the Russians were quick to send evangelists among their pagan conquerors. In 1261 a certain Mitrophan went as missionary bishop to Sarai, the Tartar capital on the Volga. Others preached, not among the Mongols, but among the primitive pagan tribes in the north-east and far north of the Russian continent. True to the example of Cyril and Methodius, these missionaries translated the Bible and Church services into the languages and dialects of the people to whom they ministered.

1. From the thirteenth-century life of Alexander Nevsky; quoted in Fedotov, *The Russian Religious Mind*, p. 383.

Saint Stephen, Bishop of Perm (?1340–96), worked among the Zyrian tribes. He spent thirteen years of preparation in a monastery, studying not only the native dialects but also Greek, to be the better fitted for the work of translation. While Cyril and Methodius had employed an adapted Greek alphabet in their Slavonic translations, Stephen made use of the native runes. He was an icon painter, and sought to show forth God as the God not of truth only, but of beauty. Like many other of the early Russian missionaries, he did not follow in the wake of military and political conquest, but was ahead of it.

Sergius of Radonezh (?1314–92), the greatest national saint of Russia, is closely connected with the recovery of the land in the fourteenth century. The outward pattern of his life recalls that of Saint Antony of Egypt. In early manhood Sergius withdrew into the forests (the northern equivalent of the Egyptian desert) and here he founded a hermitage dedicated to the Holy Trinity. After several years of solitude, his place of retreat became known, disciples gathered round him, and he grew into a spiritual guide, an 'elder' or *starets*. Finally (and here the parallel with Antony ends) he turned his group of disciples into a regular monastery, which became within his own lifetime the greatest religious house in the land. What the Monastery of the Caves was to Kievan Russia, the Monastery of the Holy Trinity was to Muscovy.

Sergius displayed the same deliberate self-humiliation as Theodosius, living (despite his noble birth) as a peasant, dressing in the poorest of clothing. 'His garb was of coarse peasant felt, old and worn, unwashed, saturated with sweat, and heavily patched.'[1] At the height of his fame, when Abbot of a great community, he still worked in the kitchen garden. Often when he was pointed out to visitors, they could not believe that it was really the celebrated Sergius. 'I came to see a prophet,' exclaimed one man in disgust, 'and you show me a beggar.'[2] Like Theodosius, Sergius played an active part in

1. Saint Epiphanius, 'The Life of Saint Sergius', in Fedotov, *A Treasury of Russian Spirituality*, pp. 69–70.
2. Epiphanius, in Fedotov, op. cit., p. 70.

politics. A close friend of the Grand Dukes of Moscow, he encouraged the city in its expansion, and it is significant that before the Battle of Kulikovo the leader of the Russian forces, Prince Dmitry Donskoy, went specially to Sergius to secure his blessing.

But while there exist many parallels in the lives of Theodosius and Sergius, two important points of difference must be noted. First, whereas the Monastery of the Caves, like most monasteries in Kievan Russia, lay on the outskirts of a city, the Monastery of the Holy Trinity was founded in the wilderness at a distance from the civilized world. Sergius was in his way an explorer and a colonist, pushing forward the boundaries of civilization and reducing the forest to cultivation. Nor is he the only example of a colonist monk at this time. Others went like him into the forests to become hermits, but in their case as in his, what started as a hermitage soon grew into a regular monastery, with a civilian town outside the walls. Then the whole process would start all over again: a fresh generation of monks in search of the solitary life would make their way into the yet more distant forest, disciples would follow, new communities would form, fresh land would be cleared for agriculture. This steady advance of colonist monks is one of the most striking features of fourteenth- and fifteenth-century Russia. From Radonezh and other centres a vast network of religious houses spread swiftly across the whole of north Russia as far as the White Sea and the Arctic Circle. Fifty communities were founded by disciples of Sergius in his own lifetime, forty more by his followers in the next generation. These explorer monks were not only colonists but missionaries, for as they penetrated farther north, they preached Christianity to the wild pagan tribes in the forests around them.

In the second place, while there is in the religious experience of Theodosius nothing that can be termed specifically mystical, in Sergius a new dimension of the spiritual life becomes evident. Sergius was a contemporary of Gregory Palamas, and it is not impossible that he knew something of the Hesychast movement in Byzantium. At any rate some of the visions granted to Sergius in prayer, which his biographer Epiphanius recorded, can only be interpreted in a mystical sense.

Sergius has been called a 'Builder of Russia', and such he was in three senses: politically, for he encouraged the rise of Moscow and the resistance against the Tartars; geographically, for it was he more than any other who inspired the great advance of monks into the forests; and spiritually, for through his experience of mystical prayer he deepened the inner life of the Russian Church. Better, perhaps, than any other Russian saint, he succeeded in balancing the social and mystical aspects of monasticism. Under his influence and that of his followers, the two centuries from 1350 to 1550 proved a golden age in Russian spirituality.

These two centuries were also a golden age in Russian religious art. During these years Russian painters carried to perfection the iconographic traditions which they had taken over from Byzantium. Icon painting flourished above all among the spiritual children of Saint Sergius. It is no coincidence that the finest of all Orthodox icons from the artistic point of view – the Holy Trinity, by Saint Andrew Rublev (?1370–?1430) – should have been painted in honour of Saint Sergius and placed in his monastery at Radonezh.

Sixty-one years after the death of Sergius, the Byzantine Empire fell to the Turks. The new Russia which took shape after Kulikovo, and which the Saint himself had done so much to build, was now called to take Byzantium's place as protector of the Orthodox world. It proved both worthy and unworthy of this vocation.

CHAPTER 5

The Church under Islam

> The stable perseverance in these our days of the Greek
> Church ... notwithstanding the Oppression and
> Contempt put upon it by the *Turk*, and the Allure-
> ments and Pleasures of this World, is a Confirmation
> no less convincing than the Miracles and Power which
> attended its first beginnings. For indeed it is ad-
> mirable to see and consider with what Constancy,
> Resolution, and Simplicity, ignorant and poor men
> keep their Faith.
>
> *Sir Paul Rycaut*, The Present State of the Greek
> and Armenian Churches (*1679*)

IMPERIUM IN IMPERIO

'IT doth go hugely against the grain to see the crescent exalted
everywhere, where the Cross stood so long triumphant': so
wrote Edward Browne in 1677, soon after arriving as Chaplain
to the English Embassy at Constantinople. To the Greeks in
1453 it must also have gone hugely against the grain. For more
than a thousand years men had taken the Christian Empire of
Byzantium for granted as a permanent element in God's provi-
dential dispensation to the world. Now the 'God-protected city'
had fallen, and the Greeks were under the rule of the infidel.

It was not an easy transition: but it was made less hard by
the Turks themselves, who treated their Christian subjects
with remarkable generosity. The Mohammedans in the fifteenth century were far more tolerant towards Christianity
than western Christians were towards one another during the
Reformation and the seventeenth century. Islam regards the
Bible as a holy book and Jesus Christ as a prophet; in Moslem
eyes, therefore, the Christian religion is incomplete but not
entirely false, and Christians, being 'People of the Book',
should not be treated as if on a level with mere pagans. Accord-

ing to Mohammedan teaching, Christians are to undergo no persecution, but may continue without interference in the observance of their faith, so long as they submit quietly to the power of Islam.

Such were the principles which guided the conqueror of Constantinople, Sultan Mohammed II. Before the fall of the city, Greeks called him 'the precursor of Antichrist and the second Sennacherib', but they found that in practice his rule was very different in character. Learning that the office of Patriarch was vacant, Mohammed summoned the monk Gennadius and installed him on the Patriarchal throne. Gennadius (?1405-?72), known as George Scholarios before he became a monk, was a voluminous writer and the leading Greek theologian of his time. He was a determined opponent of the Church of Rome, and his appointment as Patriarch meant the final abandonment of the Union of Florence. Doubtless for political reasons, the Sultan deliberately chose a man of anti-Latin convictions: with Gennadius as Patriarch, there would be less likelihood of the Greeks seeking secret aid from Roman Catholic powers.

The Sultan himself instituted the Patriarch, ceremonially investing him with his pastoral staff, exactly as the autocrats of Byzantium had formerly done. The action was symbolic: Mohammed the Conqueror, champion of Islam, became also the protector of Orthodoxy, taking over the role once exercised by the Christian Emperor. Thus Christians were assured a definite place in the Turkish order of society; but, as they were soon to discover, it was a place of guaranteed inferiority. Christianity under Islam was a second-class religion, and its adherents second-class citizens. They paid heavy taxes, wore a distinctive dress, were not allowed to serve in the army, and were forbidden to marry Moslem women. The Church was allowed to undertake no missionary work, and it was a crime to convert a Moslem to the Christian faith. From the material point of view there was every inducement for a Christian to apostatize to Islam. Direct persecution often serves to strengthen a Church; but the Greeks in the Ottoman Empire were denied the more heroic ways of witnessing to their faith, and were subjected instead to the demoralizing effects of an unrelenting social pressure.

Nor was this all. After the fall of Constantinople the Church was not allowed to revert to the situation before the conversion of Constantine; paradoxically enough, the things of Caesar now became more closely associated with the things of God than they had ever been before. For the Mohammedans drew no distinction between religion and politics: from their point of view, if Christianity was to be recognized as an independent religious faith, it was necessary for Christians to be organized as an independent political unit, an Empire within the Empire. The Orthodox Church therefore became a civil as well as a religious institution: it was turned into the *Rum Millet*, the 'Roman nation'. The ecclesiastical structure was taken over *in toto* as an instrument of secular administration. The bishops became government officials, the Patriarch was not only the spiritual head of the Greek Orthodox Church, but the civil head of the Greek nation – the *ethnarch* or *millet-bashi*. This situation continued in Turkey until 1923, and in Cyprus until the death of Archbishop Makarios III (1977).

The *millet* system performed one invaluable service: it made possible the survival of the Greek nation as a distinctive unit through four centuries of alien rule. But on the life of the Church it had two melancholy effects. It led first to a sad confusion between Orthodoxy and nationalism. With their civil and political life organized completely around the Church, it became all but impossible for the Greeks to distinguish between Church and nation. The Orthodox faith, being universal, is limited to no single people, culture, or language; but to the Greeks of the Turkish Empire 'Hellenism' and Orthodoxy became inextricably intertwined, far more so than they had ever been in the Byzantine Empire. The effects of this confusion continue to the present day.

In the second place, the Church's higher administration became caught up in a degrading system of corruption and simony. Involved as they were in worldly affairs and matters political, the bishops fell a prey to ambition and financial greed. Each new Patriarch required a *berat* from the Sultan before he could assume office, and for this document he was obliged to pay heavily. The Patriarch recovered his expenses from the episcopate, by exacting a fee from each bishop before instituting him in his diocese; the bishops in turn taxed the parish clergy, and the clergy taxed their flocks. What was once said of the Papacy was certainly true of the Ecumenical Patriarchate under the Turks: everything was for sale.

When there were several candidates for the Patriarchal throne, the Turks virtually sold it to the highest bidder; and they were quick to see that it was in their financial interests to change the Patriarch as frequently as possible, so as to multiply occasions for selling the *berat*. Patriarchs were removed and reinstated with kaleidoscopic rapidity. 'Out of 159 Patriarchs who have held office between the fifteenth and the twentieth century, the Turks have on 105 occasions driven Patriarchs from their throne; there have been 27 abdications, often involuntary; 6 Patriarchs have suffered violent deaths by hanging, poisoning, or drowning; and only 21 have died natural deaths while in office.'[1] The same man sometimes held office on four or five different occasions, and there were usually several ex-Patriarchs watching restively in exile for a chance to return to the throne. The extreme insecurity of the Patriarch naturally gave rise to continual intrigues among the Metropolitans of the Holy Synod who hoped to succeed him, and the leaders of the Church were usually separated into bitterly hostile parties. 'Every good Christian,' wrote an English resident in the seventeenth-century Levant, 'ought with sadness to consider, and with compassion to behold this once glorious Church to tear and rend out her own bowels, and give them for food to vultures and ravens, and to the wild and fierce Creatures of the World.'[2]

1. B. J. Kidd, *The Churches of Eastern Christendom*, London, 1927, p. 304.
2. Sir Paul Rycaut, *The Present State of the Greek and Armenian Churches*, London, 1679, p. 107.

But if the Patriarchate of Constantinople suffered an inward decay, outwardly its power expanded as never before. The Turks looked on the Patriarch of Constantinople as the head of *all* Orthodox Christians in their dominions. The other Patriarchates also within the Ottoman Empire – Alexandria, Antioch, Jerusalem – remained theoretically independent but were in practice subordinate. The Churches of Bulgaria and Serbia – likewise within Turkish dominions – gradually lost all independence, and by the mid eighteenth century had passed directly under the Ecumenical Patriarch's control. But in the nineteenth century, as Turkish power declined, the frontiers of the Patriarchate contracted. The nations which gained freedom from the Turks found it impracticable to remain subject ecclesiastically to a Patriarch resident in the Turkish capital and closely involved in the Turkish political system. The Patriarch resisted as long as he could, but in each case he bowed eventually to the inevitable. A series of national Churches were carved out of the Patriarchate: the Church of Greece (organized in 1833, recognized by the Patriarch of Constantinople in 1850); the Church of Romania (organized in 1864, recognized in 1885); the Church of Bulgaria (re-established in 1871, not recognized by Constantinople until 1945); the Church of Serbia (restored and recognized in 1879). The diminution of the Patriarchate has continued in the present century, chiefly as a result of war, and its membership is now but a tiny fraction of what it once was in the palmy days of Ottoman suzerainty.

The Turkish occupation had two opposite effects upon the intellectual life of the Church: it was the cause on the one hand of an immense conservatism and on the other of a certain westernization. Orthodoxy under the Turks felt itself on the defensive. The great aim was *survival* – to keep things going in hope of better days to come. The Greeks clung with miraculous tenacity to the Christian civilization which they had taken over from Byzantium, but they had little opportunity to develop this civilization creatively. Intelligibly enough, they were usually content to repeat accepted formulae, to entrench themselves in the positions which they had inherited from the past. Greek thought underwent an ossification and a hardening which one cannot but regret; yet conservatism had its advantages. In a dark and difficult period the Greeks did in fact maintain the Orthodox tradition substantially unimpaired. The Orthodox under Islam took as their guide Paul's words to Timothy: 'Guard the deposit: keep safe what has been entrusted to you' (1 Timothy vi, 20). Could they in the end have chosen a better motto?

Yet alongside this traditionalism there is another and contrary current in Orthodox theology of the seventeenth and eighteenth centuries: the current of western infiltration. It was difficult for the Orthodox under Ottoman rule to maintain a good standard of scholarship. Greeks who wished for a higher education were obliged to travel to the non-Orthodox world, to Italy and Germany, to Paris, and even as far as Oxford. Among the distinguished Greek theologians of the Turkish period, a few were self-taught, but the overwhelming majority had been trained in the west under Roman Catholic or Protestant masters.

Inevitably this had an effect upon the way in which they interpreted Orthodox theology. Certainly Greek students in the west read the Fathers, but they only became acquainted with such of the Fathers as were held in esteem by their non-Orthodox professors. Thus Gregory Palamas was still read, for his spiritual teaching, by the monks of Athos; but to most learned Greek theologians of the Turkish period he was utterly unknown. In the works of Eustratius Argenti (died ?1758), the ablest Greek theologian of his time, there is not a single citation from Palamas; and his case is typical. It is symbolic of the state of Greek Orthodox learning in the last four centuries that one of the chief works of Palamas, *The Triads in Defence of the Holy Hesychasts*, should have remained in great part unpublished until 1959.

There was a real danger that Greeks who studied in the west, even though they remained fully loyal in intention to their own Church, would lose their Orthodox mentality and become cut off from Orthodoxy as a living tradition. It was difficult for them not to look at theology through western spectacles; whether consciously or not, they used terminology and forms of argument foreign to their own Church. Orthodox theology underwent what the Russian theologian Father Georges Florovsky (1893–1979) has appropriately termed a *pseudomorphosis*. Religious thinkers of the Turkish period can be divided for the most part into two broad groups, the 'Latinizers' and the 'Protestantizers'. Yet the extent of this westernization must not be exaggerated. Greeks used the outward forms which they had learnt in the west, but in the substance of their thought the great majority remained fundamentally Orthodox. The tradition was at times distorted by being forced into alien moulds – distorted, but not wholly destroyed.

Keeping in mind this twofold background of conservatism and westernization, let us consider the challenge presented to the Orthodox world by Reformation and Counter-Reformation.

REFORMATION AND COUNTER-REFORMATION: THEIR DOUBLE IMPACT

The forces of Reform stopped short when they reached the borders of Russia and the Turkish Empire, so that the Orthodox Church has not undergone either a Reformation or a Counter-Reformation. Yet it would be a mistake to conclude that these two movements have had no influence whatever upon Orthodoxy. There were many means of contact: Orthodox, as we have seen, went to study in the west; Jesuits and Franciscans, sent out to the eastern Mediterranean, undertook missionary work among Orthodox; the Jesuits were also at work in the Ukraine; the foreign embassies at Constantinople, both of Roman Catholic and of Protestant powers, played a religious as well as a political role. During the seventeenth century these contacts led to significant developments in Orthodox theology.

The first important exchange of views between Orthodox

and Protestants began in 1573, when a delegation of Lutheran
scholars from Tübingen, led by Jakob Andreae and Martin
Crusius, visited Constantinople and gave the Patriarch, Jeremias II, a copy of the Augsburg Confession translated into
Greek. Doubtless they hoped to initiate some sort of Reformation among the Greeks; as Crusius somewhat naïvely wrote:
'If they wish to take thought for the eternal salvation of their
souls, they must join us and embrace our teaching, or else
perish eternally'! Jeremias, however, in his three *Answers* to
the Tübingen theologians (dated 1576, 1579, 1581), adhered
strictly to the traditional Orthodox position and showed no
inclination to Protestantism. To his first two letters the
Lutherans sent replies, but in his third letter the Patriarch
brought the correspondence to a close, feeling that matters had
reached a deadlock: 'Go your own way, and do not write any
more on doctrinal matters; and if you do write, then write only
for friendship's sake.' The whole incident shows the interest
felt by the Reformers in the Orthodox Church. The Patriarch's
Answers are important as the first clear and authoritative
critique of the doctrines of the Reformation from an Orthodox
point of view. The chief matters discussed by Jeremias were
free will and grace, Scripture and Tradition, the sacraments,
prayers for the dead, and prayers to the saints.

During the Tübingen interlude, Lutherans and Orthodox
both showed great courtesy to one another. A very different
spirit marked the first major contact between Orthodoxy and
the Counter-Reformation. This occurred outside the limits of
the Turkish Empire, in the Ukraine. After the destruction of
Kievan power by the Tartars, a large area in the south-west of
Russia, including the city of Kiev itself, became absorbed by
Lithuania and Poland; this south-western part of Russia is
commonly known as Little Russia or the Ukraine. The crowns
of Poland and Lithuania were united under a single ruler from
1386; thus while the monarch of the joint realm, together with
the majority of the population, was Roman Catholic, an appreciable minority of his subjects was Russian and Orthodox.
These Orthodox in Little Russia were in an uncomfortable

predicament. The Patriarch of Constantinople, to whose jurisdiction they belonged, could exercise no very effective control
in Poland; their bishops were appointed not by the Church but
by the Roman Catholic king of Poland, and were sometimes
courtiers wholly lacking in spiritual qualities and incapable of
providing any inspiring leadership. There was, however, a vigorous laity, led by several energetic Orthodox nobles, and in
many towns there were powerful lay associations, known as the
Brotherhoods (*Bratstva*).

More than once the Roman Catholic authorities in Poland
had tried to make the Orthodox submit to the Pope. With the
arrival of the Society of Jesus in the land in 1564, pressure on
the Orthodox increased. The Jesuits began by negotiating
secretly with the Orthodox bishops, who were for the most
part willing to cooperate (they were, we must remember,
the nominees of a Roman Catholic monarch). In due course,
so the Jesuits hoped, the whole Orthodox hierarchy in Poland
would agree to submit *en bloc* to the Pope, and the 'union'
could then be proclaimed publicly as a *fait accompli* before
anyone else could raise objections: hence the need for concealment in the earlier stages of the operation. But matters
did not in fact go entirely according to plan. In 1596 a council
was summoned at Brest-Litovsk to proclaim the union with
Rome, but the hierarchy was divided. Six out of eight Orthodox bishops, including the Metropolitan of Kiev, Michael
Ragoza, supported the union, but the remaining two bishops,
together with a large number of the delegates from the
monasteries and from the parish clergy, desired to remain
members of the Orthodox Church. The two sides concluded
by excommunicating and anathematizing one another.

Thus there came into existence in Poland a 'Uniate' Church,
whose members were known as 'Catholics of the Eastern Rite'.
The decrees of the Council of Florence formed the basis of the
union. The Uniates recognized the supremacy of the Pope, but
were allowed to keep their traditional practices (such as married
clergy), and they continued as before to use the Slavonic
Liturgy, although in course of time western elements crept

into it. Outwardly, therefore, there was very little to distinguish Uniates from Orthodox, and one wonders how far uneducated peasants in Little Russia understood what the quarrel was really about. Many of them, at any rate, explained the matter by saying that the Pope had now joined the Orthodox Church.

The government authorities recognized only the decisions of the Roman party at the Council of Brest, so that from their point of view the Orthodox Church in Poland had now ceased legally to exist. Those who desired to continue Orthodox were severely persecuted. Monasteries and churches were seized and given to the Uniates, against the wishes of the monks and congregations. 'Roman Catholic Polish gentry sometimes handed over the Orthodox Church of their peasants to a Jewish usurer, who could then demand a fee for allowing an Orthodox baptism or funeral.'[1] The tale of the Uniate movement in Poland makes sorrowful reading: the Jesuits began by using deceit, and ended by resorting to violence. Doubtless they were sincere men who genuinely desired the unity of Christendom, but the tactics which they employed were better calculated to widen the breach than to close it. The Union of Brest has embittered relations between Orthodoxy and Rome from 1596 until the present day.

It is small wonder that Orthodox, when they saw what was happening in Poland, should prefer Mohammedan to Roman Catholic rulers, just as Alexander Nevsky had preferred the Tartars to the Teutonic Knights. Travelling through the Ukraine in the 1650s, Paul of Aleppo, nephew and Archdeacon to the Patriarch of Antioch, reflected the typical Orthodox attitude when he wrote in his diary: 'God perpetuate the Empire of the Turks! For they take their impost and enter into no account of religion, be their subjects Christians or Nazarenes, Jews or Samaritans; whereas these accursed Poles, not content with taking taxes and tithes from their Christian subjects, subjected them to the enemies of Christ, the Jews, who did not allow them to build churches or leave them any

1. Bernard Pares, *A History of Russia*, third edition, London, p. 167.

educated priests.' The Poles he terms 'more vile and wicked than even the worshippers of idols, by their cruelty to Christians'.[1]

Persecution invigorated the Orthodox Church in the Ukraine. Although many Orthodox nobles joined the Uniates, the Brotherhoods stood firm and expanded their activities. To answer Jesuit propaganda they maintained printing presses and issued books in defence of Orthodoxy; to counteract the influence of the Jesuit schools they organized Orthodox schools of their own. By 1650 the level of learning in Little Russia was higher than anywhere else in the Orthodox world; scholars from Kiev, travelling to Moscow at this time, did much to raise intellectual standards in Great Russia. In this revival of learning a particularly brilliant part was played by Peter of Moghila, Metropolitan of Kiev from 1633 to 1647. To him we must shortly return.

One of the representatives of the Patriarchate of Constantinople at Brest in 1596 was a young Greek priest called Cyril Lukaris (1572–1638). His experiences in Little Russia inspired him with a lifelong hatred of the Church of Rome, and when he became Patriarch of Constantinople he devoted his full energies to combating all Roman Catholic influence in the Turkish Empire. It was unfortunate, though perhaps inevitable, that in his struggle against 'the Papic Church' (as the Greeks termed it) he should have become deeply involved in politics. He turned naturally for help to the Protestant embassies at Constantinople, while his Jesuit opponents for their part used the diplomatic representatives of the Roman Catholic powers. Besides invoking the political assistance of Protestant diplomats, Cyril also fell under Protestant influence in matters of theology, and his *Confession*,[2] first published at Geneva in 1629, is distinctively Calvinist in much of its teaching.

Cyril's reign as Patriarch is one long series of stormy and unedifying intrigues, and forms a lurid example of the troubled

1. *The Travels of Macarius*, ed. L. Ridding, London, 1936, p. 15.
2. By 'Confession' in this context is meant a statement of faith, a solemn declaration of religious belief.

state of the Ecumenical Patriarchate under the Ottomans. Six times deposed from office and six times reinstated, he was finally strangled by Turkish janissaries and his body cast into the Bosphorus. In the last resort there is something deeply tragic about his career, since he was possibly the most brilliant man to have held office as Patriarch since the days of Saint Photius. Had he but lived under happier conditions, freed from political intrigue, his exceptional gifts might have been put to better use.

Cyril's Calvinism was sharply and speedily repudiated by his fellow Orthodox, his *Confession* being condemned by no less than six local Councils between 1638 and 1691. In direct reaction to Cyril two other Orthodox hierarchs, Peter of Moghila and Dositheus of Jerusalem, produced Confessions of their own. Peter's *Orthodox Confession*, written in 1640, was based directly on Roman Catholic manuals. It was approved by the Council of Jassy in Romania (1642), but only after it had been revised by a Greek, Meletius Syrigos, who in particular altered the passages about the consecration in the Eucharist (which Peter attributed solely to the Words of Institution) and about Purgatory. Even in its revised form the Confession of Moghila is still the most Latin document ever to be adopted by an official Council of the Orthodox Church. Dositheus, Patriarch of Jerusalem from 1669 to 1707, also drew heavily upon Latin sources. His *Confession*, ratified in 1672 by the Council of Jerusalem (also known as the Council of Bethlehem), answers Cyril's *Confession* point by point with concision and clarity. The chief matters over which Cyril and Dositheus diverge are four: the question of free will, grace, and predestination; the doctrine of the Church; the number and nature of the sacraments; and the veneration of icons. In his statement upon the Eucharist, Dositheus adopted not only the Latin term *transubstantiation* but the Scholastic distinction between *substance* and *accidents*;[1] and in defending prayers for the dead he came very close to the Roman doctrine of Purgatory, without actually using the word Purgatory itself. On the whole, however, the

1. See p. 291, note 1.

Confession of Dositheus is less Latin than that of Moghila, and must certainly be regarded as a document of primary importance in the history of modern Orthodox theology. Faced by the Calvinism of Lukaris, Dositheus used the weapons which lay nearest to hand – Latin weapons (under the circumstances it was perhaps the only thing that he could do); but the faith which he defended with these Latin weapons was not Roman, but Orthodox.

Outside the Ukraine, relations between Orthodox and Roman Catholics were often friendly in the seventeenth century. In many places in the eastern Mediterranean, particularly in the Greek islands under Venetian rule, Greeks and Latins shared in one another's worship: we even read of Roman Catholic processions of the Blessed Sacrament, which the Orthodox clergy attended in force, wearing full vestments, with candles and banners. Greek bishops invited the Latin missionaries to preach to their flocks or to hear confessions. But after 1700 these friendly contacts grew less frequent, and by 1750 they had largely ceased. In 1724 a large part of the Orthodox Patriarchate of Antioch submitted to Rome; after this the Orthodox authorities, fearing that the same thing might happen elsewhere in the Turkish Empire, were far stricter in their dealings with Roman Catholics. The climax in anti-Roman feeling came in 1755, when the Patriarchs of Constantinople, Alexandria, and Jerusalem declared Latin baptism to be entirely invalid and demanded that all converts to Orthodoxy be baptized anew. 'The baptisms of heretics are to be rejected and abhorred,' the decree stated; they are 'waters which cannot profit ... nor give any sanctification to such as receive them, nor avail at all to the washing away of sins'. This measure remained in force in the Greek world until the end of the nineteenth century, but it did not extend to the Church of Russia; the Russians generally baptized Roman Catholic converts between 1441 and 1667, but since 1667 they have not normally done so.

The Orthodox of the seventeenth century came into contact not only with Roman Catholics, Lutherans, and Calvinists but also with the Church of England. Cyril Lukaris corresponded

THE CHURCH UNDER ISLAM

with Archbishop Abbot of Canterbury, and a future Patriarch of Alexandria, Metrophanes Kritopoulos, studied at Oxford from 1617 to 1624: Kritopoulos is the author of a *Confession*, slightly Protestant in tone, but widely used in the Orthodox Church. Around 1694 there was even a plan to establish a 'Greek College' at Gloucester Hall, Oxford (now Worcester College), and about ten Greek students were actually sent to Oxford; but the plan failed for lack of money, and the Greeks found the food and lodging so poor that many of them ran away. From 1716 to 1725 a most interesting correspondence was maintained between the Orthodox and the Non-Jurors (a group of Anglicans who separated from the main body of the Church of England in 1688, rather than swear allegiance to the usurper William of Orange). The Non-Jurors approached both the four Eastern Patriarchs and the Church of Russia, in the hope of establishing communion with the Orthodox. But the Non-Jurors could not accept the Orthodox teaching concerning the presence of Christ in the Eucharist; they were also troubled by the veneration shown by Orthodoxy to the Mother of God, the saints, and the Holy Icons. Eventually the correspondence was suspended without any agreement being reached.

Looking back on the work of Moghila and Dositheus, on the Councils of Jassy and Jerusalem, and on the correspondence with the Non-Jurors, one is struck by the limitations of Greek theology in this period: one does not find the Orthodox tradition in its *fullness*. Nevertheless the Councils of the seventeenth century made a permanent and constructive contribution to Orthodoxy. The Reformation controversies raised problems which neither the Ecumenical Councils nor the Church of the later Byzantine Empire was called to face: in the seventeenth century the Orthodox were forced to think more carefully about the sacraments, and about the nature and authority of the Church. It was important for Orthodoxy to express its mind on these topics, and to define its position in relation to the new teachings which had arisen in the west; this was the task which the seventeenth-century Councils achieved. These Councils were local, but the substance of their decisions has been accepted by the Orthodox Church as a whole. The seventeenth-century Councils, like the Hesychast Councils three hundred years before, show that creative theological work did not come to an end in the Orthodox Church after the period of the Ecumenical Councils. There are important doctrines not defined by the General Councils, which every Orthodox is bound to accept as an integral part of his faith.

Many western people learn about Orthodoxy either from studying the Byzantine period, or through the medium of Russian religious thought in the last hundred years. In both cases they tend to by-pass the seventeenth century, and to underestimate its influence upon Orthodox history.

Throughout the Turkish period the traditions of Hesychasm remained alive, particularly on Mount Athos; and at the end of the eighteenth century there was an important spiritual revival, whose effects can still be felt today. At the centre of this revival was a monk of Athos, Saint Nicodemus of the Holy Mountain ('the Hagiorite', 1748–1809), justly called 'an encyclopaedia of the Athonite learning of his time'. With the help of Saint Macarius (Notaras), Metropolitan of Corinth, Nicodemus compiled an anthology of spiritual writings called the *Philokalia*. Published at Venice in 1782, it is a gigantic work of 1,207 folio pages, containing authors from the fourth century to the fifteenth, and dealing chiefly with the theory and practice of prayer, especially the Jesus Prayer. It has proved one of the most influential publications in Orthodox history, and has been widely read not only by monks but by many living in the world. Translated into Slavonic and Russian, it was instrumental in producing a spiritual reawakening in nineteenth-century Russia.

Nicodemus was conservative, but not narrow or obscurantist. He drew on Roman Catholic works of devotion, adapting for Orthodox use books by Lorenzo Scupoli and Ignatius Loyola. He and his circle were strong advocates of frequent communion, although in his day most Orthodox communicated only a few times a year. Nicodemus was in fact vigorously attacked on this issue, but a Council at Constantinople in 1819 confirmed his teaching. Movements which are trying to introduce weekly communion in Greece today appeal to the great authority of Nicodemus.

It has been rightly said that if there is much to pity in the state of Orthodoxy during the Turkish period, there is also much to admire. Despite innumerable discouragements, the Orthodox Church under Ottoman rule never lost heart. There were of course many cases of apostasy to Islam, but in Europe at any rate they were not as frequent as might have been expected. Orthodoxy in these centuries was not lacking in martyrs, who are honoured in the Church's calendar with the special title of *New Martyrs*: many of them were Greeks who became Mohammedan and then repented, returning to Christianity once more – for which the penalty was death. The corruption in the higher administration of the Church, shocking though it was, had very little effect on the daily life of the ordinary Christian, who was still able to worship Sunday by Sunday in his parish church. More than anything else it was the Holy Liturgy which kept Orthodoxy alive in those dark days.

CHAPTER 6

Moscow and St Petersburg

The sense of God's presence – of the supernatural –
seems to me to penetrate Russian life more completely
than that of any of the western nations.
*H. P. Liddon, Canon of Saint Paul's, after a visit to
Russia in 1867*

MOSCOW THE THIRD ROME

AFTER the taking of Constantinople in 1453, there was only
one nation capable of assuming leadership in eastern Christendom. The greater part of Bulgaria, Serbia, and Romania had
already been conquered by the Turks, while the rest was
absorbed before long. Russia alone remained. To the Russians
it seemed no coincidence that at the very moment when the
Byzantine Empire came to an end, they themselves were at last
throwing off the few remaining vestiges of Tartar suzerainty:
God, it seemed, was granting them their freedom because He
had chosen them to be the successors of Byzantium.

At the same time as the land of Russia, the Russian Church
gained its independence, more by chance than from any deliberate design. Hitherto the Patriarch of Constantinople had
appointed the head of the Russian Church, the Metropolitan.
At the Council of Florence the Metropolitan was a Greek,
Isidore. A leading supporter of the union with Rome, Isidore
returned to Moscow in 1441 and proclaimed the decrees of
Florence, but he met with no support from the Russians: he
was imprisoned by the Grand Duke, but after a time was
allowed to escape, and went back to Italy. The chief see was
thus left vacant; but the Russians could not ask the Patriarch
for a new Metropolitan, because until 1453 the official Church
at Constantinople continued to accept the Florentine Union.
Reluctant to take action on their own, the Russians delayed for

several years. Eventually in 1448 a council of Russian bishops proceeded to elect a Metropolitan without further reference to Constantinople. After 1453, when the Florentine Union was abandoned at Constantinople, communion between the Patriarchate and Russia was restored, but Russia continued to appoint its own chief hierarch. Henceforward the Russian Church was autocephalous.

The idea of Moscow as successor of Byzantium was assisted by a marriage. In 1472 Ivan III 'the Great' (reigned 1462–1505) married Sophia, niece of the last Byzantine Emperor. Although Sophia had brothers and was not the legal heir to the throne, the marriage served to establish a dynastic link with Byzantium. The Grand Duke of Moscow began to assume the Byzantine titles of 'autocrat' and 'Tsar' (an adaptation of the Roman 'Caesar') and to use the double-headed eagle of Byzantium as his State emblem. Men came to think of Moscow as 'the Third Rome'. The first Rome (so they argued) had fallen to the barbarians and then lapsed into heresy; the second Rome, Constantinople, had in turn fallen into heresy at the Council of Florence, and as a punishment had been taken by the Turks. Moscow therefore had succeeded Constantinople as the Third and last Rome, the centre of Orthodox Christendom. The monk Philotheus of Pskov set forth this line of argument in a famous letter written in 1510 to Tsar Basil III:

I wish to add a few words on the present Orthodox Empire of our ruler: he is on earth the sole Emperor (Tsar) of the Christians, the leader of the Apostolic Church which stands no longer in Rome or in Constantinople, but in the blessed city of Moscow. She alone shines in the whole world brighter than the sun .... All Christian Empires are fallen and in their stead stands alone the Empire of our ruler in accordance with the Prophetical books. Two Romes have fallen, but the third stands and a fourth there will not be.[1]

This idea of Moscow the Third Rome had a certain appropriateness when applied to the Tsar: the Emperor of Byzantium had once acted as champion and protector of Orthodoxy,

1. Quoted in Baynes and Moss, *Byzantium: an Introduction*, p. 385.

and now the autocrat of Russia was called to perform the same task. But it could also be understood in other and less acceptable ways. If Moscow was the Third Rome, then should not the head of the Russian Church rank senior to the Patriarch of Constantinople? In fact this seniority has never been granted, and Russia has always ranked no higher than fifth among the Orthodox Churches, after Jerusalem. The concept of Moscow the Third Rome also encouraged a kind of Muscovite Messianism, and led Russians sometimes to think of themselves as a chosen people who could do no wrong; and if taken in a political as well as religious sense, it could be used to further the ends of Russian secular imperialism.

Now that the dream for which Saint Sergius worked – the liberation of Russia from the Tartars – had become a reality, a sad division occurred among his spiritual descendants. Sergius had united the social with the mystical side of monasticism, but under his successors these two aspects became separated. The separation first came into the open at a Church council in 1503. As this council drew to its close, Saint Nilus of Sora (Nil Sorsky, ?1433–1508), a monk from a remote hermitage in the forests beyond the Volga, rose to speak, and launched an attack on the ownership of land by monasteries (about a third of the land in Russia belonged to monasteries at this time). Saint Joseph, Abbot of Volokalamsk (1439–1515), replied in defence of monastic landholding. The majority of the Council supported Joseph; but there were others in the Russian Church who agreed with Nilus – chiefly hermits living like him beyond the Volga. Joseph's party were known as the Possessors, Nilus and the 'Transvolga hermits' as the Non-Possessors. During the next twenty years there was considerable tension between the two groups. Finally in 1525–6 the Non-Possessors attacked Tsar Basil III for unjustly divorcing his wife (the Orthodox Church grants divorce, but only for certain reasons); the Tsar then imprisoned the leading Non-Possessors and closed the Transvolga hermitages. The tradition of Saint Nilus was driven underground, and although it never entirely disappeared, its influence in the Russian Church was very much restricted. For the time being the outlook of the Possessors reigned supreme.

Behind the question of monastic property lay two different conceptions of the monastic life, and ultimately two different views of the relation of the Church to the world. The Possessors emphasized the social obligations of monasticism: it is part of the work of monks to care for the sick and poor, to show hospitality and to teach; to do these things efficiently, monasteries need money and therefore they must own land. Monks (so they argued) do not use their wealth on themselves, but hold it in trust for the benefit of others. There was a saying among the followers of Joseph, 'The riches of the Church are the riches of the poor'.

The Non-Possessors argued on the other hand that almsgiving is the duty of the laity, while a monk's primary task is to help others by praying for them and by setting an example. To do these things properly a monk must be detached from the world, and only those who are vowed to complete poverty can achieve true detachment. Monks who are landowners cannot avoid being tangled up in secular anxieties, and because they become absorbed in worldly concerns, they act and think in a worldly way. In the words of the monk Vassian (Prince Patrikiev), a disciple of Nilus:

Where in the traditions of the Gospels, Apostles, and Fathers are monks ordered to acquire populous villages and enslave peasants to the brotherhood? . . . We look into the hands of the rich, fawn slavishly, flatter them to get out of them some little village . . . We wrong and rob and sell Christians, our brothers. We torture them with scourges like wild beasts.[1]

Vassian's protest against torture and scourges brings us to a second matter over which the two sides disagreed, the treatment of heretics. Joseph upheld the view all but universal in Christendom at this time: if heretics are recalcitrant, the Church must call in the civil arm and resort to prison, torture, and if necessary fire. But Nilus condemned all forms of coercion

1. Quoted in B. Pares, *A History of Russia*, third edition, p. 93.

and violence against heretics. One has only to recall how Protestants and Roman Catholics treated one another in western Europe during the Reformation, to realize how exceptional Nilus was in his tolerance and respect for human freedom.

The question of heretics in turn involved the wider problem of relations between Church and State. Nilus regarded heresy as a spiritual matter, to be settled by the Church without the State's intervention; Joseph invoked the help of the secular authorities. In general Nilus drew a clearer line than Joseph between the things of Caesar and the things of God. The Possessors were great supporters of the ideal of Moscow the Third Rome; believing in a close alliance between Church and State, they took an active part in politics, as Sergius had done, but perhaps they were less careful than Sergius to guard the Church from becoming the servant of the State. The Non-Possessors for their part had a sharper awareness of the prophetic and other-worldly witness of monasticism. The Josephites were in danger of identifying the Kingdom of God with a kingdom of this world; Nilus saw that the Church on earth must always be a Church in pilgrimage. While Joseph and his party were great patriots and nationalists, the Non-Possessors thought more of the universality and Catholicity of the Church.

Nor did the divergences between the two sides end here: they also had different ideas of Christian piety and prayer. Joseph emphasized the place of rules and discipline, Nilus the inner and personal relation between God and the soul. Joseph stressed the place of beauty in worship, Nilus feared that beauty might become an idol: the monk (so Nilus maintained) is dedicated not only to an outward poverty, but to an absolute self-stripping, and he must be careful lest a devotion to beautiful icons or Church music comes between him and God. (In this suspicion of beauty, Nilus displays a Puritanism – almost an Iconoclasm – most unusual in Russian spirituality.) Joseph realized the importance of corporate worship and of liturgical prayer:

A man can pray in his own room, but he will never pray there as he prays in Church ... where the singing of many voices rises united towards God, where all have but one thought and one voice in the unity of love .... On high the seraphim proclaim the *Trisagion*, here below the human multitude raises the same hymn. Heaven and earth keep festival together, one in thanksgiving, one in happiness, one in joy.[1]

Nilus on the other hand was chiefly interested not in liturgical but in mystical prayer: before he settled at Sora he had lived as a monk on Mount Athos, and he knew the Byzantine Hesychast tradition at first hand.

The Russian Church rightly saw good things in the teaching of both Joseph and Nilus, and has canonized them both. Each inherited a part of the tradition of Saint Sergius, but no more than a part: Russia needed both the Josephite and the Transvolgian forms of monasticism, for each supplemented the other. It was sad indeed that the two sides entered into conflict, and that the tradition of Nilus was largely suppressed: without the Non-Possessors, the spiritual life of the Russian Church became one-sided and unbalanced. The close integration which the Josephites upheld between Church and State, their Russian nationalism, their devotion to the outward forms of worship – these things were to lead to trouble in the next century.

One of the most interesting participants in the dispute of Possessors and Non-Possessors was Saint Maximus the Greek (?1470–1556), a 'bridge figure' whose long life embraces the three worlds of Renaissance Italy, Mount Athos, and Muscovy. Greek by birth, he spent the years of early manhood in Florence and Venice, as a friend of Humanist scholars such as Pico della Mirandola; he also fell under the influence of Savonarola, and for two years was a Dominican. Returning to Greece in 1504, he became a monk on Athos; in 1517 he was invited to Russia by the Tsar, to translate Greek works into Slavonic and to correct the Russian service books, which were disfigured by

1. Quoted by J. Meyendorff, 'Une controverse sur le rôle social de l'Église. La querelle des biens ecclésiastiques au XVIe siècle en Russie', in the periodical *Irénikon*, vol. XXIX (1956), p. 29.

numerous errors. Like Nilus, he was devoted to the Hesychast ideals, and on arriving in Russia he threw in his lot with the Non-Possessors. He suffered with the rest, and was imprisoned for twenty-six years, from 1525 to 1551. He was attacked with particular bitterness for the changes which he proposed in the service books, and the work of revision was broken off and left unfinished. His great gifts of learning, from which the Russians could have benefited so much, were largely wasted in imprisonment. He was as strict as Nilus in his demand for self-stripping and spiritual poverty. 'If you truly love Christ crucified,' he wrote, ' . . . be a stranger, unknown, without country, without name, silent before your relatives, your acquaintances, and your friends; distribute all that you have to the poor, sacrifice all your old habits and all your own will.'[1]

Although the victory of the Possessors meant a close alliance between Church and State, the Church did not forfeit all independence. When Ivan the Terrible's power was at its height, the Metropolitan of Moscow, Saint Philip (died 1569), dared to protest openly against the Tsar's bloodshed and injustice, and rebuked him to his face during the public celebration of the Liturgy. Ivan put him in prison and later had him strangled. Another who sharply criticized Ivan was Saint Basil the Blessed, the 'Fool in Christ' (died 1552). Folly for the sake of Christ is a form of sanctity found in Byzantium, but particularly prominent in medieval Russia: the 'Fool' carries the ideal of self-stripping and humiliation to its furthest extent, by renouncing all intellectual gifts, all forms of earthly wisdom, and by voluntarily taking upon himself the Cross of madness. These Fools often performed a valuable social rôle: simply because they were fools, they could criticize those in power with a frankness which no one else dared to employ. So it was with Basil, the 'living conscience' of the Tsar. Ivan listened to the shrewd censure of the Fool, and so far from punishing him, treated him with marked honour.

In 1589, with the consent of the Patriarch of Constantinople,

1. Quoted by E. Denissoff, *Maxime le Grec et l'Occident*, Paris, 1943, pp. 275-6.

the head of the Russian Church was raised from the rank of Metropolitan to that of Patriarch. It was from one point of view a triumph for the ideal of Moscow the Third Rome; but it was a qualified triumph, for the Moscow Patriarch did not take first place in the Orthodox world, but fifth, after Constantinople, Alexandria, Antioch, and Jerusalem (but superior to the more ancient Patriarchate of Serbia). As things turned out, the Moscow Patriarchate was to last for little more than a century.

THE SCHISM OF THE OLD BELIEVERS

The seventeenth century in Russia opened with a period of confusion and disaster, known as the Time of Troubles, when the land was divided against itself and fell a victim to outside enemies. But after 1613 Russia made a sudden recovery, and the next forty years were a time of reconstruction and reform in many branches of the nation's life. In this work of reconstruction the Church played a large part. The reforming movement in the Church was led at first by the Abbot Dionysius of the Trinity–Saint Sergius Monastery and by Philaret, Patriarch of Moscow from 1619 to 1633 (he was the father of the Tsar); after 1633 the leadership passed to a group of married parish clergy, and in particular to the Archpriests John Neronov and Avvakum Petrovitch. The work of correcting service books, begun in the previous century by Maximus the Greek, was now cautiously resumed; a Patriarchal Press was set up at Moscow, and more accurate Church books were issued, although the authorities did not venture to make too many drastic alterations. On the parish level, the reformers did all they could to raise moral standards alike among the clergy and the laity. They fought against drunkenness; they insisted that the fasts be observed; they demanded that the Liturgy and other services in the parish churches should be sung with reverence and without omissions; they encouraged frequent preaching.

The reforming group represented much of what was best in

the tradition of Saint Joseph of Volokalamsk. Like Joseph they believed in authority and discipline, and saw the Christian life in terms of ascetic rules and liturgical prayer. They expected not only monks but parish priests and laity – husband, wife, children – to keep the fasts and to spend long periods at prayer each day, either in church or before the icons in their own homes. Those who would appreciate the severity and self-discipline of the reforming circle should read the vivid and extraordinary autobiography of the Archpriest Avvakum (1620–82). In one of his letters Avvakum records how each evening, after he and his family had recited the usual evening prayers together, the lights would be put out: then he recited 600 prayers to Jesus and 100 to the Mother of God, accompanied by 300 prostrations (at each prostration he would lay his forehead on the ground, and then rise once more to a standing position). His wife, when with child (as she usually was), recited only 400 prayers with 200 prostrations. This gives some idea of the exacting standards observed by devout Russians in the seventeenth century.

The reformers' programme made few concessions to human weakness, and was too ambitious ever to be completely realized. Nevertheless Muscovy around 1650 went far to justify the title 'Holy Russia'. Orthodox from the Turkish Empire who visited Moscow were amazed (and often filled with dismay) by the austerity of the fasts, by the length and magnificence of the services. The whole nation appeared to live as 'one vast religious house'.[1] Archdeacon Paul of Aleppo, who stayed in Russia from 1654 to 1656, found that banquets at Court were accompanied not by music but by readings from the Lives of the Saints, as at meals in a monastery. Services lasting seven hours or more were attended by the Tsar and the whole Court: 'Now what shall we say of these duties, severe enough to turn children's hair grey, so strictly observed by the Emperor, Patriarch, grandees, princesses, and ladies, standing upright on their legs from morning to evening? Who would believe that they should thus go beyond the devout anchorites of the

1. N. Zernov, *Moscow the Third Rome*, p. 51.

desert?'[1] The children were not excluded from these rigorous observances: 'What surprised us most was to see the boys and little children ... standing bareheaded and motionless, without betraying the smallest gesture of impatience.'[2] Paul found Russian strictness not entirely to his taste. He complains that they permit no 'mirth, laughter, and jokes', no drunkenness, no 'opium eating', and no smoking: 'For the special crime of drinking tobacco they even put men to death.'[3] It is an impressive picture which Paul and other visitors to Russia present, but there is perhaps too much emphasis on externals. One Greek remarked on his return home that Muscovite religion seemed to consist largely in bell-ringing.

In 1652–3 there began a fatal quarrel between the reforming group and the new Patriarch, Nicon (1605–81). A peasant by origin, Nicon was probably the most brilliant and gifted man ever to become head of the Russian Church; but he suffered from an overbearing and authoritarian temper. Nicon was a strong admirer of things Greek: 'I am a Russian and the son of a Russian,' he used to say, 'but my faith and my religion are Greek.'[4] He demanded that Russian practices should be made to conform at every point to the standard of the four ancient Patriarchates, and that the Russian service books should be altered wherever they differed from the Greek.

This policy was bound to provoke opposition among those who belonged to the Josephite tradition. They regarded Moscow as the Third Rome, and Russia as the stronghold and norm of Orthodoxy; and now Nicon told them that they must in all respects copy the Greeks. But was not Russia an independent Church, a fully grown member of the Orthodox family, entitled to hold to her own national customs and traditions? The Russians certainly respected the memory of the Mother Church of Byzantium from which they had received the faith, but they did not feel the same reverence for contemporary Greeks. They

1. 'The Travels of Macarius', in W. Palmer, *The Patriarch and the Tsar*, London, 1873, vol. 11, p. 107.
2. *The Travels of Macarius*, edited Ridding, p. 68.
3. ibid., p. 21.   4. ibid., p. 37.

remembered the 'apostasy' of the Greeks at Florence, and they knew something of the corruption and disorders within the Patriarchate of Constantinople under Turkish rule.

Had Nicon proceeded gently and tactfully, all might yet have been well: Patriarch Philaret had already made some corrections in the service books without arousing opposition. Nicon, however, was not a gentle or a tactful man, but pressed on with his programme regardless of the feelings of others. In particular he insisted that the sign of the Cross, at that time made by the Russians with two fingers, should now be made in the Greek fashion with three. This may seem a trivial matter; but it must be remembered how great an importance Orthodox in general and Russians in particular have always attached to ritual actions, to the symbolic gestures whereby the inner belief of a Christian is expressed. In the eyes of simple believers a change in the symbol constituted a change in the faith. The divergence over the sign of the Cross also raised in concrete form the whole question of Greek *versus* Russian Orthodoxy. The Greek form with three fingers was more recent than the Russian form with two: why should the Russians, who remained loyal to the ancient ways, be forced to accept a 'modern' Greek innovation?

Neronov and Avvakum, together with many other clergy, monks, and lay people, defended the old Russian practices and refused to accept Nicon's changes or to use the new service books which he issued. Nicon was not a man to tolerate any disagreement, and he had his opponents exiled and imprisoned: in some cases they were eventually put to death. Yet despite persecution, the opposition continued; although Neronov finally submitted, Avvakum refused to give way, and after ten years of exile and twenty-two years of imprisonment (twelve of them spent in an underground hut) he was finally burnt at the stake. His supporters regarded him as a saint and martyr for the faith. Those who like Avvakum defied the official Church with its Niconian service books eventually formed a separate sect (*raskol*) known as the *Old Believers* (it would be more exact to call them Old Ritualists). Thus there arose in seventeenth-century Russia a movement of Dissent; but if we compare it with English Dissent of the same period, we notice two great differences. First, the Old Believers – the Russian Dissenters – differed from the official Church solely in ritual, not in doctrine; and secondly, while English Dissent was radical – a protest against the official Church for not carrying reform far enough – Russian Dissent was the protest of conservatives against an official Church which in their eyes had carried reform too far.

The schism of the Old Believers has continued to the present day. Before 1917 their numbers were officially assessed at two million, but the true figure may well have been over five times as great. They are divided into two main groups, the *Popovtsy*, who have retained the priesthood and who since 1846 have also possessed their own succession of bishops; and the *Bezpopovtsy*, who have no priests.

There is much to admire in the *Raskolniki*. They numbered in their ranks the finest elements among the parish clergy and the laity of seventeenth-century Russia. Historians in the past have done them a serious injustice by regarding the whole dispute merely as a quarrel over the position of a finger, over texts, syllables, and false letters. The true cause of the schism lay elsewhere, and was concerned with something far more profound. The Old Believers fought for the two-finger sign of the Cross, for the old texts and customs, not simply as ends in themselves, but because of the matter of principle which was herein involved: they saw these things as embodying the ancient tradition of the Church, and this ancient tradition, so they held, had been preserved in its full purity by Russia and by Russia alone. Can we say that they were entirely wrong? The two-finger sign of the Cross was in fact more ancient than the three-finger form; it was the Greeks who were the innovators, the Russians who remained loyal to the old ways. Why then should the Russians be forced to adopt the modern Greek practice? Certainly, in the heat of controversy the Old Believers pushed their case to extremes, and their legitimate reverence for 'Holy Russia' degenerated into a fanatical nationalism; but Nicon also went too far in his uncritical admiration for all things Greek.

'We have no reason to be ashamed of our *Raskol*,' wrote Khomiakov. ' . . . It is worthy of a great people, and could inspire respect in a stranger; but it is far from embracing all the richness of Russian thought.'[1] It does not embrace the richness of Russian thought because it represents but a single aspect of Russian Christianity – the tradition of the Possessors. The defects of the Old Believers are the Josephite defects writ large: too narrow a nationalism, too great an emphasis on the externals of worship. Nicon too, despite his Hellenism, is in the end a Josephite: he demanded an absolute uniformity in the externals of worship, and like the Possessors he freely invoked the help of the civil arm in order to suppress all religious opponents. More than anything else, it was his readiness to resort to persecution which made the schism definitive. Had the development of Church life in Russia between 1550 and 1650 been less one-sided, perhaps a lasting separation would have been avoided. If men had thought more (as Nilus did) of tolerance and freedom instead of using persecution, then a reconciliation might have been effected; and if they had attended more to mystical prayer, they might have argued less bitterly about ritual. Behind the division of the seventeenth century lie the disputes of the sixteenth.

As well as establishing Greek practices in Russia, Nicon pursued a second aim: to make the Church supreme over the State. In the past the theory governing relations between Church and State had been the same in Russia as in Byzantium – a dyarchy or symphony of two coordinated powers, *sacerdotium* and *imperium*, each supreme in its own sphere. In the Assumption Cathedral of the Kremlin there were placed two equal thrones, one for the Patriarch and one for the Tsar. In practice the Church had enjoyed a wide measure of independence and influence in the Kievan and Mongol periods. But under the Moscow Tsardom, although the theory of two equal

1. See A. Gratieux, *A. S. Khomiakov et le mouvement slavophile*, Paris, 1939, vol. II, p. 165.

powers remained the same, in practice the civil power came to control the Church more and more; the Josephite policy naturally encouraged this tendency. Nicon attempted to reverse the situation. Not only did he demand that the Patriarch's authority be absolute in religious matters, but he also claimed the right to intervene in civil affairs, and assumed the title 'Great Lord', hitherto reserved to the Tsar alone. Tsar Alexis had a deep respect for Nicon, and at first submitted to his control. 'The Patriarch's authority is so great,' wrote Olearius, visiting Moscow in 1654, 'that he in a manner divides the sovereignty with the Grand Duke.'[1]

But after a time Alexis began to resent Nicon's interference in secular affairs. In 1658 Nicon, perhaps in hopes of restoring his influence, decided upon a curious step: he withdrew into semi-retirement, but did not resign the office of Patriarch. For eight years the Russian Church remained without an effective head, until at the Tsar's request a great Council was held at Moscow in 1666–7 over which the Patriarchs of Alexandria and Antioch presided. The Council decided in favour of Nicon's *reforms*, but against his *person*: Nicon's changes in the service books and above all his ruling on the sign of the Cross were confirmed, but Nicon himself was deposed and exiled, a new Patriarch being appointed in his place. The Council was therefore a triumph for Nicon's policy of imposing Greek practices on the Russian Church, but a defeat for his attempt to set the Patriarch above the Tsar. The Council reasserted the Byzantine theory of a harmony of equal powers.

But the decisions of the Moscow Council upon the relations of Church and State did not remain long in force. The pendulum which Nicon had pushed too far in one direction soon swung back in the other with redoubled violence. Peter the Great (reigned 1682–1725) altogether suppressed the office of Patriarch, whose powers Nicon had so ambitiously striven to aggrandize.

1. Palmer, *The Patriarch and the Tsar*, vol. II, p. 407.

THE SYNODICAL PERIOD (1700–1917)

Peter was determined that there should be no more Nicons. In 1700, when Patriarch Adrian died, Peter took no steps towards the appointment of a successor; and in 1721 he proceeded to issue the celebrated *Spiritual Regulation*, which declared the Patriarchate to be abolished, and set up in its place a commission, the Spiritual College or Holy Synod. This was composed of twelve members, three of whom were bishops, and the rest drawn from the heads of monasteries or from the married clergy.

The constitution of the Synod was not based on Orthodox Canon Law, but copied from the Protestant ecclesiastical synods in Germany. Its members were not chosen by the Church but nominated by the Emperor; and the Emperor who nominated could also dismiss them at will. Whereas a Patriarch, holding office for life, could perhaps defy the Tsar, a member of the Holy Synod was allowed no scope for heroism: he was simply retired. The Emperor was not called 'Head of the Church', but he was given the title 'Supreme Judge of the Spiritual College'. Meetings of the Synod were not attended by the Emperor himself, but by a government official, the Chief Procurator. The Procurator, although he sat at a separate table and took no part in the discussions, in practice wielded considerable power over Church affairs and was in effect if not in name a 'Minister for Religion'.

The *Spiritual Regulation* sees the Church not as a divine institution but as a department of State. Based largely on secular presuppositions, it makes little allowance for what were termed in the English Reformation 'the Crown rights of the Redeemer'. This is true not only of its provisions for the higher administration of the Church, but of many of its other rulings. A priest who learns, while hearing confessions, of any scheme which the government might consider seditious, is ordered to violate the secrecy of the sacrament and to supply the police with names and full details. Monasticism is bluntly termed 'the origin of innumerable disorders and disturbances' and placed under many restrictions. New monasteries are not to be founded without special permission; monks are forbidden to live as hermits; no woman under the age of fifty is allowed to take vows as a nun.

There was a deliberate purpose behind these restrictions on the monasteries, the chief centres of social work in Russia up to this time. The abolition of the Patriarchate was part of a wider process: Peter sought not only to deprive the Church of leadership, but to eliminate it from all participation in social work. Peter's successors circumscribed the work of the monasteries still more drastically. Elizabeth (reigned 1741–62) confiscated most of the monastic estates, and Catherine II (reigned 1762–96) suppressed more than half the monasteries, while on such houses as remained open she imposed a strict limitation to the number of monks. The closing of the monasteries was little short of a disaster in the more distant provinces of Russia, where they formed virtually the only cultural and charitable centres. But although the social work of the Church was grievously restricted, it never completely ceased.

The *Spiritual Regulation* makes lively reading, particularly in its comments on clerical behaviour. We are told that priests and deacons 'being drunk, bellow in the Streets, or what is worse, in their drink whoop and hollow in Church'; bishops are told to see that the clergy 'walk not in a dronish lazy manner, nor lie down in the Streets to sleep, nor tipple in Cabacks, nor boast of the Strength of their Heads'.[1] One fears that despite the efforts of the reforming movement in the previous century, these strictures were not entirely unjustified.

There is also some vivid advice to preachers:

A Preacher has no Occasion to shove and heave as tho' he was tugging at an Oar in a Boat. He has no need to clap his Hands, to set his Arms a Kimbo, nor to bounce or spring, nor to giggle and laugh, nor any Reason for Howlings and hideous Lamentations. For tho' he should be never so much griev'd in Spirit, yet

1. The *Spiritual Regulation*, translated by Thomas Consett in *The Present State and Regulations of the Church of Russia*, London, 1729, pp. 157–8.

ought he to suppress his Tears all he can, because these Emotions are all superfluous and indecent, and disturb an Audience.[1]

So much for the *Spiritual Regulation*. Peter's religious reforms naturally aroused opposition in Russia, but it was ruthlessly silenced. Outside Russia the redoubtable Dositheus made a vigorous protest; but the Orthodox Churches under Turkish rule were in no position to intervene effectively, and in 1723 the four ancient Patriarchates accepted the abolition of the Patriarchate of Moscow and recognized the constitution of the Holy Synod.

The system of Church government which Peter the Great established continued in force until 1917. The Synodical period in the history of Russian Orthodoxy is usually represented as a time of decline, with the Church in complete subservience to the State. Certainly a superficial glance at the eighteenth century would serve to confirm this verdict. It was an age of ill-advised westernization in Church art, Church music, and theology. Those who rebelled against the dry scholasticism of the theological academies turned, not to the teachings of Byzantium and ancient Russia, but to religious or pseudo-religious movements in the contemporary west: Protestant mysticism, German pietism, Freemasonry,[2] and the like. Prominent among the higher clergy were Court prelates such as Ambrose (Zertiss-Kamensky), Archbishop of Moscow and Kaluga, who at his death in 1771 left (among many other possessions) 252 shirts of fine linen and nine eye-glasses framed in gold.

But this is only one side of the picture in the eighteenth century. The Holy Synod, however objectionable its theoretical constitution, in practice governed efficiently. Reflective Churchmen were well aware of the defects in Peter's reforms, and submitted to them without necessarily agreeing with them. Theology was westernized, but standards of scholarship were

1. Consett, op. cit., p. 90. The picturesqueness of the style is due more to Consett than to his Russian original.

2. Orthodox are strictly forbidden, on pain of excommunication, to become Freemasons.

high. Behind the façade of westernization, the true life of Orthodox Russia continued without interruption. Ambrose Zertiss-Kamensky represented one type of Russian bishop, but there were other bishops of a very different character, true monks and pastors, such as Saint Tikhon of Zadonsk (1724–83), Bishop of Voronezh. A great preacher and a fluent writer, Tikhon is particularly interesting as an example of one who, like most of his contemporaries, borrowed heavily from the west, but who remained at the same time firmly rooted in the classic tradition of Orthodox spirituality. He drew upon German and Anglican books of devotion; his detailed meditations upon the physical sufferings of Jesus are more typical of Roman Catholicism than of Orthodoxy; in his own life of prayer he underwent an experience similar to the Dark Night of the Soul, as described by western mystics such as Saint John of the Cross. But Tikhon was also close in outlook to Theodosius and Sergius, to Nilus and the Non-Possessors. Like so many Russian saints, both lay and monastic, he took a special delight in helping the poor, and he was happiest when talking with simple people – peasants, beggars, and even criminals.

The second part of the Synodical period, the nineteenth century, so far from being a period of decline, was a time of great revival in the Russian Church. Men turned away from religious and pseudo-religious movements in the contemporary west, and fell back once more upon the true spiritual forces of Orthodoxy. Hand in hand with this revival in the spiritual life went a new enthusiasm for missionary work, while in theology, as in spirituality, Orthodoxy freed itself from a slavish imitation of the west.

It was from Mount Athos that this religious renewal took its origin. A young Russian at the theological academy of Kiev, Paissy Velichkovsky (1722–94), horrified by the secular tone of the teaching, fled to Mount Athos and there became a monk. In 1763 he went to Romania and became Abbot of the monastery of Niamets, which he made a great spiritual centre, gathering round him more than 500 brethren. Under his guidance, the community devoted itself specially to the work of translating

Greek Fathers into Slavonic. At Athos Paissy had learnt at first hand about the Hesychast tradition, and he was in close sympathy with his contemporary Nicodemus. He made a Slavonic translation of the *Philokalia*, which was published at Moscow in 1793. Paissy laid great emphasis upon the practice of continual prayer – above all the Jesus Prayer – and on the need for obedience to an elder or *starets*. He was deeply influenced by Nilus and the Non-Possessors, but he did not overlook the good elements in the Josephite form of monasticism: he allowed more place than Nilus had done to liturgical prayer and to social work, and in this way he attempted, like Sergius, to combine the mystical with the corporate and social aspect of the monastic life.

Paissy himself never returned to Russia, but many of his disciples travelled thither from Romania and under their inspiration a monastic revival spread across the land. Existing houses were reinvigorated, and many new foundations were made: in 1810 there were 452 monasteries in Russia, whereas in 1914 there were 1,025. This monastic movement, while outward-looking and concerned to serve the world, also restored to the centre of the Church's life the tradition of the Non-Possessors, largely suppressed since the sixteenth century. It was marked in particular by a high development of the practice of spiritual direction. Although the 'elder' has been a characteristic figure in many periods of Orthodox history, nineteenth-century Russia is *par excellence* the age of the *starets*.

The first and greatest of the *startsi* of the nineteenth century was Saint Seraphim of Sarov (1759–1833), who of all the saints of Russia is perhaps the most immediately attractive to non-Orthodox Christians. Entering the monastery of Sarov at the age of nineteen, Seraphim first spent sixteen years in the ordinary life of the community. Then he withdrew to spend the next twenty years in seclusion, living at first in a hut in the forest, then (when his feet swelled up and he could no longer walk with ease) enclosed in a cell in the monastery. This was his training for the office of eldership. Finally in 1815 he opened the doors of his cell. From dawn until evening he received all who came to him for help, healing the sick, giving advice, often supplying the answer before his visitor had time to ask any questions. Sometimes scores or hundreds would come to see him in a single day. The outward pattern of Seraphim's life recalls that of Antony of Egypt fifteen centuries before: there is the same withdrawal in order to return. Seraphim is rightly regarded as a characteristically Russian saint, but he is also a striking example of how much Russian Orthodoxy has in common with Byzantium and the universal Orthodox tradition throughout the ages.

Seraphim was extraordinarily severe to himself (at one point in his life he spent a thousand successive nights in continual prayer, standing motionless throughout the long hours of darkness on a rock), but he was gentle to others, without ever being sentimental or indulgent. Asceticism did not make him gloomy, and if ever a saint's life was illuminated by joy, it was Seraphim's. He practised the Jesus Prayer, and like the Byzantine Hesychasts he was granted the vision of the Divine and Uncreated Light. In Seraphim's case the Divine Light actually took a visible form, outwardly transforming his body. One of Seraphim's 'spiritual children', Nicholas Motovilov, described what happened one winter day as the two of them were talking together in the forest. Seraphim had spoken of the need to acquire the Holy Spirit, and Motovilov asked how a man could be sure of 'being in the Spirit of God':

Then Father Seraphim took me very firmly by the shoulders and said: 'My son, we are both at this moment in the Spirit of God. Why don't you look at me?'

'I cannot look, Father,' I replied, 'because your eyes are flashing like lightning. Your face has become brighter than the sun, and it hurts my eyes to look at you.'

'Don't be afraid,' he said. 'At this very moment you yourself have become as bright as I am. You yourself are now in the fullness of the Spirit of God; otherwise you would not be able to see me as you do.'

Then bending his head towards me, he whispered softly in my ear: 'Thank the Lord God for His infinite goodness towards

131

us. . . . But why, my son, do you not look me in the eyes? Just look, and don't be afraid; the Lord is with us.'

After these words I glanced at his face, and there came over me an even greater reverent awe. Imagine in the centre of the sun, in the dazzling light of its midday rays, the face of a man talking to you. You see the movement of his lips and the changing expression of his eyes, you hear his voice, you feel someone holding your shoulders; yet you do not see his hands, you do not even see yourself or his body, but only a blinding light spreading far around for several yards and lighting up with its brilliance the snow-blanket which covers the forest glade and the snow-flakes which continue to fall unceasingly . . .

'What do you feel?' Father Seraphim asked me.

'An immeasurable well-being,' I said.

'But what sort of well-being? How exactly do you feel well?'

'I feel such a calm,' I answered, 'such peace in my soul that no words can express it.'

'This,' said Father Seraphim, 'is that peace of which the Lord said to His disciples: My peace I give to you; not as the world gives do I give to you [John xiv, 27], the peace which passes all understanding [Philippians iv, 7] . . . What else do you feel?'

'Infinite joy in all my heart.'

And Father Seraphim continued: 'When the Spirit of God comes down to man and overshadows him with the fullness of His presence, then the man's soul overflows with unspeakable joy, for the Holy Spirit fills with joy whatever He touches . . .'[1]

So the conversation continues. The whole passage is of extraordinary importance for understanding the Orthodox doctrine of deification and union with God. It shows how the Orthodox idea of sanctification includes the body: it is not Seraphim's (or Motovilov's) soul only, but the whole body which is transfigured by the grace of God. We may note that neither Seraphim nor Motovilov is in a state of ecstasy; both can talk in a coherent way and are still conscious of the outside world, but both are filled with the Holy Spirit and surrounded by the light of the age to come.

1. *Conversation of Saint Seraphim on the Aim of the Christian Life*, printed in *A Wonderful Revelation to the World*, Jordanville (N.Y.), 1953, pp. 23–5.

Seraphim had no teacher in the art of direction and he left no successor. After his death the work was taken up by another community, the hermitage of Optino. From 1829 until 1923, when the monastery was closed by the Bolsheviks, a succession of *startsi* ministered here, their influence extending like that of Seraphim over the whole of Russia. The best known of the Optino elders are Leonid (1768–1841), Macarius (1788–1860), and Ambrose (1812–91). While these elders all belonged to the school of Paissy and were all devoted to the Prayer of Jesus, each of them had a strongly marked character of his own: Leonid, for example, was simple, vivid, and direct, appealing specially to peasants and merchants, while Macarius was highly educated, a Patristic scholar, a man in close contact with the intellectual movements of the day. Optino influenced a number of writers, including Gogol, Khomiakov, Dostoyevsky, Soloviev, and Tolstoy.[1] The remarkable figure of the elder Zossima in Dostoyevsky's novel *The Brothers Karamazov* was based partly on Father Macarius or Father Ambrose of Optino, although Dostoyevsky says that he was inspired primarily by the life of Saint Tikhon of Zadonsk.

'There is one thing more important than all possible books and ideas,' wrote the Slavophil Ivan Kireyevsky, 'to find an Orthodox *starets*, before whom you can lay each of your thoughts, and from whom you can hear not your own opinion, but the judgement of the Holy Fathers. God be praised, such *startsi* have not yet disappeared in Russia.'[2]

Through the *startsi*, the monastic revival influenced the life of the whole people. The spiritual atmosphere of the time is vividly expressed in an anonymous book, *The Way of a Pilgrim*, which describes the experiences of a Russian peasant who

1. The story of Tolstoy's relations with the Orthodox Church is extremely sad. In later life he publicly attacked the Church with great violence, and the Holy Synod after some hesitation excommunicated him (February 1901). As he lay dying in the stationmaster's house at Astapovo, one of the Optino elders travelled to see him, but was refused admittance by Tolstoy's family.

2. Quoted by Metropolitan Seraphim (of Berlin and Western Europe), *L'Église orthodoxe*, Paris, 1952, p. 219.

tramped from place to place practising the Jesus Prayer. For those who know nothing of the Jesus Prayer, there can be no better introduction than this little work. *The Way of a Pilgrim* shows how the Prayer is not limited to monasteries, but can be used by everyone, in every form of life. As he travelled, the Pilgrim carried with him a copy of the *Philokalia*, presumably the Slavonic translation by Paissy. Bishop Theophan the Recluse (1815–94) during the years 1876–90 issued a greatly expanded translation of the *Philokalia* in five volumes, this time not in Slavonic but in Russian.

Hitherto we have spoken chiefly of the movement centring on the monasteries. But among the great figures of the Russian Church in the nineteenth century there was also a member of the married parish clergy, John Sergiev (1829–1908), usually known as Father John of Kronstadt, because throughout his ministry he worked in the same place, Kronstadt, a naval base and suburb of Saint Petersburg. Father John is best remembered for his work as a parish priest – visiting the poor and the sick, organizing charitable work, teaching religion to the children of his parish, preaching continually, and above all praying with and for his flock. He had an intense awareness of the power of prayer, and as he celebrated the Liturgy he was entirely carried away: 'He could not keep the prescribed measure of liturgical intonation: he called out to God; he shouted; he wept in the face of the visions of Golgotha and the Resurrection which presented themselves to him with such shattering immediacy.'[1] The same sense of immediacy can be felt on every page of the spiritual autobiography which Father John wrote, *My Life in Christ*. Like Saint Seraphim, he possessed the gifts of healing, of insight, and of spiritual direction.

Father John insisted on frequent communion, although in Russia at this date it was very unusual for the laity to communicate more than four or five times a year. Because he had no time to hear individually the confessions of all who came for communion, he established a form of public confession,

1. Fedotov, *A Treasury of Russian Spirituality*, p. 348.

with everybody shouting their sins aloud simultaneously. He turned the iconostasis into a low screen, so that altar and celebrant might be visible throughout the service. In his emphasis on frequent communion and his reversion to the more ancient form of chancel screen, Father John anticipated liturgical developments in contemporary Orthodoxy. In 1964 he was proclaimed a saint by the Russian Church in Exile.

In nineteenth-century Russia there was a striking revival of missionary work. Since the days of Mitrophan of Sarai and Stephen of Perm, Russians had been active missionaries, and as Muscovite power advanced eastward, a great field was opened up for evangelism among the native tribes and among the Mohammedan Mongols. But although the Church never ceased to send out preachers to the heathen, in the seventeenth and eighteenth centuries missionary efforts had somewhat languished, particularly after the closing of monasteries by Catherine. But in the nineteenth century the missionary challenge was taken up with fresh energy and enthusiasm: the Academy of Kazan, opened in 1842, was specially concerned with missionary studies; native clergy were trained; the scriptures and the Liturgy were translated into a wide variety of languages. In the Kazan area alone the Liturgy was celebrated in twenty-two different languages or dialects.

It is significant that one of the first leaders in the missionary revival, Archimandrite Macarius (Glukharev, 1792–1847), was a student of Hesychasm and knew the disciples of Paissy Velichkovsky: the missionary revival had its roots in the revival of the spiritual life. The greatest of the nineteenth-century missionaries was Innocent (John Veniaminov, 1797–1879), Bishop of Kamchatka and the Aleutian Islands, who was proclaimed a saint in 1977. His diocese included some of the most inhospitable regions of the world; it extended across the Bering Straits to Alaska, which at that time belonged to Russia. Innocent played an important part in the development of American Orthodoxy, and millions of American Orthodox today can look on him as one of their chief 'Apostles'.

In the field of theology, nineteenth-century Russia broke away from its excessive dependence upon the west. This was due chiefly to the work of Alexis Khomiakov (1804–60), leader of the Slavophil circle and perhaps the first original theologian in the history of the Russian Church. A country landowner and a retired cavalry captain, Khomiakov belonged to the tradition of lay theologians which has always existed in Orthodoxy. Khomiakov argued that all western Christianity, whether Roman or Protestant, shares the same assumptions and betrays the same fundamental point of view, while Orthodoxy is something entirely distinct. Since this is so (Khomiakov continued), it is not enough for Orthodox to borrow their theology from the west, as they had been doing since the seventeenth century; instead of using Protestant arguments against Rome, and Roman arguments against the Protestants, they must return to their own authentic sources, and rediscover the true Orthodox tradition, which in its basic presuppositions is neither Roman nor Reformed, but unique. As his friend G. Samarin put it, before Khomiakov 'our Orthodox school of theology was not in a position to define either Latinism or Protestantism, because in departing from its own Orthodox standpoint, it had itself become divided into two, and each of these halves had taken up a position *opposed* indeed to its opponent, Latin or Protestant, but not *above* him. It was Khomiakov who first looked upon Latinism and Protestantism from the point of view *of the Church*, and therefore from a *higher* standpoint: and this is the reason why he was also able to define them.'[1] Khomiakov was particularly concerned with the doctrine of the Church, its unity and authority; and here he made a lasting contribution to Orthodox theology.

Khomiakov during his lifetime exercised little or no influence on the theology taught in the academies and seminaries, but here too there was an increasing independence from the west. By 1900 Russian academic theology was at its height, and there were a number of theologians, historians, and liturgists, thoroughly trained in western academic disciplines, yet not

1. Quoted in Birkbeck, *Russia and the English Church*, p. xlv.

allowing western influences to distort their Orthodoxy. In the years following 1900 there was also an important intellectual revival outside the theological schools. Since the time of Peter the Great, unbelief had been common among Russian 'intellectuals', but now a number of thinkers, by various routes, found their way back to the Church. Some were former Marxists, such as Sergius Bulgakov (1871–1944) (later ordained priest) and Nicholas Berdyaev (1874–1948), both of whom subsequently played a prominent part in the life of the Russian emigration in Paris.

When one reflects on the lives of Tikhon and Seraphim, on the Optino *startsi* and John of Kronstadt, on the missionary and theological work in nineteenth-century Russia, it can be seen how unfair it is to regard the Synodical period simply as a time of decline. One of the greatest of Russian Church historians, Professor Kartashev (1875–1960), has rightly said:

The subjugation was ennobled from within by Christian humility. . . . The Russian Church was suffering under the burden of the régime, but she overcame it from within. She grew, she spread and flourished in many different ways. Thus the period of the Holy·Synod could be called the most brilliant and glorious period in the history of the Russian Church.[1]

On 15 August 1917, six months after the abdication of Emperor Nicholas II, when the Provisional Government was in power, an All-Russian Church Council was convened at Moscow, which did not finally disperse until September of the following year. More than half the delegates were laymen – the bishops and clergy present numbered 250, the laity 314 – but (as Canon Law demanded) the final decision on specifically religious questions was reserved to the bishops alone. The Council carried through a far-reaching programme of reform, its chief act being to abolish the Synodical form of government established by Peter the Great, and to restore the Patriarchate. The election of the Patriarch took place on 5 November 1917.

1. Article in the periodical *The Christian East*, vol. XVI (1936), pp. 114 and 115.

In a series of preliminary ballots, three candidates were selected; but the final choice among these three was made by lot. At the first ballot Antony (Khrapovitsky), Archbishop of Kharkov (1863–1936), came first with 101 votes; then Arsenius, Archbishop of Novgorod, with 27 votes; and thirdly Tikhon (Beliavin), Metropolitan of Moscow (1866–1925), with 23 votes. But when the lot was drawn, it was the last of these three candidates, Tikhon, who was actually chosen as Patriarch.

Outside events gave a note of urgency to the deliberations. At the earlier sessions members could hear the sound of Bolshevik artillery shelling the Kremlin, and two days before the election of the new Patriarch, Lenin and his associates gained full mastery of Moscow. The Church was allowed no time to consolidate the work of reform. Before the Council came to a close in the summer of 1918, its members learnt with horror of the brutal murder of Vladimir, Metropolitan of Kiev, by the Bolsheviks. Persecution had already begun.

CHAPTER 7

The Twentieth Century, I:
Greeks and Arabs

THE Orthodox Church of today exists in two contrasting situations: outside the communist sphere lie the four ancient Patriarchates and Greece, under communism are the Slav Churches and Romania. Whereas communism only impinges upon the periphery of the Roman Catholic and the Protestant worlds, in the case of the Orthodox Church the vast majority of its members live in a communist state. At the present moment there are probably between sixty and ninety million practising Orthodox – the number of baptized Orthodox is considerably higher – and of these more than eighty-five per cent are in communist countries.

Following this obvious line of division, in this chapter we shall consider the Orthodox Churches outside the communist bloc, and in the next the position of Orthodoxy in the 'second world'. A third chapter is devoted to the Orthodox 'dispersion' in other places, and to Orthodox missionary activities at the present time.

Of the seven Orthodox Churches not under communist rule, four – Constantinople, Greece, Cyprus, Sinai – are predominantly or exclusively Greek; one – Alexandria – is partly Greek, partly Arab and African; the remaining two – Antioch and Jerusalem – are mainly Arab, although at Jerusalem the higher administration of the Church is in Greek hands.

(1) The *Patriarchate of Constantinople*, which in the tenth century contained 624 dioceses, is today enormously reduced in size. At present within the Patriarch's jurisdiction are:

   (i)   Turkey;
  (ii)   Crete and various other islands in the Aegean;

   (iii)   All Greeks of the dispersion, together with certain Russian, Ukrainian, Polish, and Albanian dioceses in emigration (on these see Chapter 9);

   (iv)   Mount Athos;

   (v)   Finland.

This amounts in all to about three million persons, more than half of whom are Greeks dwelling in North America.

At the end of the First World War, Turkey contained a population of some 1,500,000 Greeks, but the greater part of these were either massacred or deported at the end of the disastrous Greco-Turkish War of 1922, and today (apart from the island of Imbros) the only place in Turkey where Greeks are allowed to live is Istanbul (Constantinople) itself. Even in Constantinople, Orthodox clergy (with the exception of the Patriarch) are forbidden to appear in the streets in clerical dress. The Greek community in the city has dwindled since the anti-Greek (and anti-Christian) riot of 6 September 1955, when in a single night sixty out of the eighty Orthodox Churches at Constantinople were gutted or sacked, the total damage to Christian property being reckoned at £50,000,000. Since then, many Greeks have fled from fear or else have been forcibly deported, and there is a grave danger that the Turkish government will eventually expel the Patriarchate. Athenagoras, Patriarch during 1948–72 – indefatigable as a worker for Christian unity – and his successor Patriarch Dimitrios have shown great patience and dignity in this tragic situation.

The Patriarchate had a celebrated theological school on the island of Halki near Constantinople, which in the 1950s began to acquire a somewhat international character, with students not only from Greece but from the Near East in general. But unfortunately from 1971 onwards the Turkish authorities prevented the school from admitting any new students, and there is at present very little prospect that it will be reopened.

Mount Athos, like Halki, is not merely Greek but international. Of the twenty ruling monasteries, at the present day seventeen are Greek, one Russian, one Serbian, and one Bul-

garian; in Byzantine times one of the twenty was Georgian, and
there were also Latin houses. Besides the ruling monasteries
there are several other large houses, and innumerable smaller
settlements known as *sketes* or *kellia*; there are also hermits,
most of whom live above alarming precipices at the southern
tip of the peninsula, in huts or caves often accessible only by
decaying ladders. Thus the three forms of the monastic life,
dating back to fourth-century Egypt – the community life, the
semi-eremitic life, and the hermits – continue side by side on
the Holy Mountain today. It is a remarkable illustration of the
continuity of Orthodoxy.

Athos faces many problems, the most obvious and serious
being the spectacular decline in numbers. Compare the figures
for 1903 and 1965:

	1903	1965
Greeks	3,276	1,290
Russians	3,496	62
Bulgarians	307	17
Serbs	16	28
Romanians	286	94
Georgians	51	None
	7,432	1,491

It is likely that numbers will continue to decline, for the
majority of the monks today are old men. Although there have
been times in the past – for example, the early nineteenth
century – when monks were even fewer than at present, yet
the suddenness of the decrease in the past fifty years is most
alarming.

In many parts of the Orthodox world today, and not least in
certain circles in Greece itself, the monastic life is viewed with
indifference and contempt, and this is in part responsible for
the lack of new vocations on Athos. Another cause is the political situation: in 1903 more than half the monks were Slavs or
Romanians, but after 1917 the supply of novices from Russia
was cut off, while since 1945 the same has happened with

Bulgaria and Romania. The Russian monastery of Saint Panteleimon, which in 1904 had 1,978 members, in 1959 numbered less than 60; the vast Russian *skete* of Saint Elias now has less than five monks, while that of Saint Andrew is entirely closed; the spacious buildings of Zographou, the Bulgarian house, are virtually deserted, and at the Romanian *skete* of Saint John the Baptist there is a mere handful of monks. In 1966, after prolonged negotiations, the Greek government eventually allowed five monks from the U.S.S.R. to enter Saint Panteleimon, and four monks from Bulgaria to enter Zographou: but clearly recruitment on a far vaster scale is necessary. Of the non-Greek communities, the Serbian monastery alone is in a slightly better position, as some young men have recently been allowed to come from Yugoslavia to be professed as monks.

In Byzantine times the Holy Mountain was a centre of theological scholarship, but today most of the monks come from peasant families and have little education. This, though not a new situation, has certain unfortunate consequences. It would be sad indeed were Athos to modernize itself at the expense of the traditional and timeless values of Orthodox monasticism; but so long as the monasteries remain intellectually isolated, they cannot make their full (and very necessary) contribution to the life of the Church at large. There are signs that leaders on Athos are aware of the dangers of this isolation and are seeking ways to overcome it. The Athonite School of Theology was reopened in 1953, in the hope of attracting and training a somewhat different type of novice. Father Theoklitos, of the monastery of Dionysiou, goes regularly to Athens and Thessalonica to speak at meetings, and has written an important book on the monastic life, *Between Heaven and Earth*, as well as a study of Saint Nicodemus of the Holy Mountain. Father Gabriel, for many years Abbot of Dionysiou, is also widely known and respected in Greece as a whole.

But it would be wrong to judge Athos or any other monastic centre by numbers or literary output alone, for the true criterion is not size or scholarship but the quality of spiritual life.

If in Athos today there are signs in some places of an alarming decadence, yet there can be no doubt that the Holy Mountain still continues to produce saints, ascetics, and men of prayer formed in the classic traditions of Orthodoxy. One such monk was Father Silvan (1866–1938), at the Russian monastery of Saint Panteleimon: of peasant background, a simple and humble man, his life was outwardly uneventful, but he left behind him some deeply impressive meditations, which have since been published in several languages.[1] Another such monk was Father Joseph (died 1959), a Greek who lived in a semi-eremitic settlement – the New Skete – in the south of Athos, and gathered round him a group of monks who under his guidance practised the continual recitation of the Jesus Prayer. So long as Athos numbers among its members men such as Silvan and Joseph, it is by no means failing in its task.[2]

The Orthodox *Church of Finland* owes its origin to monks from the Russian monastery of Valamo on Lake Ladoga, who preached among the pagan Finnish tribes in Karelia during the Middle Ages. The Finnish Orthodox were dependent on the Russian Church until the Revolution, but since 1923 they have been under the spiritual care of the Patriarchate of Constantinople, although the Russian Church did not accept this situation until 1957. The vast majority of Finns are nominally Lutheran, and the 66,000 Orthodox comprise only 1·5 per cent of the population. There is an Orthodox seminary at Kuopio. 'With its active youth, concerned with international

1. See Archimandrite Sophrony, *The Monk of Mount Athos* and *Wisdom from Mount Athos*, London, 1973–4 (most valuable).
2. The text above describes the situation as it existed on Athos during 1960–66. Since then there has been a notable improvement. Although the non-Greek monasteries have only been able to receive a few fresh recruits, in several Greek houses there has been a striking increase in numbers, and many of the new monks are gifted and well-educated. The revival is particularly evident in Simonos Petras, Philotheou, Grigoriou, and Stavronikita. In all of these monasteries there are outstanding abbots.

and ecumenical contacts, anxious to appear a western and European community, while at the same time safeguarding its Orthodox traditions, the Church of Finland is perhaps destined to play an important role in the western witness of Orthodoxy.'[1]

(2)   The *Patriarchate of Alexandria* has been a small Church ever since the separation of the Monophysites in the fifth century, when the great majority of Christians in Egypt rejected the Council of Chalcedon. Today there are about 10,000 Orthodox in Egypt, and perhaps 150,000–250,000 elsewhere in Africa. The head of the Alexandrian Church is known officially as 'Pope and Patriarch': in Orthodox usage, the title 'Pope' is not limited solely to the Bishop of Rome. The Patriarch and most of his clergy are Greek. The whole of the African continent falls under the charge of the Patriarch, and since Orthodox are just now beginning to undertake missionary work in Central Africa, it may well be that the ancient Church of Alexandria, however attenuated at present, will expand in new and unexpected ways during the years to come. (On missions in Africa, see Chapter 9.)

(3)   The *Patriarchate of Antioch* numbers some 320,000 Orthodox in Syria and the Lebanon, and perhaps a further 150,000 in Iraq and America. (Roman Catholics, Uniate and Latin, number about 640,000 in Syria and the Lebanon.) The Patriarch, who lives in Damascus, has been an Arab since 1899, but before that time he and the higher clergy were Greek, although the majority of the parish clergy and the people of the Antiochene Patriarchate were and are Arab.

Some thirty years ago a leading Orthodox in the Lebanon, Father (now Bishop) George Khodre, said: 'Syria and the Lebanon form a dark picture among Orthodox countries.' Indeed, until recently the Patriarchate of Antioch could without injustice be taken as a striking example of a 'sleeping'

1. J. Meyendorff, *L'Église orthodoxe hier et aujourd'hui*, Paris, 1960, p. 157.

Church. Today there are signs of an awakening, chiefly as a result of the Orthodox Youth Movement in the Patriarchate, a most remarkable and inspiring organization, originally founded by a small group of students in 1941–2. The Youth Movement runs catechism schools and Bible seminars, as well as issuing an Arabic periodical and other religious material. It undertakes social work, combating poverty and providing medical assistance. It encourages preaching and is attempting to restore frequent communion; and under its influence two small but outstanding religious communities have been founded at Tripoli and Deir-el-Harf. In the Youth Movement at Antioch, as in the 'home missionary' movements of Greece, a leading part is played by the laity.

(4) The *Patriarchate of Jerusalem* has always occupied a special position in the Church: never large in numbers, its primary task has been to guard the Holy Places. As at Antioch, Arabs form the majority of the people; they number today about 60,000 but are on the decrease, while before the war of 1948 there were only 5,000 Greeks within the Patriarchate and at present there are very much fewer (? not more than 500). But the Patriarch of Jerusalem is still a Greek, and the Brotherhood of the Holy Sepulchre, which looks after the Holy Places, is completely in Greek control.

Before the Bolshevik Revolution, a notable feature in the life of Orthodox Palestine was the annual influx of Russian pilgrims, and often there were more than 10,000 of them staying in the Holy City at the same time. For the most part they were elderly peasants, to whom this pilgrimage was the most notable event in their lives: after a walk of perhaps several thousand miles across Russia, they took ship at the Crimea and endured a voyage of what to us today must seem unbelievable discomfort, arriving at Jerusalem if possible in time for Easter.[1] The

1. See Stephen Graham, *With the Russian Pilgrims to Jerusalem*, London, 1913. The author travelled himself with the pilgrims, and gives a revealing picture of Russian peasants and their religious outlook.

Russian Spiritual Mission in Palestine, as well as looking after the Russian pilgrims, did most valuable pastoral work among the Arab Orthodox and maintained a large number of schools. This Russian Mission has naturally been sadly reduced in size since 1917, but has not entirely disappeared, and there are still three Russian convents at Jerusalem; two of them receive Arab girls as novices.

(5)   The *Church of Greece* continues to occupy a central place in the life of the country as a whole. Writing in the early 1950s, a sympathetic Anglican observer remarked: 'Hellas, when all is said as to the spread of secularism and indifference, remains a Christian nation in a sense of which we in the west can have but little conception.'[1] In the 1951 census, out of a total population of 7,632,806, the Orthodox numbered 7,472,559, other Christians no more than 41,107; in addition there were 112,665 Mohammedans, 6,325 Jews, 29 persons of other religions, and 121 atheists. Today there is much more indifference than in the 1950s, and the Socialist government elected in 1981 began to take steps towards a separation of Church and State; but the Church remains deeply influential.

Greek dioceses of today, as in the primitive Church, are small: there are 78 (contrast Russia before 1917, with 67 dioceses for 100 million faithful) and in north Greece many dioceses contain less than 100 parishes. In ideal and often in reality, the Greek bishop is not merely a distant administrator, but an accessible figure with whom his flock can have personal contact, and in whom the poor and simple freely confide, calling daily in large numbers for practical as well as spiritual advice. The Greek bishop delegates far less to his parish clergy than a bishop in the west, and in particular he still reserves to himself much of the task of preaching, though he is assisted in this by a small staff of monks or educated laymen, working under his direction.

1. P. Hammond, *The Waters of Marah*, p. 25.

Thus by no means all the married parish clergy of Greece in the past preached sermons; nor is this surprising, since few had received a regular theological training. In pre-Revolutionary Russia all parish priests had passed through a theological seminary, but in Greece in the year 1920, of 4,500 married clergy, less than 1,000 had received more than an ordinary elementary school education. Hitherto the priest of the Greek countryside has been closely integrated with the local community: usually he is a native of the village which he serves; after ordination, as well as being priest, he still continues with his previous work, whatever that may be – carpentry, shoemaking, or more commonly farming; he is not a man of higher learning than the laity round him; very possibly he has never attended a seminary. This system has had certain undeniable advantages, and in particular it has meant that the Greek Church has avoided a cultural gulf between pastor and people, such as has existed in England for several centuries. But with the rise in educational standards in Greece during recent years, a change in this system has become necessary: today priests clearly need a more specialized training, and it seems likely that henceforward most, if not all, Greek ordinands will be sent to study in a seminary.

The two older universities of Greece, at Athens and Thessalonica, both contain Faculties of Theology. Non-Orthodox are often surprised to find that the great majority of professors in both faculties are laymen, and that most of the students have no intention of being ordained; but Orthodox consider it entirely natural that the laity as well as the clergy should take an interest in theology. Many students afterwards teach religion in secondary schools, and it is usually the local schoolmasters whom the bishops choose as their lay preachers. Only a few of these students become parish clergy; a few others are professed as monks, though it is likely that only a minority of these graduate monks will live as resident members of a monastery: in most cases they will work on the bishop's staff, or perhaps become preachers.

The theological professors of Greece have produced a considerable body of important work during the past half century: one thinks at once of Chrestos Androutsos, author of a famous *Dogmatic Theology* first published in 1907, and more recently of men such as P. N. Trembelas, P. I. Bratsiotis, I. N. Karmiris, B. Ioannides, and Ieronymos Kotsonis, the recent Archbishop of Athens, an expert on Canon Law. But while fully acknowledging the notable achievements of modern Greek theology, one cannot deny that it possesses certain shortcomings. Many Greek theological writings, particularly if compared with work by members of the Russian emigration, seem a little arid and academic in tone. The situation mentioned in an earlier chapter has continued to the present century, and most Greek theologians have studied for a time at a foreign university, usually in Germany; and sometimes German religious thought seems to have influenced their work at the expense of their own Orthodox tradition. Theology in Greece today suffers from the divorce between the monasteries and the intellectual life of the Church: it is a theology of the university lecture room, but not a *mystical* theology, as in the days of Byzantium when theological scholarship flourished in the monastic cell as well as in the university. Nevertheless in Greece at the present time there are encouraging signs of a more flexible approach to theology, and of a living recovery of the spirit of the Fathers.

What of the monastic life? In male communities, the shortage of young monks is as alarming on the mainland of Greece as it was on Athos until recently, and many houses are in danger of being closed altogether. There are very few educated men in the communities. But this gloomy prospect is relieved by striking exceptions, such as the recently founded monastery of the Paraclete at Oropos (Attica). Some older communities still attract novices – for example, Saint John the Evangelist on the island of Patmos (under the Ecumenical Patriarch). In Meteora some notable efforts to revive the monastic life were made by the late Metropolitan Dionysius of Trikkala. Here there are a series of monastic houses, perched on rocky pinnacles in a remote part of Thessaly, which were partially repopulated in the 1960s by young and well-educated monks. But the constant flow of tourists rendered monastic life impossible, and in the 1970s almost all the monks moved to Mount Athos.

But while the situation of male communities is often critical, the female communities are in a far more lively condition, and the number of nuns is rapidly increasing. Some of the most active convents are of quite recent origin, such as the Convent of the Holy Trinity on Aegina, dating from 1904, whose founder, Nektarios (Kephalas), Metropolitan of Pentapolis (1846–1920), has already been canonized; or the Convent of Our Lady of Help at Chios, established in 1928, which now has fifty members. The Convent of the Annunciation at Patmos, started in 1936 by Father Amphilochios (died 1970; perhaps the greatest *pnevmatikos* or spiritual father in post-war Greece), already has two daughter houses, at Rhodes and Kalymnos.[1]

In the past twenty years a surprising number of classic works of monastic spirituality have been reprinted in Greece, including a new edition of the *Philokalia*. It seems that there is a revived interest in the ascetic and spiritual treasures of Orthodoxy, a development which bodes well for the future of the monasteries.

Religious art in Greece is undergoing a most welcome transformation. The debased westernized style, universal at the beginning of the present century, has largely been abandoned in favour of the older Byzantine tradition. A number of churches at Athens and elsewhere have recently been decorated with a full scheme of icons and frescoes, executed in strict conformity with the traditional rules. The leader of this artistic renewal, Photius Kontoglou (1896–1965), was noted for his uncompromising advocacy of Byzantine art. Typical of his outlook is his comment on the art of the Italian Renaissance: 'Those who

1. In this connexion one must also mention the impressive Old Calendarist Convent of Our Lady at Keratea in Attica, founded in 1925, which now has between two and three hundred nuns. (On the Old Calendarists, see p. 309.)

see in a secular way say that it progressed, but those who see in a religious way say that it declined.'[1]

Greece possesses an Orthodox counterpart to Lourdes: the island of Tinos, where in 1823 a miracle-working icon of the Virgin and Child was discovered, buried underground in the foundations of a ruined church. A large pilgrimage shrine stands today on the site, which is visited in particular by the sick, and many cases of miraculous healing have occurred. There are always great crowds on the island for the Feast of the Assumption (15 August).

In the Greek Church of the present century there has been a striking development of 'home missionary' movements, devoted to evangelistic and educational work. *Apostoliki Diakonia* ('Apostolic Service'), the official organization concerned with the 'Home Mission', was founded in 1930. Alongside it there are a number of parallel movements which, while cooperating with the bishops and other Church authorities, spring from private initiative – *Zoe*, *Sotir*, the *Orthodox Christian Unions*, and others. The oldest, most influential, and most controversial of these movements, *Zoe* ('Life'), also known as the 'Brotherhood of Theologians', was started by Father Eusebius Matthopoulos in 1907. It is in fact a kind of semi-monastic order, since all its members must be unmarried, although they take no formal vows and are free to leave the Brotherhood at any time. About a quarter of the Brotherhood are monks (none of whom live regularly in a monastery) and the rest laymen. One wonders how far *Zoe*, with its monastic structure, points the way to future developments in the Orthodox Church. In the past the primary task of an eastern monk has been prayer; but, besides this traditional type of monasticism, is there not also room in Orthodoxy for 'active' religious orders, parallel to the Dominicans and Franciscans in the west, and dedicated to the work of evangelism in the world?

These 'home missionary' movements, especially *Zoe*, lay

1. C. Cavarnos, *Byzantine Sacred Art: Selected Writings of the contemporary Greek icon painter Fotis Kontoglous*, New York, 1957, p. 21

great stress on Bible study and encourage frequent communion. Between them they publish an impressive number of periodicals and books, with a very wide circulation. Under their leadership and guidance there exist today about 9,500 catechism schools (in 1900 there were few if any such schools in Greece), and it is reckoned that fifty-five per cent of Greek children – in some parishes a far higher proportion – regularly attend catechism classes. Besides these schools, a wide programme of youth work is undertaken: 'The period of adolescence,' to quote an Anglican writer, 'when so overwhelming a portion of our own children lose all vital contact with the Church, is commonly that at which the young Greek Christian begins to play an active part in the life of his local community.'[1]

The influence of these 'home missionary' movements has declined considerably in the 1960s and 1970s, and in particular the words just quoted – written more than twenty-five years ago – unfortunately would need today to be qualified.

(6) The ancient *Church of Cyprus*, independent since the Council of Ephesus (431), has at present 600 priests and over 450,000 faithful. The Turkish system, whereby the head of the Church is also the civil leader of the Greek population, was continued by the British when they took over the island in 1878. This explains the double part, both political and religious, played by Makarios, the recent head of the Cypriot Church, 'ethnarch' and President as well as Archbishop.

(7) The *Church of Sinai* is in some ways a 'freak' in the Orthodox world, consisting as it does in a single monastery, Saint Catherine's, at the foot of the Mountain of Moses. There is some disagreement about whether the monastery should be termed an 'autocephalous' or merely an 'autonomous' Church (see p. 14). The abbot, who is always an archbishop, is elected by the monks and consecrated by the Patriarch of Jerusalem; the monastery is entirely independent of outside control. Sad to say, there are today fewer than twenty monks.

1. P. Hammond, *The Waters of Marah*, p. 133.

CHAPTER 8

The Twentieth Century, II:
Orthodoxy and the Militant Atheists

'Those who desire to see Me shall pass through
tribulation and despair.'
Epistle of Barnabas vii, 11

'THE ASSAULT UPON HEAVEN'

WHEN the Bolsheviks seized power in October 1917, the
Church of Russia found itself in a position for which there was
no exact precedent in Orthodox history. The Roman Empire,
although it persecuted Christians, was not an atheist state,
opposed to all religion as such. The Turks, while non-Christians, were still worshippers of One God and, as we have seen,
allowed the Church a large measure of toleration. But communism is committed by its fundamental principles to an
aggressive and militant atheism. A communist government cannot rest satisfied merely with a separation of Church and State,
but it seeks either by direct or indirect means to overthrow
all organized Church life and to extirpate all religious belief.
'The Party cannot be neutral towards religion,' wrote Stalin.
'It conducts an anti-religious struggle against all and any religious prejudices.'[1] So the communists believed in 1917, and so
they believe today; but while their doctrine has remained the
same, their tactics have varied. Sometimes they have used
direct persecution, sometimes they have preferred indirect
methods.

The terms of the Soviet Constitution have grown progressively more severe. The Constitution of 1918 allowed
'freedom of religious and anti-religious propaganda' (Article
13); in 1929 this was changed to 'freedom of religious *belief* and

1. *Works*, Moscow, 1953, vol. x, p. 132.

of anti-religious *propaganda*', while the present Constitution (1977) permits 'freedom of religious *worship* and of anti-religious propaganda' (Article 52). Thus the Constitution allows the Church freedom of worship, but no freedom of propaganda: for the Church, as the *Great Soviet Encyclopedia* puts it, is 'a union of believers created and existing *solely for the purpose of worship*'.

This emphasis upon worship is deliberate. The Soviet government, particularly since 1943, has permitted a number of church buildings to remain open for services, but both before and after 1943 it has subjected Christianity to a systematic and relentless policy of cultural strangulation. The Church can worship, but is not allowed to maintain charitable or social work; it can train a certain number of candidates for the priesthood, but otherwise is forbidden to undertake educational activities. Let us consider briefly what this means for Russian Christians today.

Atheist ideas are supposed to be taught in every school and by every teacher:

A Soviet teacher must be guided by the principle of the Party spirit of science; he is obliged not only to be an unbeliever himself, but also to be an active propagandist of Godlessness among others, to be the bearer of the ideas of militant proletarian atheism. Skilfully and calmly, tactfully and persistently, the Soviet teacher must expose and overcome religious prejudices in the course of his activity in school and outside school, day in and day out.[1]

How can a parish priest counteract this anti-religious propaganda? He can preach sermons during Church services (and this the Russian clergy of today, like Father John of Kronstadt, do with great assiduity), but he cannot give religious instruction at any other time or in any other way. He is forbidden to organize discussion or study groups, either among young people or adults; he cannot form a parish library, since the only books

1. F. N. Oleschuk (formerly Secretary of the League of Militant Atheists) in *Uchitelskaya Gazeta*, 26 November 1949.

which he is permitted to keep in church are service books; there are no suitable pamphlets which he can distribute to his people, since ecclesiastical publications in Russia are rigidly restricted. He cannot even give them Bibles to read: since 1956 the Russian Orthodox Church has on a few occasions been allowed to reprint the text of Scripture, but the number of copies available is tragically inadequate – fortunate indeed are the lay people who have a Bible of their own. In particular the parish priest is denied the possibility of holding catechism classes or Sunday schools; for the legal code strictly prohibits the giving of organized religious instruction to children or young people, and infringements of this rule are punished severely. This hardly constitutes 'religious freedom' in any normal sense of the word.

Nor is the teaching of atheism in schools the only method of propaganda which communists have employed. Former churches have been turned into 'museums of religion and atheism', many of which are now closed, but a few still remain open, most notably the museum in the former Kazan Cathedral at Leningrad. In the twenties and thirties an astonishing quantity of atheist periodicals and pamphlets were distributed, lecturers were sent out to every part of the U.S.S.R., and the 'League of Militant Atheists' was formed, with a nation-wide organization. The League was abolished in 1942, but its functions were taken over after the war by the 'All-Union Society for the Dissemination of Scientific and Political Knowledge', founded in 1947. Although not on such a large scale as before the war, anti-religious periodicals, pamphlets, and lectures are still vigorously maintained: in 1954, for example, 120,679 anti-religious lectures were given in the Soviet Union, while in 1958 the number had risen to 300,000. But there are constant protests in the Soviet press today about the lack of interest in atheist propaganda, particularly among young people.

Before the last war, anti-religious processions of a crude and blasphemous character used to be held in the streets, above all at Easter and Christmas. A Russian who saw these atheist celebrations has written:

There were no protests from the silent streets – the years of terror had done their work – but nearly everyone tried to turn off the road when they met this shocking procession. I, personally, as a witness of the Moscow carnival, may certify that there was not a drop of popular pleasure in it. The parade moved along empty streets and its attempts at creating laughter or provocation were met with dull silence on the part of the occasional witnesses.[1]

The matters of which we have spoken hitherto might be termed 'indirect' methods of persecution. But the communists have resorted to direct persecution as well, and even the 'freedom of religious worship' turns out on closer inquiry to be precarious. When the Decree on the Separation of Church and State was published on 5 February 1918, the Church ceased to possess any legal rights. The Decree deprived it of the power to hold property. All seminaries and theological academies were ordered to be closed down (since 1945 a few have been reopened). All Church buildings, lands, and moneys were declared to be national property; local authorities at their discretion could allow congregations to use their former places of worship, but if these local authorities, 'at the request of the workers', decided to close a church, the worshippers could do nothing to stop them. From 1918 until 1939, churches were methodically desecrated, closed, and destroyed, often against the wishes of the overwhelming majority of the population and at times in the face of their active opposition.

The communists, moreover, have attacked not only property but persons. In the years between the two World Wars the Christians of Russia underwent sufferings which in extent and in cruelty equalled anything endured by the early Christians. Since the 1917 Revolution was specifically anti-religious, all active Christians in Russia could be classed as 'counter-revolutionaries' and treated accordingly. At one time as many as 150 bishops were in prison at the same moment (before 1917 the total number of diocesan and assistant bishops in the

1. G. P. Fedotov, *The Russian Church since the Revolution*, London, 1928, p. 47.

Russian Empire was less than 130). In 1918 and 1919 alone, about twenty-eight bishops were killed; between 1923 and 1926 some fifty more were murdered by the Bolsheviks. Parish clergy and monks also suffered severely: by 1926, according to information supplied by a bishop living in Russia at the time, some 2,700 priests, 2,000 monks, and 3,400 nuns and other ordained persons had been killed, while *émigré* writers today calculate that since 1917, among priests alone, at least 12,000, and possibly far more, have been executed or have died through ill-treatment. These figures cannot of course be checked in detail, but in any case the number of deaths has been very large. It will never be known how many laity suffered impoverishment, prison sentences, or death because of their faith. In the words of the Archpriest Avvakum: 'Satan has obtained our radiant Russia from God, that she may become red with the blood of martyrs.'[1]

What effect did communist propaganda and persecution have upon the Church? In many places there was an amazing quickening of the spiritual life. Cleansed of worldly elements, freed from the burden of insincere members who had merely conformed outwardly for social reasons, purified as by fire, the true Orthodox believers gathered themselves together and resisted with heroism and humility. 'In every place where the faith has been put to the test,' a Russian of the emigration writes, 'there have been abundant outpourings of grace, the most astonishing miracles – icons renewing themselves before the eyes of astonished spectators; the cupolas of churches shining with a light not of this world.' 'Nevertheless,' the same author rightly adds, 'all this was scarcely noticed. The glorious aspect of what had taken place in Russia remained almost without interest for the generality of mankind. ... The crucified and buried Christ will always be judged thus by those who are blind to the light of his resurrection.'[2] It is not surprising that

1. From Avvakum's *Life*; see Fedotov, *A Treasury of Russian Spirituality*, p. 167.

2. Lossky, *The Mystical Theology of the Eastern Church*, pp. 245–6. The miraculous 'renewal of icons', to which Lossky refers, has

enormous numbers should have deserted the Church in the hour of persecution, for this has always happened, and will doubtless happen again. Far more surprising is the fact that so many remained faithful.

OFFICIAL CHURCH—STATE RELATIONS IN RUSSIA: THE ATTITUDE OF THE HIERARCHY

There can be no doubt about the devotion of the New Martyrs and Confessors of Russia. More open to criticism is the official policy of the ecclesiastical hierarchy, which has by degrees adopted an increasingly conciliatory attitude towards the atheist government. But the reservations which one may feel about the hierarchy must in no sense be taken as a reflection upon the Russian Orthodox people as a whole.

The official *rapprochement* between the Church and communism reached a more or less definitive form in 1943–5, since when there have been no significant changes. The main features of the present situation are as follows:

(1) The Church is 'loyal' to the Soviet government. This means not only that it refrains from any criticism of the authorities, but also that it is pledged *actively* to support communist policies and propaganda at home and abroad, particularly communist foreign policy (Greek civil war, Korea, Hungary, and so on).[1]

(2) In return the State has greatly relaxed direct forms of persecution, although such persecution has not entirely ceased. The forced closing of churches and the imprisonment of clergy still continue, but since 1945 cases have occurred less

---

occurred in a number of places under communist rule. Icons and frescoes, darkened and disfigured with age, have suddenly and without any human intervention resumed fresh and bright colours.

1. Pro-Soviet propaganda by the Moscow Patriarchate has often bewildered Orthodox in other lands. Thus during the Greek civil war, the people of Greece were surprised to find that an Orthodox Patriarch should speak out in support of the communist partisans who desecrated Orthodox churches and crucified Orthodox priests.

frequently, and there have been far fewer instances of actual martyrdom.

(3) The policy of cultural strangulation has not been abandoned. The Soviet government continues to regard religion as an enemy to be combated on the ideological level, while the Church is not allowed to hit back.

(4) In theory the Church is granted 'freedom of inner government'. In practice the State has many means whereby it can interfere in religious affairs.[1]

Let us consider the stages prior to the existing position. At the outset Patriarch Tikhon was firm and uncompromising towards the Bolsheviks. On 1 February 1918 he excommunicated those whom he termed 'the enemies of Christ, open or disguised', 'the godless rulers of the darkness of our time':

By the authority conferred upon us by God we forbid you to approach the Holy Sacraments, and if you still call yourselves Christians we anathematize you. . . . As for you, faithful sons of the Church, we call upon you to stand in defence of our holy Mother, now outraged and oppressed . . . and should it become necessary to suffer for the cause of Christ, we call upon you to follow us on the way of suffering. . . . And you, my brother bishops and priests . . . without delay organize religious associations, call upon them to range themselves among the spiritual combatants who will resist physical force with the power of the Spirit. We firmly believe that the enemies of the Church of Christ will be broken and scattered by the power of the Cross, for the promise of Him who bore the Cross is unalterable: *I will build my Church and the gates of Hell shall not prevail against it.* (Matthew xvi, 18.)

This excommunication was confirmed by the All-Russian Council of 1917–18 and has never been revoked. Later in 1918 Tikhon publicly condemned the murder of Emperor Nicholas II, while in a famous letter on the first anniversary of the October Revolution he wrote:

1. This analysis is taken (with some changes) from N. S. Timasheff, 'The Russian Orthodox Church Today', in *Saint Vladimir's Seminary Quarterly* (New York), vol. 2 (new series), no. 3 (1958), pp. 40–50.

It is not for us to judge earthly powers. . . . However, to you who use your power for the persecution and destruction of the inno- cent, we issue our word of warning: celebrate the anniversary of your rise to power by releasing the imprisoned, by ceasing from bloodshed, violence, and havoc, and by removing restric- tions upon the faith; devote yourselves not to destruction but to the building up of order and law; give to the people the respite from civil warfare which they have both desired and deserved. For otherwise the righteous blood which you have shed will cry out against you. *For all they who take the sword shall perish by the sword.* (Matthew xxvi, 52.)

But though Tikhon spoke with vehemence in these pro- nouncements, he did not take sides in any strictly political ques- tion. He condemned bloodshed and injustice, and he protested against attacks upon the Church; but he passed no judgement on communist social and economic measures as such. He ex- communicated the Bolsheviks not because he disagreed with them politically, but because they were professed atheists; and he urged the faithful to resist not with military but with spiritual weapons.

Yet Tikhon's attitude, even if not political, was scarcely likely to prove acceptable to the communists. If they could not exterminate religious belief at once, then they wanted a Church so far as possible subservient to their policy; indeed they real- ized that a subservient Church might well prove more useful than no Church at all. Thus as well as attacking Orthodoxy from the outside – by propagating atheism, by closing churches, by killing and imprisoning the clergy – they also brought pressure to bear on Orthodox life from within. From May 1922 to June 1923 Tikhon was kept in prison, and while there he was persuaded to hand over the control of the Church to a group of married clergy, which unknown to him was acting in cooperation with the communist authorities. This group, which came to be known as the 'Renewed' or 'Living Church', initiated a sweeping programme of ecclesiastical reform; some of the enactments were directly contrary to Canon Law (for example, married bishops), but even though other reforms were not objectionable in themselves, the whole movement was compromised by its crypto-communist character. Tikhon, as soon as he realized what was happening, denounced the Living Church and refused to have any dealings with it; but several Orthodox Churches abroad were deceived for a time, and in particular the Ecumenical Patriarchate during the 1920s extended a certain measure of official recognition to the Living Church. But within Russia itself most of the faithful soon appreciated the true nature of the Living Church and ceased to support it; as a result the government quickly lost interest in the movement, since it had been deprived of its value as a tool of communist policy. The Living Church in time split into several groups, and after 1926 was no longer of any great importance. The first attempt by the Bolsheviks to create within the Church a party obedient to their interests proved a fiasco.

But the communists continued to bring pressure on the Church in other ways. How far Tikhon was 'brainwashed' while in custody we shall never know, but after his imprisonment he spoke in a more conciliatory tone than he had done in 1917–18: this is particularly evident in his 'Confession' (issued shortly before his release from prison) and in his 'Will' (signed on the day of his death, 7 April 1925).[1] Yet if these later statements are carefully examined, it will be found that despite the change in tone, there is no change in principle from his earlier pronouncements. He remained, as before, non-political. As he put it in 1923:

The Russian Orthodox Church is non-political, and henceforward does not want to be either a Red or a White Church; it should and will be the One Catholic Apostolic Church, and all attempts coming from any side to embroil the Church in the political struggle should be rejected and condemned.

1. Many Russian writers doubt the authenticity of the 'Will', regarding it as a communist forgery. Tikhon died suddenly, under mysterious circumstances. Perhaps a martyr, and certainly a confessor for the faith, he is widely venerated as a saint by Orthodox both within Russia and outside.

Faced by communist attempts to infiltrate into the Church and to influence it from within, Tikhon continued to demand a true and fair separation between Church and State. He desired a Church politically neutral but not politically subservient, and to his death he strove to guard Russian Orthodoxy from any interference in its inner life.

Tikhon realized that when he died it would not be possible for a Council to assemble freely, as in 1917, and to elect a new Patriarch. He therefore designated his own successor, appointing three *locum tenentes* or 'Guardians' of the Patriarchal throne: Metropolitans Cyril, Agathangel, and Peter. The first two were already in prison at the time of Tikhon's death, so that in April 1925 Peter, Metropolitan of Krutitsy, became Patriarchal *locum tenens*. In December 1925 Peter was arrested and exiled to Siberia, where he remained until his death in 1936. After Peter's arrest, Sergius (Starogorodsky), Metropolitan of Nizhni-Novgorod, took over the leadership in his stead, with the curious title 'Deputy to the *locum tenens*'. Sergius had joined the Living Church in 1922, but in 1924 had made his submission to Tikhon, who restored him to his former position.

At first Sergius continued the policy adopted by Tikhon in the last years of his Patriarchate. In a declaration issued on 10 June 1926, while emphasizing that the Church respected the laws of the Soviet Union, he said that bishops could not be expected to enter into any special undertaking to prove their loyalty. He continued: 'We cannot accept the duty of watching over the political tendencies of our co-religionists.' This was in effect a request for a true separation between Church and State: Sergius wanted to keep the Church out of politics, and therefore declined to make it an agent of Soviet policy. In this same declaration he also spoke openly of the incompatibility and the 'contradictions' existing between Christianity and communism. 'Far from promising reconciliation with the irreconcilable and from pretending to adapt our faith to communism, we will remain from the religious point of view what we are, that is, members of the traditional Church.'

But in 1927 – a crucial year for Church–State relations in Russia – Sergius changed his position. He spent from December 1926 to March 1927 in prison,[1] and on his release he requested the Soviet authorities to legalize the Patriarchal Synod over which he presided and to permit him to live at Moscow; these requests were promptly granted by the authorities (May 1927). It was a development which caused some alarm: legalization seemed to open the door to Soviet interference, since what a totalitarian government authorizes it can also control. Then on 29 July 1927 Sergius issued a new declaration, significantly different from his declaration of the previous year. He said nothing this time about the 'contradictions' between Christianity and communism; he no longer pleaded for a separation between Church and State, but associated the two as closely as possible:

We wish to be Orthodox and at the same time to recognize the Soviet Union as our civil fatherland, whose joys and successes are our joys and successes, and whose failures are our failures. Every blow directed against the Union ... we regard as a blow directed against us.

In 1926 Sergius had declined to watch over the political tendencies of his co-religionists; but he now demanded from the clergy abroad 'a written promise of their complete loyalty to the Soviet government'.

This 1927 declaration caused great distress to many Orthodox both within and outside Russia. It seemed that Sergius had compromised the Church in a way that Tikhon had never done. In identifying the Church so closely with a government dedicated wholeheartedly to the overthrow of all religion, he appeared to be attempting the very thing which in 1926 he had refused to do – to reconcile the irreconcilable. The victory of atheism would certainly be a joy and success for the Soviet State: would it also be a joy and success for the Church? The

1. Perhaps he was 'brainwashed', just as Tikhon may have been. We must allow for this possibility when evaluating Sergius's later actions.

dissolution of the League of Militant Atheists would be a blow to the communist government, but scarcely a blow to the Church. How could the Russian clergy abroad be expected to sign a written promise of complete loyalty to the Soviet government, when many of them had now become citizens of another country? It is hardly surprising that Metropolitan Antony (Khrapovitsky), Presiding Bishop of the Russian Church in Exile, should have replied to Sergius by quoting 2 Corinthians vi, 14–15: 'Can light consort with darkness? Can Christ agree with Belial, or a believer with an unbeliever?' 'The Church,' he continued, 'cannot bless anti-Christian, much less atheistical politics.' Metropolitan Evlogy, appointed by Tikhon as Exarch for Western Europe, was also much disturbed by this demand, and tried to avoid supplying any written statement of loyalty, while still maintaining relations with Sergius.

Inside Russia the policy of Sergius also provoked lively disapproval. Certainly there were some who supported Sergius, but there were many who strongly opposed him, and had he summoned a council of his fellow bishops in 1927 (of course the conditions at the time made such a thing impossible), it is doubtful whether a majority would have supported him. Chief among the opponents of the 1927 declaration was the Patriarchal *locum tenens* himself, Metropolitan Peter. 'I have trusted Metropolitan Sergius,' he is reported to have said, 'and now I see that I was mistaken.' And to Sergius himself Peter is said to have written: 'If you yourself lack the strength to protect the Church, you should step aside and turn over your office to a stronger person.' To the end of his life Peter of Krutitsy refused to accept the 1927 declaration, although promised release from exile if he would only agree to do so; and since Sergius was merely acting as Peter's deputy, it is thus not clear what authority the document can be considered to possess. The declaration was also attacked by other Church leaders, including Cyril, Metropolitan of Kazan; Agathangel, Metropolitan of Yaroslavl (both of whom Tikhon had nominated as *locum tenentes* along with Peter); Joseph, Metropolitan of Saint Petersburg; and Seraphim, Archbishop of Kostroma.

Most of those who disagreed with Sergius were swiftly eliminated by the secret police, and the extent of the opposition to the deputy *locum tenens* was not realized by many because it was largely silenced.

Especially important in this connection is the statement drawn up in the summer of 1927 by the bishops interned at Solovky on the White Sea. True to the position of Tikhon – and of Sergius before 1927 – they expressed their complete loyalty to the State *in secular matters*, but they demanded a true separation of Church and State, such as should respect the internal freedom of the Church, and they emphasized the basic incompatibility between communist ideology and the Christian faith.

For those who could not accept the 1927 declaration of Sergius, and who were convinced that the Church would be sacrificing its integrity if it made the concessions now demanded of it by the Soviet State, there remained but one course: to work underground, to 'disappear into the Catacombs', where they could practise their faith without interference, unknown to Sergius and the communist authorities. A leading part in the formation of the 'Catacomb Church' was played by Maximus, Bishop of Serpukhov. Known in the world as Michael Shishilenko, by profession a doctor, he had been private physician and a close friend to Patriarch Tikhon. According to Maximus, Tikhon had prophesied that communist interference in Church life would increase after his death, and had told Maximus to form an underground religious organization if State pressure on the official Church became intolerable. In 1927 Maximus took Tikhon's advice, and was secretly professed a monk and consecrated bishop. Maximus was put to death in 1930, but others continued his work: a large number of bishops, monks, and married priests took an ordinary job during the day, but by night or in the early morning held secret services when and where they could. Two accounts of such services have already been quoted, at the beginning of the first chapter.[1]

1. The Catacomb Church is also known as the 'Tikhon Church', because it claims to represent the true Russian Orthodox Church, in

Meanwhile Sergius, undeterred by opposition, continued to follow the path which he believed to be right. He was forced to make many humiliating concessions to the State, and in particular to spread false information about 'religious freedom': for example, in an interview given during 1930 to foreign journalists he went so far as to claim that there had never been any persecution of religion in the Soviet Union. It is of course possible that many things were published in his name without his consent or knowledge. Some have sought to justify his conduct by suggesting that he underwent a sort of 'martyrdom', deliberately taking on himself the sin of lying in order to protect his flock from destruction. Others have not found this explanation satisfactory, but have felt that Sergius involved the Church in a soul-destroying policy of systematic duplicity. In the words of Metropolitan Anastasy, head of the Russian Church in Exile:

Our descendants will be ashamed when they compare the language of our chief hierarchs at the present day, when addressing those in power, with the language of the first Christians to the Emperors of Rome and their representatives . . . .

To please the Soviet power, the chief hierarchs are not ashamed to propagate a flagrant lie, by saying that there have never been religious persecutions in Russia under the Soviet power. In this way they commit sacrilege, by turning to derision the multitude of Russian martyrs, openly calling them political criminals. A lie is always abominable and repugnant. . . . If one who is called to be a faithful witness to Christ lies knowingly to his conscience, to men, and to God, he becomes in truth guilty of contempt of the Holy Spirit. . . .

It is not without reason that the expressions 'Soviet Church' and 'Soviet Patriarch' have now become common in the mouth of Russians.[1]

---

succession to Patriarch Tikhon.

1. See, for the full text of this letter, the periodical *Russie et Chrétienté*, 1946, no. 1, pp. 123-30.

For the time being the submissive policy of Sergius brought little apparent advantage. Despite legalization and despite the declaration of 1927, the closure of churches and the liquidation of clergy continued, and there were particularly virulent waves of persecution in 1929–30 and 1937–8. But in 1943 the outward situation changed. The Soviet government, hard pressed in the war, desperately needed the support of the entire nation, and so was prepared to grant some concessions to its Christian subjects, who formed an appreciable proportion of the population. From the start, the official Church under Sergius had in fact pledged its wholehearted assistance in the war effort, and in return the communists were willing to show – for the moment, at any rate – an increased toleration. There was also a further factor which influenced the government. When the German armies invaded Russia, the inhabitants in many places welcomed them as 'liberators': admittedly, the Russians were soon disillusioned, but that at any rate was their initial reaction. And the Nazis, in the parts of Russia which they captured, permitted and even encouraged the restoration of religious life. In the Kiev diocese, for example, where 1,710 parishes existed before the Revolution, only two churches were officially functioning in 1939, but after a year of German occupation 708 churches had been reopened.[1] The Soviet government, alarmed by the prospect of further desertions to the Nazi side, naturally felt it advisable to treat the Church as generously as the Germans were doing.

But if the position of Christianity in Russia now became easier, none of the laws against religion were repealed. The Church in Russia, though tolerated, enjoys no security, since its members know that the concessions can be withdrawn as easily as they were granted. Communist principles have not changed, and should the Soviet authorities judge it expedient, there is nothing to prevent them from reverting to the pre-war situation.

One of the first major concessions which Stalin made was the

1. In 1955 there were still 586 parishes in the Kiev diocese, but since then many churches have certainly been closed.

restoration of the Patriarchate, vacant since Tikhon's death in 1925. In September 1943 Sergius, deputy *locum tenens* from 1925 to 1936 and *locum tenens* since 1936, was elected Patriarch by a small council of nineteen bishops. Already an old man, he died the following year, and in February 1945 Alexis (Shimansky), Metropolitan of Leningrad, a close supporter of Sergius since 1927, was elected Patriarch in his place. Alexis (died 1970) and his successor Patriarch Pimen, elected in 1971, have adhered firmly to the *modus vivendi* effected by Sergius with the government.[1]

Besides the restoration of the Patriarchate, Stalin also permitted the reopening of many churches, and of a few monasteries and theological schools. Between 1941 and 1947 the external aspect of the Church in Russia was utterly transformed, and the following figures[2] tell their own story:

	1914	1941	1947
Churches	54,457	4,255	22–25,000
Active priests	57,105	5,665	33,000
Monasteries and convents	1,498	38	80
Theological academies	4	None	2
Theological seminaries	57	None	8
Other religious schools	40,150	None	None

The figures for churches and priests in 1941 and 1947 cannot of course be checked: perhaps the former are too low, and perhaps (what is much more likely) the latter are too high. The sudden increase in priests is partly explained by the fact that in 1941 many were in hiding, but resumed priestly work at the end of the war; also areas were incorporated into the U.S.S.R. in 1945 where the churches had not been closed.

One fact stands out clearly from the statistics: apart from

1. Of course they do not stand alone. The same conciliatory policy towards communist authorities has been adopted by many other Christian leaders within Eastern Europe, both Protestant and Roman Catholic.

2. Taken from J. Meyendorff, *L'Église orthodoxe hier et aujourd'hui*, p. 135.

colleges for the training of priests no Church schools existed in 1947, nor do any exist today. The policy of cultural strangulation continues to be enforced as strictly as ever: cut off from the cultural and intellectual movements of the time, excluded from social and educational work, forbidden to answer anti-religious propaganda, the Church exists in a growing isolation which may in the end prove more deadly than open persecution. It is particularly difficult for the Church to exert any effective influence over children and youth. Yet if the Holy Liturgy saved Greek Orthodoxy under the Turks, it may be hoped that freedom of worship will preserve the Orthodox faith under communism. Time alone can show.

Even to exist in this isolation, the Church is forced to pay a heavy price. Church leaders are obliged to act as propagandists for Soviet home and foreign policy, and to take a prominent part in such things as the communist-sponsored 'Peace' Movement. The *Journal of the Moscow Patriarchate* (the only Church publication permitted, apart from calendars, service books, collections of sermons, and a theological review) regularly includes political articles on the 'struggle for peace' and the like. The *Journal* used also to contain frequent attacks against the Roman Catholic Church, closely similar in tone to the political articles. Often these attacks on Rome were by writers who when treating other topics displayed real learning and depth of Christian feeling. How can we explain the violent and unscholarly manner in which they spoke of their fellow Christians? 'One can hardly doubt that these contributions show the effect of direct pressure from without: unadulterated theology could hardly descend to such a level.'[1]

Nor is this the full account of the price paid for a severely limited toleration. While the ecclesiastical administration under the restored Patriarchate appears to function in a normal manner, the laws of the U.S.S.R. in fact allow the State in-

1. A. Schmemann, 'The Revival of Theological Studies in the U.S.S.R.', in *Religion in the U.S.S.R.*, edited Boris Iwanow, Munich, 1960, p. 42. Attacks on Rome in the *Journal* began to diminish after Stalin's death, and since Vatican II they have ceased altogether.

numerable ways of interfering. No Church Council, large or small, can be assembled, and no new parish can be organized, without government consent; no one, from the Patriarch to the humblest parish priest, can assume any ecclesiastical office without the approval of the civil authority. Priests, like other professional men, require a licence to exercise their profession, and this licence can at any time be withdrawn. The communists therefore have at their disposal an elaborate machinery for eliminating undesirable bishops or priests and replacing them with 'safe' men. It is not impossible that there is extensive communist infiltration into the ranks of the Russian clergy at the present time. The Soviet authorities would find little difficulty in sending their agents to theological seminaries and so securing their ordination, but how far they in fact resort to such tactics we do not of course know.

The price which the leaders of the Russian Church have agreed to pay is indeed a heavy one. Has the Moscow Patriarchate chosen aright? Would it have been better to adopt the way of martyrdom, as the Catacomb Church has done? How, in other words, ought a Christian under militant atheist rule to bear witness to his faith? These are questions to which Orthodox today give varying answers. None can doubt the agonizing position in which leaders of the Russian Church have been placed since 1917, but not all agree that the path which Sergius, Alexis, and Pimen have followed is the best. Some feel that they have adopted the only practicable policy in trying to guard their flock from continued persecution, and in seeking at all costs to preserve an outward organization, with churches open for public worship, with monasteries and theological schools. Others, both within Russia and outside, would reply that it is not outward organization that matters, but inward integrity; and they view with sorrow and indignation the way in which (so it seems to them) the shepherds of the Christian flock have agreed to collaborate with the enemies of Christ.

Need the church leaders in fact adopt so submissive an attitude? Could they not, without forfeiting a working relationship with the State, adopt a far more independent stand?

THE PRESENT STATE OF THE CHURCH IN RUSSIA
AND OTHER COMMUNIST COUNTRIES

The Church of Russia. No official statistics are available, but several visitors to the U.S.S.R. or spokesmen for the Moscow Patriarchate have recently estimated that about ten per cent of the population go to church on any given Sunday – that is, between twenty and thirty million people. This means that in proportion to the total population, Church attendance in Russia after forty years of communism is higher than in many countries of western Europe. Believing Christians in Russia may well be appreciably more numerous than regular worshippers: there are many people – school teachers, university students, men and women in professional posts or government offices – who (for altogether creditable and unselfish reasons) do not wish it to be known that they are Christians, and who therefore only go to church at Christmas or Easter, when the vast crowds make concealment easier.

In large towns, at any rate, the churches are full (information about religion in country districts is scanty). In an Orthodox church the congregation usually stand, and there are few if any chairs or pews, so that a surprisingly large number can be fitted into a comparatively small space. A central town church normally has two celebrations of the Liturgy each Sunday morning, with perhaps two or three thousand present at each. At such a church there may be fifty to a hundred baptisms a week: Church authorities reckon that about half the children born in Moscow are baptized, while the proportion is lower in other towns but higher in the countryside. It is thus clear that many who are not themselves churchgoers still bring their babies for baptism; the Soviet press complains from time to time that prominent members of the Party or Komsomol go to church at night, and have their children secretly baptized.

But the town churches, though well attended, are few and far between: in 1955 there were only fifty-five in Moscow, for seven million inhabitants, and fourteen in Leningrad, for three million. Kiev has fared better, with twenty-six churches in 1955 for one million inhabitants, but in 1960 it was reported that only eight of these were still open. In other large towns the situation is even worse: Kharkov (930,000 inhabitants) has three churches, Kazan (643,000 inhabitants) and Perm (628,000) have only two each, while some of the newly built Soviet towns have none at all. If the figure given in 1947 is correct – 22,000 open churches in the U.S.S.R. – then the proportion of churches to the population must be far higher in smaller towns or in the countryside. Many of the city parishes are large centres, with perhaps five or ten clergy and twenty other paid staff working full time; people naturally prefer to attend big and crowded churches, since there is less danger of observation. Congregations include more women than men and more old people than young; this is a disquieting feature, but one by no means peculiar to the Church in Russia. There may be truth in the words of a Russian priest, who replied, when asked what would happen in thirty years' time when all the old women were dead: 'There will be another generation of old women.' It is sometimes said that many, whom atheist propaganda alienated from Christianity in adolescence, are now returning to the Church in middle age; but of this it is difficult to judge.

In the 1950s the two theological academies and eight seminaries contained 1,000–1,500 students, thus providing an annual supply of perhaps 200–300 ordinands. But in the 1960s, owing to renewed state pressure, the number of students and ordinands was considerably reduced. There seems to be no shortage of candidates for ordination (mainly young men of peasant or working-class background, but including some university graduates); the applications for admission to the seminaries far exceed the number of places which the Church authorities are allowed to offer. Certainly bishops are also ordaining to the priesthood men who have not passed through the seminaries. In some Russian dioceses there are summer schools for older clergy who have no theological degree, while priests can also take pastoral courses by correspondence. The monasteries and convents have a number of young members and novices; at the end of the Second World War, monks were allowed to return, among other places, to the Monastery of the Caves at Kiev and to the Trinity–St Sergius Monastery at Radonezh (or Zagorsk, as it is now called).

Christians in Russia, though often poor, give with great generosity, so that the Church – unable to spend its money on schools or charities – is beginning to suffer from a blight of wealth. The fabric of the church buildings is beautifully maintained, and the clergy are well paid and housed: city priests usually receive a salary equal to that of a university lecturer. Beyond doubt the clergy work extremely hard, and deserve what they are paid: yet one wonders whether the communists may not be glad to see an economic division between priest and people, with the pastor enjoying a far better standard of living than most of his flock.

Despite the relative stability of Church–State relations since 1943, the outward appearance of calm is undoubtedly deceptive. It is true that on 10 November 1954 the Central Committee of the Communist Party issued a resolution, signed by Khrushchev and entitled 'On Mistakes in the conduct of Scientific–Atheistic Propaganda among the population'; this condemned violent persecution and offensive attacks on religious belief, and insisted that the anti-religious struggle be carried out on a high ideological level. Since 1958, however, atheist propaganda has been intensified, and is not by any means restricted to matters of high ideology. The Soviet press for 1959 contained several 'exposures' of individual bishops and monasteries; monks in general were denounced at some length as 'money grabbers', 'idlers', 'libertines', 'sexual perverts', and so on. Theological colleges were singled out for particular attack, perhaps to prepare public opinion for their closure. 'Does an honest man go to a theological school, in our century of science and technology?' one writer inquires. '. . . The rector and inspector select any sort of rabble . . . lovers of an easy, dishonest life . . . criminals who should be remoulded by work.' In fact, the hours of rising at the seminaries are early, the programme crowded, and the discipline fairly strict – surely not a congenial régime for the lover of an easy life!

Besides propaganda, the government began, in the years following 1959, to use more direct methods: organized hooliganism during Church services, the imprisonment of prominent Churchmen for 'tax offences' or the like, the suppression of seminaries and monasteries, the forced closing of churches. By 1963 this campaign against the Church had developed into a full-scale persecution. Of the eight seminaries reopened around 1945, only three were still functioning in 1966; of the eighty monasteries existing in 1947, only about sixteen remained open in the 1970s. The Monastery of the Caves at Kiev was closed once more. At the Monastery of Saint Job of Pochaev the monks were treated with particular brutality. In 1961 this community numbered 140: in 1963 only 36 remained. At least one monk was beaten to death in prison, others – though in good health – were taken regularly to hospital for injections, and several were temporarily put out of the way in lunatic asylums. As a result, however, of protests in the west, the attacks diminished after a time. In 1960–63 there were also massive closures of parish churches; the number of 'functioning' churches – said to be 22,000–25,000 in 1947 – had probably dwindled by the later 1970s to less than 7,000. In many places priests have been forbidden to give communion to children of school age, although such a prohibition directly infringes the 'freedom of worship' guaranteed by the Constitution.

Renewed persecution has had the effect of stiffening the opposition of many priests and lay people. In 1965 Archbishop Hermogen of Kaluga and also two Moscow priests, Fathers Nicholas Eshliman and Gleb Yakunin, appealed to the church authorities to be firmer in resisting government pressures. In the late 1960s and the 1970s similar protests were made by laymen such as Anatoly Krasnov-Levitin and Lev Regelson. Individual voices have been silenced, but the movement of protest continues.

In addition to this opposition movement within the official Church, the 'Catacomb Church' – refusing all contact with Patriarch Pimen and all compromise with the atheist state – still continues to exist, but little is known about it.

In the new countries which fell under their control at the end of the Second World War, the communists have attempted to establish a *modus vivendi* with the Orthodox Church similar to that prevailing in Russia since 1943. There has been no wholesale closure of churches; recalcitrant clergy have been imprisoned but as a rule not put to death, since the communists have found from experience in Russia that martyrdom only makes believers more stubborn. Church publications are permitted more freely than in the U.S.S.R., and the Church has retained a number of theological seminaries and academies; but it is excluded from all social or charitable work, and in most cases also from any part in education. Atheist propaganda is maintained as in Russia, especially among the youth, and the Church is faced by the same difficulties in reaching children and young people. At the same time the Church is used by the government to further the cause of communism, and semipolitical 'confederations of priests' have been formed in many places under state patronage. Clergy are usually required to take an oath of loyalty. In Czechoslovakia, for instance, the 1949 law on Church and State obliges each priest to swear 'to do everything within my ability to support the efforts at reconstruction for the welfare of the people'; in Romania, a priest undertakes 'to defend the Romanian People's Republic against its enemies abroad and at home'. The Churches of Romania and Bulgaria continue to receive financial help from the government.

In accepting this situation, the (Orthodox) hierarchy certainly runs the risk of appearing, in the eyes of its own faithful and of those abroad, simply as a body of officials in the service of a government whose ultimate and avowed aim is to destroy 'religious prejudices'.[1]

1. J. Meyendorff, *L'Église orthodoxe hier et aujourd'hui*, p. 143.

Of the various Orthodox Churches under communist rule, it is the *Church of Serbia* which has shown the greatest independence in its dealings with the State since the war, yet for a time it appeared to be the Serbian Church which was also confronting the most serious difficulties in its own internal life. Visitors reported that the churches, although full in Belgrade, were often poorly attended elsewhere. There was a lack of candidates for ordination, and a grave shortage of young monks, although as in Greece the communities for women greatly increased in number. In the later 1960s and the 1970s the situation has in many ways improved. But the State has tried to weaken the Church by subdivision, and in 1967, despite the opposition of the Serbian Patriarchate, an autocephalous *Church of Macedonia* was set up. This has not been recognized by any other Orthodox Church.

The *Church of Bulgaria* since 1945 has closely followed the policy of the Moscow Patriarchate *vis-à-vis* the State, and laws passed in 1949 gave the civil authorities far-reaching powers of interference in its inner life. By the 1970s, however, the Church had gained a larger measure of freedom. Attendance at services, though often poor, seems to be reviving in some areas, but there is a lack of young priests, and of monks and nuns.

The *Church of Romania* from 1948 onwards followed a policy of close cooperation with the communist authorities; at the same time, spiritually and theologically it underwent a major renewal. In Romania, curiously enough, there has never been a formal act of separation between Church and State; the *Europa Year Book* for 1960 not inappropriately sums up the situation by saying: 'Religion in Romania is disestablished, but the Romanian Orthodox Church is recognized as the national Church.' Justinian, Patriarch from 1948 until his death in 1977, at times identified himself to a surprising degree with Marxist ideology; but he was also a devoted pastor, deeply loved by his Orthodox flock. His successor Justin continues to work in close cooperation with the State.

Churches are very well attended in Romania, and most of them still remain open: it is said that 220 churches function in Bucharest (compared with under fifty in Moscow). There are six seminaries, with a total of 1,400 students, and two university institutes for higher theological study, with a total of 1,100 students; at least nine religious periodicals are published, several of them with a standard of theological scholarship superior to anything published in Russia since 1917. By contrast with most Orthodox countries in the present century, monasticism in Romania has flourished, and in 1958 there were between seven and ten thousand monks and nuns, many of them young and with good education. Monastic life in contemporary Romania is based on the best traditions of Hesychasm, with an emphasis on the Jesus Prayer; the spirit of Paissy Velichkovsky is still very much alive. In 1946 and the years following, the first four volumes appeared of a Romanian version of the *Philokalia*, edited by Father Staniloae: far more than a mere translation, this edition was accompanied by long and scholarly commentaries, making use of western spiritual writers and of western critical research.[1]

The vitality of the Romanian Church has from time to time led the government to take repressive action. The publication of the *Philokalia*, for example, was suspended in 1948 and not resumed until 1976 (in 1981 the tenth volume appeared – in all, over 4,500 pages). The state authorities have often made it difficult for the monasteries – and more particularly the communities for men – to receive novices, and by 1979 the total number of monks and nuns had fallen to about three thousand. But there is no shortage of candidates for the priesthood, and in almost every diocese new parish churches are being built each year. Of all the Orthodox Churches, not excluding the Greek, it is the Romanian that is undoubtedly the most vigorous in its outward life, and the best supported by the people.

1. See Un moine de l'Église orthodoxe de Roumanie, 'L'avènement philocalique dans l'Orthodoxie roumaine', in the periodical *Istina*, 1958, pp. 295–328, 443–74.

Besides the great Churches of Russia, Serbia, Bulgaria, and Romania, there are four lesser Orthodox Churches under communist rule. The *Church of Georgia*, founded in the fourth century by Saint Nina 'the Equal of the Apostles', remained for a long time dependent on the Patriarchate of Antioch, becoming autocephalous in the eighth century. Incorporated into the Russian Church in 1811, it became independent once more after the February Revolution of 1917. Christianity in Georgia, as in the rest of the U.S.S.R., has been heavily persecuted, and today the Church is much reduced in size. 'I shall give you some statistics from which you can draw your own conclusions,' said the Catholicos Callistratos to an American reporter in 1951. 'Out of 2,455 churches in Georgia, there are now only 100 functioning, and the same number of priests are now performing their duties.'[1] These few priests try to serve a population of more than two million. In many places without a priest, the people now gather round the ruins of their former church and hold a service on their own. There is a small seminary for training clergy, and one monastery.

The *Church of Albania*, formerly part of the Patriarchate of Constantinople, became autocephalous in 1937. The total population of the country is over 1,500,000, of whom about twenty per cent are said to be Orthodox (ten per cent are Roman Catholics, the majority of the rest Mohammedans). There has been severe persecution since 1945, and in 1967 Albanian communist sources stated that all Christian churches had now been closed.

The *Church of Poland* (autocephalous since 1924) and the *Church of Czechoslovakia* (autocephalous since 1951), while in theory self-governing, are both closely dependent on the Moscow Patriarchate. The Czechoslovak Church is made up largely of former Uniates, most of whom joined the Orthodox Church in 1950 under Communist pressure. In 1968 an appreciable number returned to Roman Catholicism.

1. Interview with Harrison Salisbury of the *New York Times*, published in *Georgian Opinion*, New York, 1956, no. 8. The number of functioning churches is now about two hundred.

For a time, relations were cool between the Ecumenical Patriarch and the Churches of Poland and Czechoslovakia. This was not surprising in view of what had happened in these countries since 1945. In Poland, for example, at the end of the Second World War the canonical head of the Polish Orthodox Church, Metropolitan Dionysius, was supplanted by a bishop dependent on the Moscow Patriarchate, but so long as Dionysius lived, Constantinople declined to recognize the intruder. The situation has now been regularized.

A few words must be added about the fate of the Uniates since 1945. On several occasions before that date, substantial numbers of Uniates returned to Orthodoxy: three dioceses were received back in 1839, and a further group in 1875; between 1891 and 1914 about 120 Uniate parishes in North America became Orthodox; around 1930, 25,000 Uniates in Czechoslovakia joined the Orthodox Church. In 1839 and perhaps also in 1875 there was a certain amount of pressure, direct or indirect, from the Russian civil authorities, but in America and Czechoslovakia the move was entirely free and in no sense the result of government interference. But the main bulk of Uniates in eastern Europe, numbering more than 5,000,000 in 1945 – over 3,500,000 in the Ukraine and Czechoslovakia, and 1,500,000 in Romania – were still loyal to the Pope when they passed under communist rule at the end of the Second World War. Between 1946 and 1950, however, these Uniate Churches under communist rule ceased to exist officially, their members being incorporated *en bloc* into the Orthodox Church.

How far was the return of the Uniates to Orthodoxy voluntary? Leaders of the Russian and Romanian Churches say that the great majority of Uniate priests and congregations genuinely desired to join the Orthodox Church, although it is admitted that there was a 'hardbitten' minority who refused to be reconciled. Roman Catholic sources, on the other hand, suggest that the movement for reunion with the Orthodox had very little popular support, but was largely the result of communist pressure, and (in many cases) of direct coercion and police terrorism. In our present state of knowledge it is extremely difficult to decide between these contrary opinions, but on the whole the truth seems to lie more with the Roman Catholic view. There was considerable unrest among the Uniates of eastern Europe in the inter-war period, and many may therefore have welcomed the opportunity to become Orthodox; one must not forget the precedent of the Uniates in North America and elsewhere who freely chose Orthodoxy. Yet at the same time one cannot but suspect that there were many others who wished to continue subject to the Pope, and who in consequence have suffered severely for their religious convictions.[1] Orthodox leaders under communist rule have been placed in an unenviably equivocal situation, for they appear to have profited from the persecution of other Christians by the atheist government. Among the charges that can be made against the Moscow Patriarchate, there can be few if any so serious as this.

The struggle between religion and materialism in communist countries is still far from a final resolution, and many features in the present situation remain exceedingly obscure. Yet this much at least is evident: extreme gloom and extreme optimism are equally unjustified. There are some in the west who speak as if religion in communist areas were already dead, and the Church a living corpse. This is certainly not true; but it is equally misleading to assume, as others do, that the Church has nothing to fear from communism. Hitherto Orthodox believers have shown in the face of fierce persecution an astonishing power of spiritual resistance; but in the long run the subtler and more insidious forms of pressure to which the Church is today exposed may prove more devastating than any direct attacks.

1. This is surely borne out by events in Czechoslovakia in 1968, when the vast majority of the former Uniates returned to Roman Catholicism as soon as they were given the opportunity.

CHAPTER 9

The Twentieth Century, III:
Diaspora and Mission

JURISDICTIONAL DIVISIONS

IN the past Orthodoxy has appeared, from the cultural and geographical point of view, almost exclusively as an 'eastern' Church. Today this is rapidly ceasing to be so. Outside the boundaries of the traditional Orthodox countries there now exists a large Orthodox 'dispersion', its chief centre in North America, but with branches in every part of the world. In numbers and influence Greeks and Russians predominate, but the 'diaspora' is by no means limited to them alone: Serbs, Romanians, Arabs, Bulgarians, Albanians, and others all have a place.

The origins of this Orthodox diaspora extend some way back. Russian missionaries first settled on the North American continent in 1794; and some time earlier than this, in 1677, the first Greek Church was opened in London, in the then fashionable district of Soho. It had a brief but troubled career, and was closed in 1682. Henry Compton, the Anglican Bishop of London, forbade the Greeks to have a single icon in the church and demanded that their clergy omit all prayers to the saints, disown the Council of Jerusalem (1672), and repudiate the doctrine of Transubstantiation. When the Patriarch of Constantinople protested against these conditions to the English Ambassador, Sir John Finch, the latter retorted that it was 'illegal for any public Church in England to express Romish beliefs, and that it was just as bad to have them professed in Greek as in Latin'![1] When the Greeks next opened a church in London

1. See E. Carpenter, *The Protestant Bishop*, London, 1956, pp. 357–64.

in 1838, they were fortunately not subject to these irksome restrictions.

But if the fact of an Orthodox diaspora is not itself new, only within the last sixty years has it attained such dimensions as to make the presence of Orthodox a significant factor in the religious life of non-Orthodox countries. Even today, as a result of national and jurisdictional divisions, the influence of the diaspora is not nearly as great as it might otherwise be.

The most important single event in the story of the dispersion has been the Bolshevik Revolution, which drove into exile more than a million Russians, including the cultural and intellectual *élite* of the nation. Before 1914 the majority of Orthodox *émigrés*, whether Greek or Russian, were poor and little educated – people travelling west to trade or to look for work. But the great wave of exiles after the Revolution contained many men qualified to make contact with the west on a scholarly level, who could present Orthodoxy to the non-Orthodox world in a way that most earlier immigrants manifestly could not. The output of the Russian emigration, particularly in its first years, was astonishing: in the two decades between the World Wars, so it has been calculated, they published 10,000 books and 200 journals, not counting literary and scientific reviews. Today the Russian emigration is outnumbered by the Greek, and the Greeks, too, have begun to play an active part in the intellectual life of their adopted countries: in the United States, for example, a number of Greeks hold academic posts and a 'Hellenic University' is now being established at Boston.

The Greek diaspora, as we have seen, is under the Patriarch of Constantinople. The Russian diaspora is divided ecclesiastically into four groups or 'jurisdictions':

(1) *The Synod of the Russian Church in Exile* (also known as 'the Russian Church Outside Russia', 'the Karlovtzy Synod', 'the Synod') – over 17 bishops, perhaps 250 parishes.
(2) *The Moscow Patriarchate* – about 10 bishops, perhaps 70 parishes.

(3) *The Russian Archdiocese of Western Europe*, under the jurisdiction of the Ecumenical Patriarchate (also known as the 'Paris jurisdiction') – 2 bishops, perhaps 40 parishes.
(4) *The Orthodox Church in America* (until 1970 'The Russian Orthodox Greek Catholic Church of America', 'The Metropolia'; no longer solely Russian) – 12 bishops, 550 parishes.

The story of Russian jurisdictional divisions is both tragic and complicated, and it can only be summarized briefly here. On 20 November 1920 Patriarch Tikhon, doubtless foreseeing that he would be imprisoned and deprived of the free exercise of his office, issued a decree authorizing Russian bishops to set up temporary independent organizations of their own, should it become impossible to maintain normal relations with the Patriarchate. After the collapse of the White Russian armies, over a million Russians found themselves in exile, including many priests and several bishops. It was clearly impossible for the Patriarch to supervise the religious life of the exiles, and so the bishops outside Russia applied the conditions of Tikhon's 1920 decree. In 1921, at the invitation of the Patriarch of Serbia, they held a Council at Sremski-Karlovci (Karlovtzy) in Yugoslavia, at which a temporary ecclesiastical administration for Russian Orthodox in exile was worked out. Supreme control was vested in a Synod of bishops who were to meet annually at Karlovtzy; an Administrative Board was also set up, comprising representatives of the clergy and laity.

The decisions of the Karlovtzy Council of 1921 were at first accepted by every Russian bishop at that time outside the borders of Russia. But Tikhon, on 5 May 1922, issued a decree abolishing the Administrative Board, and ordering Metropolitan Evlogy to work out a new scheme for the Russian Church abroad. Evlogy (1864–1946), the Russian bishop in Paris, was Exarch in western Europe; he had attended the Council of 1921 and signed the decisions. When he issued this decree, Tikhon was already in communist hands, so that there is some reason to believe he was acting under pressure and unable to express his true mind. Evlogy and the other bishops at the Karlovtzy Synod of 1922 duly worked out a new administration for the Russian Church in exile. Tikhon made no protest against these arrangements, and the Karlovtzy bishops claimed that he accepted the new constitution. Sergius, Alexis, and Pimen, however, have several times condemned the Karlovtzy administration, and the Moscow Patriarchate continues to the present day to regard it as entirely illegal and uncanonical. The Synod, for its part, does not recognize as valid the elections of Patriarch Sergius and his successors; and it has ignored the condemnations published by Moscow, looking upon them as political documents devoid of any spiritual authority. Between the wars the Synod met regularly at Karlovtzy; after the Second World War it moved to Munich, and since 1949 its centre has been in New York. The Synod was headed at first by Antony (Khrapovitsky), formerly Metropolitan of Kiev; from 1936 until 1964 the presiding bishop was Metropolitan Anastasy; the present head is Metropolitan Philaret. In the last fifteen years this group has become increasingly isolated from the rest of the Orthodox Church.

A small number of *émigré* Russians, instead of recognizing the Karlovtzy administration, preferred to remain in direct contact with the Moscow Patriarchate, thus forming the second of the four jurisdictions mentioned above. This group has never been large (very few clergy in exile were willing to comply with the demand of Sergius in 1927, and to provide a written statement of loyalty to the Soviet régime); but in 1945 several bishops and parishes in western Europe joined this Moscow jurisdiction.

The two remaining groups were formed by bishops who at first supported the Karlovtzy Synod, but who left it in 1926. The Paris jurisdiction owed its origin to the Russian Exarch in Paris, Metropolitan Evlogy. At first, as we have seen, he co-operated with the bishops at Karlovtzy, but after 1926 he ceased to attend the Synod. Then in 1930 he was disowned by Sergius because he prayed for the Christians under persecution in Russia (Sergius held that there were no persecuted Christians in Russia). Finding himself isolated, in 1931 Evlogy placed himself and his parishes under the spiritual care of the Ecumenical Patriarch. In 1934 Evlogy was privately reconciled to Metropolitan Antony, and in the following year he went to Karlovtzy for a special 'reunion' conference, at which the schism between him and the Synod was healed; but he subsequently renounced this agreement. Eventually, in 1945, shortly before his death, he submitted to the Patriarch of Moscow. But the great majority of his flock did not feel able to follow him, and remained under the jurisdiction of the Ecumenical Patriarch. So matters continued until 1965, when the Patriarch of Constantinople – acting apparently under Russian pressure – suddenly announced that he could no longer continue his Russian Exarchate; and he recommended its members to join the jurisdiction of Moscow. This, not surprisingly, the overwhelming majority were unwilling to do, and they chose rather to constitute themselves into an independent group. In 1971 they were received back into the jurisdiction of the Ecumenical Patriarchate.

Finally there is the fourth group, the North American Metropolia. After the Revolution, the Russians in America stood in a slightly different position from the *émigrés* elsewhere, since here alone in the countries outside Russia, there was a regularly constituted Russian diocese before 1917, with a resident bishop. Metropolitan Platon of New York (1866–1934), like Evlogy, separated from the Karlovtzy Synod in 1926; he had already – in 1924 – severed contact with the Moscow Patriarchate, so that after 1926 the Russians in the United States formed *de facto* an autonomous group. At the 'reunion' conference in Yugoslavia in 1935 Platon's successor, Metropolitan Theophilus, rejoined the Karlovtzy jurisdiction. In 1946, however, at the Synod of Cleveland, a division occurred among the Russians in America. Five of the nine bishops present at this Synod, and a minority of the delegates from the parishes, decided to remain subject to the Karlovtzy–Munich group under Anastasy; but the other four bishops (including Theophilus himself), with a large majority of the parochial delegates, decided to submit to the Moscow Patriarchate, on condition that the Patriarchate allowed them to retain their 'complete autonomy as it exists at present'. At that time the Patriarchate was unable to consent to this. In 1970, however, the Moscow Patriarchate granted the Metropolia not just autonomy but autocephaly, declaring it to be the 'Autocephalous Orthodox Church in America' (the 'OCA'). But this grant of autocephaly has not yet been recognized by Constantinople, or by most of the other Orthodox Churches. The present head of the OCA is Metropolitan Theodosius. The OCA has not only Russian but Albanian, Romanian and Bulgarian parishes.

The Russian Church in Exile is strongly critical of the submissive attitude adopted by Church authorities in Russia today towards the atheist government; so are many members of the Russian Archdiocese of W. Europe and the OCA. Often it is claimed that the differences between Russian groupings in emigration are primarily political, that the Russian Church in Exile is 'white' or 'Tsarist', the Moscow Patriarchate 'red', and the other two somewhere in between. This is a very misleading way of looking at the matter. Certainly the Russian Church in Exile venerates the memory of Emperor Nicholas II, and its members hope that God may one day allow a Christian government to be restored in Russia; but it refuses to submit to the Moscow Patriarchate not for political but for religious reasons. The basic question at issue is this: How should the Church and the Christian bear witness, when confronted by a militant atheist government? And that is not a political but a spiritual problem.

WESTERN ORTHODOXY

Let us look briefly at the Orthodox communities in western Europe and in North America. In 1922 the Greeks created an Exarchate for western Europe, with its centre in London. The first Exarch, Metropolitan Germanos (1872–1951), was widely known for his work for Christian unity, and played a leading part in the Faith and Order Movement between the wars. In 1963 this Exarchate was divided into four separate dioceses, with bishops at London, Paris, Bonn, and Vienna;

further dioceses were later formed in Scandinavia and Belgium, and most recently of all (1892) in Switzerland. There are about 130 Greek parishes in western Europe with permanent churches and resident clergy, and in addition a number of smaller Church groups.

The chief centres of Russian Orthodoxy in western Europe are Munich and Paris. At Paris the celebrated Theological Institute of Saint Sergius (under the Paris jurisdiction of Russians), founded in 1925, has acted as an important point of contact between Orthodox and non-Orthodox. Particularly during the inter-war period, the Institute numbered among its professors an extraordinarily brilliant group of scholars. Those formerly or at present on the staff of Saint Sergius include Archpriest Sergius Bulgakov (1871–1944), the first Rector; Bishop Cassian (1892–1965), his successor; A. Kartashev (1875–1960), G. P. Fedotov (1886–1951), P. Evdokimov (1901–70), Father Boris Bobrinskoy and the Frenchman, Olivier Clément. Three professors, Fathers Georges Florovsky, Alexander Schmemann, and John Meyendorff, moved to America, where they played a decisive role in the development of American Orthodoxy. A list of books and articles published by teachers at the Institute between 1925 and 1947 runs to ninety-two pages, and includes seventy full-scale books – a remarkable achievement, rivalled by the staffs of few theological academies (however large) in any Church. Saint Sergius is also noted for its choir, which has done much to revive the use of the ancient ecclesiastical chants of Russia. Almost entirely Russian between the two wars, the Institute now draws the majority of its students from other nationalities: in 1981, for example, of the thirty-four students, there were seven Russians (all except one brought up in France), seven Greeks, five Serbs, one Georgian, one Romanian, seven French, two Belgians, two from Africa, and one each from Holland and Israel. Courses are now mainly in French.

In western Europe during the post-war period there has also been an active group of Orthodox theologians belonging to the Moscow Patriarchate, including Vladimir Lossky

(1903–58), Archbishop Basil (Krivocheine) of Brussels, Archbishop Alexis (van der Mensbrugghe) (1899–1980) and Archbishop Peter (l'Huillier) (now in the U.S.A.), the last two being converts to Orthodoxy. Another convert, the Frenchman Father Lev (Gillet) (1892–1980), a priest of the Ecumenical Patriarchate, wrote many books as 'A Monk of the Eastern Church'.

There is an active youth organization in Paris, the *Russian Student Christian Movement*, founded in 1923, and a Russian press, the 'Y.M.C.A. Press' (sponsored by the American Y.M.C.A.), which has published a large number of important religious books.

Several Russian monasteries exist in Germany and France. The largest is the women's monastery dedicated to the Lesna icon of the Mother of God, at Provemont in Normandy (Russian Church in Exile); there is a smaller monastery for women at Bussy-en-Othe, in Yonne (Russian Archdiocese of Western Europe). In Great Britain there is the Monastery of Saint John the Baptist at Tolleshunt Knights, Essex (Ecumenical Patriarchate), founded by Archimandrite Sophrony, a disciple of Father Silvan of Mount Athos, with Russian, Greek, Romanian, German and Swiss monks, and with a women's community nearby. There are also the Convent of the Annunciation in London (Russian Church in Exile), with a Russian abbess and Arab sisters, and a few smaller foundations elsewhere.

In North America there are between two and three million Orthodox, subdivided into at least fifteen national or jurisdictional groups, and with a total of more than forty bishops. Before the First World War the Orthodox of America, whatever their nationality, looked to the Russian Archbishop for leadership and pastoral care, since among the Orthodox nations it was the Russians who first established churches in the New World. Eight monks, chiefly from Valamo on Lake . Ladoga, originally arrived in Alaska in 1794: one on these, Father Herman of Spruce Island, was canonized in 1970. The work in Alaska was greatly encouraged by Innocent Veniaminov, who worked in Alaska and Eastern Siberia from 1823 to 1868, first as a priest and then as bishop. He translated Saint

Mathew's Gospel, the Liturgy, and a catechism into Aleutian. In 1845 he created a seminary at Sitka in Alaska, and in 1859 an auxiliary bishopric was set up there, which became an independent missionary see when Alaska was sold to the U.S. in 1867. In Alaska today, out of a total population of 200,000, there are perhaps 20,000 Orthodox, most of whom are natives; the seminary was reopened in 1973.

Meanwhile in the second part of the nineteenth century, numbers of Orthodox began to settle outside Alaska in other parts of North America. In 1872 the diocese was transferred from Sitka to San Francisco, and in 1905 to New York, although an auxiliary bishop was still attached to Alaska. At the turn of the century, the number of Orthodox was greatly increased by a group of Uniate parishes which was reconciled to Orthodoxy. The future Patriarch Tikhon was Archbishop of North America for nine years (1898–1907). After 1917, when relations with the Church of Russia became confused, each national group formed itself into a separate organization and the present multiplicity of jurisdictions arose. Many see, in Moscow's grant of autocephaly to the OCA, a hopeful first step towards the restoration of Orthodox unity in America.

The Greek Orthodox in North America number over one million, with more than 400 parishes. They are headed by Archbishop Jakovos, who presides over a synod of ten bishops (one lives in Canada, and another in South America). The Greek Theological School of the Holy Cross at Boston has some 110 students, most of them candidates for the priesthood. The bishops in the Greek Archdiocese in America have come in most cases from Greece, but almost all the parish clergy were born and brought up in the U.S.A. There are two or three small monasteries in the Greek Archdiocese; the much larger Monastery of the Transfiguration at Boston, Mass., originally under the Greeks, is now within the Russian Church in Exile.

The Russians have four theological seminaries in America: Saint Vladimir's in New York and Saint Tikhon's in South Canaan, Pennsylvania (both of these belong to the OCA); Holy Trinity Seminary at Jordanville, N.Y. (Russian Church in

Exile); and Christ the Saviour Seminary in Johnstown, Pennsylvania (Carpatho-Russian diocese). There are several Russian monasteries, the largest being Holy Trinity, Jordanville, with thirty monks and ten novices. The monastery, as well as maintaining a seminary for theological students, has an active printing press, which produces liturgical books in Church Slavonic, and other books and periodicals in Russian or English. The monks also farm, and have built their own church, decorated by two members of the community with icons and frescoes in the best tradition of Russian religious art.

Orthodox life in America today displays a most encouraging vitality. New parishes are continually being formed and new churches built. In some places there is a shortage of priests, but whereas a generation ago Orthodox clergy in America were often ordained hastily, with little training, today in almost every jurisdiction most if not all ordinands have a theological degree. Orthodox theologians in America are few and often overworked, but their number is gradually increasing. Holy Cross and Saint Vladimir's both produce substantial periodicals in the English language.

The chief problem which confronts American Orthodoxy is that of nationalism and its place in the life of the Church. Among members of many jurisdictions there is a strong feeling that the present subdivision into national groups is hindering both the internal development of Orthodoxy in America and its witness before the outside world. There is a danger that excessive nationalism will alienate the younger generation of Orthodox from the Church. This younger generation have known no country but America, their interests are American, their primary (often their only) language is English: will they not drift away from Orthodoxy, if their Church insists on worshipping in a foreign tongue, and acts as a repository for cultural relics of the 'old country'?

Such is the problem, and many would say that there is only one ultimate solution: to form a single and autocephalous 'American Orthodox Church'. This vision of an American autocephalous Church has its most ardent advocates in the

OCA, which sees itself as the nucleus of such a Church, and among the Syrians. But there are others, especially among the Greeks, the Serbs, and the Russian Church in Exile, who view with reserve this emphasis upon *American* Orthodoxy. They are deeply conscious of the value of the Christian civilizations developed over many centuries by the Greek and Slavonic peoples, and they feel that it would be a disastrous impoverishment for the younger generation, if their Church were to sacrifice this great inheritance and to become completely 'Americanized'. Yet can the good elements in the national traditions be preserved, without at the same time obscuring the universality of Orthodoxy?

Most of those who favour unification are of course alive to the importance of national traditions, and realize the dangers to which the Orthodox minority in America would be exposed if it cut itself off from its national roots and became immersed in the secularized culture of contemporary America. They feel that the best policy is for Orthodox parishes at present to be 'bilingual', holding services both in the language of the Mother Country and in English. In fact, this 'bilingual' situation is now becoming usual in many parts of America. All jurisdictions in principle allow the use of the English language at services and in practice are coming to employ it more and more; English is particularly common in the OCA and the Syrian Archdiocese. For a long time the Greeks, anxious to preserve their Hellenic heritage as a living reality, insisted that the Greek language alone should be used at all services; but in the 1970s this situation changed, and in many parishes English is now employed almost as much as Greek.

Over the past few years there have been increasing signs of cooperation between national groups. In 1954 the Council of Eastern Orthodox Youth Leaders of America was formed, in which the majority of Orthodox youth organizations participate. Since 1960 a committee of Orthodox bishops, representing most (but not all) the national jurisdictions, has been meeting in New York under the presidency of the Greek Archbishop (this committee existed before the war, but had fallen into abeyance over many years). So far this committee, known as the 'Standing Conference' or 'SCOBA', has not been able to contribute as much to Orthodox unity as was originally hoped. The grant of autocephaly to the OCA gave rise at the time to sharp controversy, and the underlying problems thus created remain as yet unsolved; but in practice inter-Orthodox collaboration still continues.

A small minority in an alien environment, the Orthodox of the diaspora have found it a hard task even to ensure their survival. But some of them, at any rate, realize that besides mere survival they have a wider task. If they really believe the Orthodox faith to be the true Catholic faith, they cannot cut themselves off from the non-Orthodox majority around them, but they have a duty to tell others what Orthodoxy is. They must bear witness before the world. The diaspora has a 'missionary' vocation. As the Synod of the Russian Church in Exile said in its Letter of October 1953, Orthodox have been scattered across the world with God's permission, so that they can 'announce to all peoples the true Orthodox faith and prepare the world for the Second Coming of Christ'.[1]

What does this mean for Orthodox? It does not of course imply proselytism in the bad sense. But it means that Orthodox – without sacrificing anything good in their national traditions – need to break away from a narrow and exclusive nationalism: they must be ready to present their faith to others, and must not behave as if it were something restricted to Greeks or Russians, and of no relevance to anybody else. They must rediscover the *universality* of Orthodoxy.

If Orthodox are to present their faith effectively to other people, two things are necessary. First, they need to understand their own faith better: thus the fact of the diaspora has

1. This emphasis on the Second Coming will surprise many Christians of the present day, but it would not have seemed strange to Christians in the first century. The events of the last fifty years have led to a strong eschatological consciousness in many Russian Orthodox circles.

forced Orthodox to examine themselves and to deepen their own Orthodoxy. Secondly, they need to understand the situation of those to whom they speak. Without abandoning their Orthodoxy, they must *enter into the experience* of other Christians, seeking to appreciate the distinctive outlook of western Christendom, its past history and present difficulties. They must take an active part in the intellectual and religious movements of the contemporary west – in Biblical research, in the Patristic revival, in the Liturgical Movement, in the movement towards Christian unity, in the many forms of Christian social action. They need to 'be present' in these movements, making their special Orthodox contribution, and at the same time through their participation learning more about their own tradition.

It is normal to speak of 'Eastern Orthodoxy'. But many Orthodox in Europe or America now regard themselves as citizens of the countries where they have settled; they and their children, born and brought up in the west, consider themselves not 'eastern' but 'western'. Thus a 'Western Orthodoxy' has come into existence. Besides born Orthodox, this Western Orthodoxy includes a small but growing number of converts (almost a third of the clergy of the Syrian Archdiocese in America are converts). Most of these Western Orthodox use the Byzantine Liturgy of Saint John Chrysostom (the normal Communion Service of the Orthodox Church) in French, English, German, Dutch, Spanish, or Italian. There are, for example, a number of French and German Orthodox parishes, as well as (under the Patriarchate of Moscow) a Dutch Orthodox Mission – all of them following the Byzantine rite. But some Orthodox feel that Western Orthodoxy, to be truly itself, should use specifically western forms of prayer – not the Byzantine Liturgy, but the old Roman or Gallican Liturgies. People often talk about 'the Orthodox Liturgy' when they mean the *Byzantine* Liturgy, as if that and that alone were Orthodox; but they should not forget that the ancient Liturgies of the west, dating back to the first ten centuries, also have their place in the fullness of Orthodoxy.

This conception of a western-rite Orthodoxy has not remained merely a theory. The Orthodox Church of the present day contains an equivalent to the Uniate movement in the Church of Rome. In 1937, when a group of former Old Catholics in France under Monsignor Louis-Charles Winnaert (1880–1937) were received into the Orthodox Church, they were allowed to retain the use of the western rite. This group was originally in the jurisdiction of the Moscow Patriarchate, and was for many years headed by Bishop Jean de S. Denys (Evgraph Kovalevsky) (1905–70). At present it is under the Church of Romania. There are several small western-rite Orthodox groups in the U.S.A. Various experimental Orders of the Mass for use by western-rite Orthodox have been drawn up, in particular by Archbishop Alexis (van der Mensbrugghe).

In the past the different autocephalous Churches – often through no fault of their own – have been too much isolated from one another. At times the only formal contact has been the regular exchange of letters between the heads of Churches. Today this isolation still continues, but both in the diaspora and in the older Orthodox Churches there is a growing desire for cooperation. Orthodox participation in the World Council of Churches has played its part here: at the great gatherings of the 'Ecumenical Movement', the Orthodox delegates from different autocephalous Churches have found themselves ill-prepared to speak with a united voice. Why, they have asked, does it require the World Council of Churches to bring us Orthodox together? Why do we ourselves never meet to discuss our common problems? The urgent need for co-operation is also felt by many Orthodox youth movements, particularly in the diaspora. Valuable work has been done here by *Syndesmos*, an international organization founded in 1953, in which Orthodox youth groups of many different countries collaborate.

In the attempts at cooperation a leading part is naturally played by the senior hierarch of the Orthodox Church, the Ecumenical Patriarch. After the First World War the Patriarchate of Constantinople contemplated gathering a 'Great Council' of the whole Orthodox Church, and as a first step towards this, plans were made for a 'Pro-Synod' which was to prepare the agenda for the Council. A preliminary Inter-Orthodox Committee met on Mount Athos in 1930, but the Pro-Synod itself never materialized, largely owing to obstruction from the Turkish government. Around 1950 the Ecumenical Patriarch Athenagoras revived the idea, and after repeated postponements a 'Pan-Orthodox Conference' eventually met at Rhodes in September 1961. Further Pan-Orthodox Conferences have met at Rhodes (1963, 1964) and Geneva (1968, 1976, 1982). The chief items on the agenda of the 'Great Council', when and if it eventually meets, will probably be the problems of Orthodox disunity in the west, the relations of Orthodoxy with other Christian Churches ('ecumenism'), and the application of Orthodox moral teaching in the modern world.

MISSIONS

We have already spoken of the missionary witness of the diaspora, but it remains to say something of Orthodox missionary work in the stricter sense of preaching to the heathen. Since the time of Joseph de Maistre it has been fashionable in the west to say that Orthodoxy is not a missionary Church. Certainly Orthodox have often failed to perceive their missionary responsibilities; yet de Maistre's charge is not entirely just. Anyone who reflects on the mission of Cyril and Methodius, on the work of their disciples in Bulgaria and Serbia, and on the story of Russia's conversion, will realize that Byzantium can claim missionary achievements as great as those of Celtic or Roman Christianity in the same period. Under Turkish rule it became impossible to undertake missionary work of an open kind; but in Russia, where the Church remained free, missions continued uninterrupted – although there were periods of diminished activity – from Stephen of Perm (and even before) to Innocent of Kamchatka and the beginnings of the twentieth century. It is easy for a westerner to forget how vast a missionary field the Russian continent embraced. Russian missions extended outside Russia, not only to Alaska (of which we have spoken already), but to China, Japan, and Korea.

What of the present? Under the Bolsheviks, as under the Turks, open missionary work is impossible. But the missions founded by Russia in China, Japan, and Korea still exist, while a new Orthodox mission has shot up suddenly and spontaneously in Central Africa. At the same time both the Orthodox in America and the older Churches in the eastern Mediterranean, who do not suffer from the same disabilities as their brethren in communist countries, are beginning to show a new missionary awareness.

The Chinese mission at Peking was set up in 1715, and its origins go back earlier still, to 1686, when a group of Cossacks entered service in the Chinese Imperial Guard and took their chaplain with them. Mission work, however, was not undertaken on any scale until the end of the nineteenth century, and by 1914 there were still only some 5,000 converts, although there were already Chinese priests and a seminary for Chinese theological students. (It has been the constant policy of Orthodox missions to build up a native clergy as quickly as possible.) After the 1917 Revolution, so far from ceasing, missionary work increased considerably, since a large number of Russian *émigrés*, including many clergy, fled eastward from Siberia. In China and Manchuria in 1939 there were 200,000 Orthodox (mostly Russians, but including some converts) with five bishops and an Orthodox university at Harbin.

Since 1945 the situation has changed utterly. The communist government in China, when it ordered all non-Chinese missionaries to leave the country, gave no preferential treatment to the Russians: the Russian clergy, together with most of the faithful, have either been 'repatriated' to the U.S.S.R., or have escaped to America. In the 1950s there was at least one Chinese Orthodox bishop, with some 20,000 faithful; how much of Chinese Orthodoxy survives today it is difficult to tell. Since 1957 the Chinese Church, despite its small size, has been autonomous; since the Chinese government allows no foreign missions, this is probably the only means whereby it can hope to survive. Isolated in Red China, this tiny Orthodox community has a thorny path before it.

The Japanese Orthodox Church was founded by Father (later Archbishop) Nicholas Kassatkin (1836–1912), canonized in 1970. Sent in 1861 to serve the Russian Consulate in Japan, he decided from the start to work not only among Russians but among Japanese, and after a time he devoted himself exclusively to missionary work. He baptized his first convert in 1868, and four years later two Japanese Orthodox were ordained priests. Curiously enough, the first Japanese Orthodox bishop, John Ono (consecrated 1941), a widower, was son-in-law to the first Japanese convert. After a period of discouragement between the two World Wars, Orthodoxy in Japan is now reviving. There are today about forty parishes, with 25,000 faithful. The seminary at Tokyo, closed in 1919, was reopened in 1954. Practically all the clergy are Japanese, but one of the two bishops is American. There is a small but steady stream of converts – about 200–300 in each year, mostly young people in their twenties or thirties, some with higher education. The Orthodox Church in Japan is autonomous or self-governing in its internal life, while remaining under the general spiritual care of its Mother Church, the Moscow Patriarchate. Though limited in numbers, it can justly claim to be no longer a foreign mission but an indigenous Church of the Japanese people.

The Russian mission in Korea, founded in 1898, has always been on a much smaller scale. The first Korean Orthodox priest was ordained in 1912. In 1934 there were 820 Orthodox in Korea, but today there would seem to be less. The mission suffered in 1950 during the Korean civil war, when the church was destroyed; but it was rebuilt in 1953, and a larger church was constructed in 1967. At present the mission is under the charge of the Greek diocese of New Zealand.

Besides these Asian Orthodox Churches, there is now an exceedingly lively African Orthodox Church in Uganda and Kenya. Entirely indigenous from the start, African Orthodoxy did not arise through the preaching of missionaries from the traditional Orthodox lands, but was a spontaneous movement among Africans themselves. The founders of the African Orthodox movement were two native Ugandans, Rauben Sebanja Mukasa Spartas (born 1899, bishop 1972, died 1982) and his friend Obadiah Kabanda Basajjakitalo. Originally brought up as Anglicans, they were converted to Orthodoxy in the 1920s, not as a result of personal contact with other Orthodox, but through their own reading and study. Over the past forty years Rauben and Obadiah have energetically preached their new-found faith to their fellow Africans, building up a community which, according to some reports, numbers more than 100,000, mostly in Kenya. In 1982, after the death of Bishop Rauben, there were two African bishops.

At first the canonical position of Ugandan Orthodoxy was in some doubt, as originally Rauben and Obadiah established contact with an organization emanating from the United States, the 'African Orthodox Church', which, though using the title 'Orthodox', has in fact no connexion with the true and historical Orthodox communion. In 1932 they were both ordained by a certain Archbishop Alexander of this Church, but towards the end of that same year they became aware of the dubious status of the 'African Orthodox Church', whereupon they severed all relations with it and approached the Patriarchate of Alexandria. But only in 1946, when Rauben visited Alexandria in person, did the Patriarch formally recognize the African Orthodox community in Uganda, and definitely take it under his care. In recent years the bond with Alexandria has been considerably strengthened, and since 1959 one of the Metropolitans of the Patriarchate – a Greek – has been charged with special responsibility for missionary work in Central Africa. African Orthodox have been sent to study theology in Greece, and since 1960 more than eighty Africans have been ordained as deacons and priests (until that year, the only priests were the two founders themselves). In 1982 a seminary for training priests was opened at Nairobi. Many African Orthodox have high ambitions, and are anxious to cast their net still wider. In the words of Father Spartas: 'And, me-thinks, that in no time this Church is going to embrace all the Africans at large and thereby become one of the leading Churches in Africa.'[1] The rise of Orthodoxy in Uganda has of course to be seen against the background of African national-ism: one of the obvious attractions of Orthodox Christianity in Ugandan eyes is the fact that it is entirely unconnected with the colonial régimes of the past hundred years. Yet, despite certain political undertones, Orthodoxy in Central Africa is a genuinely religious movement.

The enthusiasm with which these Africans have embraced Orthodoxy has caught the imagination of the Orthodox world at large, and has helped to arouse missionary interest in many places. Paradoxically, in Africa hitherto it has been the Africans who have taken the initiative and converted themselves to Orthodoxy. Perhaps the Orthodox, encouraged by the Ugan-dan precedent, will now establish missions elsewhere on their own initiative, instead of waiting for the Africans to come to them. The 'missionary' situation of the diaspora has made Orthodox better aware of the meaning of their own tradition: may not a closer involvement in the task of evangelizing non-Christian countries have the same effect?

Every Christian body is today confronted by grave problems, but the Orthodox have perhaps greater difficulties to face than most. In contemporary Orthodoxy it is not always easy 'to recognize victory beneath the outward appearance of failure, to discern the power of God fulfilling itself in weakness, the true Church within the historic reality'.[2] But if there are obvious weaknesses, there are also many signs of life. Whatever the doubts and ambiguities of Church–State relations in com-munist countries, today as in the past Orthodoxy has its martyrs and confessors. The decline of Orthodox monasticism,

1. Quoted in F. B. Welbourn, *East African Rebels*, London, 1961, p. 83; this book gives a critical but not unsympathetic account of Orthodoxy in Uganda.

2. V. Lossky, *The Mystical Theology of the Eastern Church*, p. 246.

unmistakable in many areas, is not by any means universal; and there are centres which may prove the source of a future monastic resurrection. The spiritual treasures of Orthodoxy – for example, the *Philokalia* and the Jesus Prayer – so far from being forgotten, are used and appreciated more and more. Orthodox theologians are few in number, but some of them – often under the stimulus of western learning – are rediscovering vital elements in their theological inheritance. A short-sighted nationalism is hindering the Church in its work, but there are growing attempts at cooperation. Missions are still on a very small scale, but Orthodoxy is showing a greater awareness of their importance. No Orthodox who is realistic and honest with himself can feel complacent about the present state of his Church; yet despite its many problems and manifest human shortcomings, Orthodoxy can at the same time look to the future with confidence and hope.

Part Two

FAITH AND WORSHIP

CHAPTER 10

Holy Tradition:
The Source of the Orthodox Faith

Guard the deposit. *1 Timothy vi, 20*

Tradition is the life of the Holy Spirit
in the Church. *Vladimir Lossky*

THE INNER MEANING OF TRADITION

ORTHODOX history is marked outwardly by a series of sudden breaks: the capture of Alexandria, Antioch, and Jerusalem by Arab Mohammedans; the burning of Kiev by the Mongols; the two sacks of Constantinople; the October Revolution in Russia. Yet these events, while they have transformed the external appearance of the Orthodox world, have never broken the inward continuity of the Orthodox Church. The thing that first strikes a stranger on encountering Orthodoxy is usually its air of antiquity, its apparent changelessness. He finds that Orthodox still baptize by threefold immersion, as in the primitive Church; they still bring babies and small children to receive Holy Communion; in the Liturgy the deacon still cries out: 'The doors! The doors!' – recalling the early days when the church's entrance was jealously guarded, and none but members of the Christian family could attend the family worship; the Creed is still recited without any additions.

These are but a few outward examples of something which pervades every aspect of Orthodox life. Recently when two Orthodox scholars were asked to summarize the distinctive characteristic of their Church, they both pointed to the same thing: its changelessness, its determination to remain loyal to the past, its sense of *living continuity* with the Church of ancient times.[1] Two and a half centuries before, the Eastern Patriarchs said exactly the same to the Non-Jurors:

> We preserve the Doctrine of the Lord uncorrupted, and firmly adhere to the Faith he delivered to us, and keep it free from blemish and diminution, as a Royal Treasure, and a monument of great price, *neither adding any thing, nor taking any thing from it.*[2]

This idea of living continuity is summed up for the Orthodox in the one word *Tradition.* 'We do not change the everlasting boundaries which our fathers have set,' wrote John of Damascus, 'but *we keep the Tradition, just as we received it.*'[3]

Orthodox are always talking about Tradition. What do they mean by the word? A tradition, says the Oxford Dictionary, is an opinion, belief, or custom handed down from ancestors to posterity. Christian Tradition, in that case, is the faith which Jesus Christ imparted to the Apostles, and which since the Apostles' time has been handed down from generation to generation in the Church.[4] But to an Orthodox Christian, Tradition means something more concrete and specific than this. It means the books of the Bible; it means the Creed; it means the decrees of the Ecumenical Councils and the writings of the Fathers; it means the Canons, the Service Books, the Holy Icons – in fact, the whole system of doctrine, Church government, worship, and art which Orthodoxy has articulated over the ages. The Orthodox Christian of today sees himself as heir and guardian to a great inheritance received from the past, and he believes that it is his duty to transmit this inheritance unimpaired to the future.

Note that the Bible forms a part of Tradition. Sometimes Tradition is defined as 'the oral teaching of Christ, not recorded in writing by his immediate disciples' (Oxford Dic-

1. See Panagiotis Bratsiotis and Georges Florovsky, in *Orthodoxy, A Faith and Order Dialogue*, Geneva, 1960.
2. Letter of 1718, in G. Williams, *The Orthodox Church of the East in the Eighteenth Century*, p. 17.
3. *On Icons*, II, 12 (*P. G.* xciv, 1297B).
4. Compare Paul in 1 Corinthians xv, 3.

tionary). Not only non-Orthodox but many Orthodox writers
have adopted this way of speaking, treating Scripture and
Tradition as two different things, two distinct sources of the
Christian faith. But in reality there is only one source, since
Scripture exists *within* Tradition. To separate and contrast the
two is to impoverish the idea of both alike.

Orthodox, while reverencing this inheritance from the past,
are also well aware that not everything received from the past
is of equal value. Among the various elements of Tradition, a
unique pre-eminence belongs to the Bible, to the Creed, to the
doctrinal definitions of the Ecumenical Councils: these things
the Orthodox accept as something absolute and unchanging,
something which cannot be cancelled or revised. The other
parts of Tradition do not have quite the same authority. The
decrees of Jassy or Jerusalem do not stand on the same level
as the Nicene Creed, nor do the writings of an Athanasius, or
a Symeon the New Theologian, occupy the same position as
the Gospel of Saint John.

Not everything received from the past is of equal value, nor
is everything received from the past necessarily true. As one
of the bishops remarked at the Council of Carthage in 257:
'The Lord said, I am truth. He did not say, I am custom.'[1]
There is a difference between 'Tradition' and 'traditions':
many traditions which the past has handed down are human
and accidental – pious opinions (or worse), but not a true part
of the one Tradition, the essential Christian message.

It is necessary to question the past. In Byzantine and post-
Byzantine times, Orthodox have not always been sufficiently
critical in their attitude to the past, and the result has frequently been stagnation. Today this uncritical attitude can no
longer be maintained. Higher standards of scholarship, increasing contacts with western Christians, the inroads of secularism and atheism, have forced Orthodox in this present
century to look more closely at their inheritance and to distinguish more carefully between Tradition and traditions. The
task of discrimination is not always easy. It is necessary to

1. *The Opinions of the Bishops on the Baptizing of Heretics*, 30.

avoid alike the error of the Old Believers and the error of the 'Living Church': the one party fell into an extreme conservatism which suffered no change whatever in traditions, the other into a Modernism or theological liberalism which undermined Tradition. Yet despite certain manifest handicaps, the Orthodox of today are perhaps in a better position to discriminate aright than their predecessors have been for many centuries; and often it is precisely their contact with the west which is helping them to see more and more clearly what is essential in their own inheritance.

True Orthodox fidelity to the past must always be a *creative* fidelity; for true Orthodoxy can never rest satisfied with a barren 'theology of repetition', which, parrot-like, repeats accepted formulae without striving to understand what lies behind them. Loyalty to Tradition, properly understood, is not something mechanical, a dull process of handing down what has been received. An Orthodox thinker must see Tradition *from within*, he must enter into its inner spirit. In order to live within Tradition, it is not enough simply to give intellectual assent to a system of doctrine; for Tradition is far more than a set of abstract propositions – it is a life, a personal encounter with Christ in the Holy Spirit. Tradition is not only kept by the Church – it lives in the Church, it is the life of the Holy Spirit in the Church. The Orthodox conception of Tradition is not static but dynamic, not a dead acceptance of the past but a living experience of the Holy Spirit in the present. Tradition, while inwardly changeless (for God does not change), is constantly assuming new forms, which supplement the old without superseding them. Orthodox often speak as if the period of doctrinal formulation were wholly at an end, yet this is not the case. Perhaps in our own day new Ecumenical Councils will meet, and Tradition will be enriched by fresh statements of the faith.

This idea of Tradition as a living thing has been well expressed by Georges Florovsky:

Tradition is the witness of the Spirit; the Spirit's unceasing revelation and preaching of good tidings. ... To accept and understand Tradition we must live within the Church, we must be conscious of the grace-giving presence of the Lord in it; we must feel the breath of the Holy Ghost in it. . . . Tradition is not only a protective, conservative principle; it is, primarily, the principle of growth and regeneration. . . . Tradition is the constant abiding of the Spirit and not only the memory of words.[1]

Tradition is the witness of the Spirit: in the words of Christ, 'When the Spirit of truth has come, he will guide you into all truth' (John xvi, 13). It is this divine promise that forms the basis of the Orthodox devotion to Tradition.

THE OUTWARD FORMS

Let us take in turn the different outward forms in which Tradition is expressed:

(1) *The Bible*

(a) *The Bible and the Church.* The Christian Church is a Scriptural Church: Orthodoxy believes this just as firmly, if not more firmly than Protestantism. The Bible is the supreme expression of God's revelation to man, and Christians must always be 'People of the Book'. But if Christians are People of the Book, the Bible is the Book of the People; it must not be regarded as something set up *over* the Church, but as something that lives and is understood *within* the Church (that is why one should not separate Scripture and Tradition). It is from the Church that the Bible ultimately derives its authority, for it was the Church which originally decided which books form a part of Holy Scripture; and it is the Church alone which can interpret Holy Scripture with authority. There are many

1. 'Sobornost: the Catholicity of the Church', in *The Church of God*, edited E. L. Mascall, pp. 64–5. Compare G. Florovsky, 'Saint Gregory Palamas and the Tradition of the Fathers', in the periodical *Sobornost*, series 4, no. 4, 1961, pp. 165–76; and V. Lossky, 'Tradition and Traditions', in Ouspensky and Lossky, *The Meaning of Icons*, pp. 13–24. To both these essays I am heavily indebted.

sayings in the Bible which by themselves are far from clear, and the individual reader, however sincere, is in danger of error if he trusts his own personal interpretation. 'Do you understand what you are reading?' Philip asked the Ethiopian eunuch; and the eunuch replied: 'How can I, unless someone guides me?' (Acts viii, 30–1). Orthodox, when they read the Scripture, accept the guidance of the Church. When received into the Orthodox Church, a convert promises: 'I will accept and understand Holy Scripture in accordance with the interpretation which was and is held by the Holy Orthodox Catholic Church of the East, our Mother.'[1]

(b) *The Text of the Bible: Biblical Criticism.* The Orthodox Church has the same New Testament as the rest of Christendom. As its authoritative text for the Old Testament, it uses the ancient Greek translation known as the Septuagint. When this differs from the original Hebrew (which happens quite often), Orthodox believe that the changes in the Septuagint were made under the inspiration of the Holy Spirit, and are to be accepted as part of God's continuing revelation. The best-known instance is Isaiah vii, 14 – where the Hebrew says 'A *young woman* shall conceive and bear a son', which the Septuagint translates 'A *virgin* shall conceive', etc. The New Testament follows the Septuagint text (Matthew i, 23).

The Hebrew version of the Old Testament contains thirty-nine books. The Septuagint contains in addition ten further books, not present in the Hebrew, which are known in the Orthodox Church as the 'Deutero-Canonical Books'.[2] These were declared by the Councils of Jassy (1642) and Jerusalem (1672) to be 'genuine parts of Scripture'; most Orthodox scholars at the present day, however, following the opinion of Athanasius and Jerome, consider that the Deutero-Canonical

1. On Bible and Church, see especially Dositheus, *Confession*, Decree ii.
2. 3 Esdras; Tobit; Judith; 1, 2, and 3 Maccabees; Wisdom of Solomon; Ecclesiasticus; Baruch; Letter of Jeremias. In the west these books are often called the 'Apocrypha'.

Books, although part of the Bible, stand on a lower footing than the rest of the Old Testament.

Christianity, if true, has nothing to fear from honest inquiry. Orthodoxy, while regarding the Church as the authoritative interpreter of Scripture, does not forbid the critical and historical study of the Bible, although hitherto Orthodox scholars have not been prominent in this field.

(c) *The Bible in worship.* It is sometimes thought that Orthodox attach less importance than western Christians to the Bible. Yet in fact Holy Scripture is read constantly at Orthodox services: during the course of Matins and Vespers the entire Psalter is recited each week, and in Lent twice a week;[1] Old Testament lessons (usually three in number) occur at Vespers on the eves of many feasts; the reading of the Gospel forms the climax of Matins on Sundays and feasts; at the Liturgy a special Epistle and Gospel are assigned for each day of the year, so that the whole New Testament (except the Revelation of Saint John) is read at the Eucharist. The *Nunc Dimittis* is used at Vespers; Old Testament canticles, with the *Magnificat* and *Benedictus*, are sung at Matins; the Lord's Prayer is read at every service. Besides these specific extracts from Scripture, the whole text of each service is shot through with Biblical language, and it has been calculated that the Liturgy contains 98 quotations from the Old Testament and 114 from the New.[2]

Orthodoxy regards the Bible as a verbal icon of Christ, the Seventh Council laying down that the Holy Icons and the Book of the Gospels should be venerated in the same way. In every church the Gospel Book has a place of honour on the altar; it is carried in procession at the Liturgy and at Matins on Sundays and feasts; the faithful kiss it and prostrate themselves

1. Such is the rule laid down by the service books. In practice, in ordinary parish churches Matins and Vespers are not recited daily, but only at weekends and on feasts; and even then, unfortunately, the portions appointed from the Psalter are often abbreviated or (worse still) omitted entirely.

2. P. Evdokimov, *L'Orthodoxie*, p. 241, note 96.

before it. Such is the respect shown in the Orthodox Church for the Word of God.

(2) *The Seven Ecumenical Councils: The Creed*

The doctrinal definitions of an Ecumenical Council are infallible. Thus in the eyes of the Orthodox Church, the statements of faith put out by the Seven Councils possess, along with the Bible, an abiding and irrevocable authority.

The most important of all the Ecumenical statements of faith is the *Nicene-Constantinopolitan Creed*, which is read or sung at every celebration of the Eucharist, and also daily at Nocturns and at Compline. The other two Creeds used by the west, the *Apostles' Creed* and the '*Athanasian Creed*', do not possess the same authority as the Nicene, because they have not been proclaimed by an Ecumenical Council. Orthodox honour the Apostles' Creed as an ancient statement of faith, and accept its teaching; but it is simply a local western Baptismal Creed, never used in the services of the Eastern Patriarchates. The 'Athanasian Creed' likewise is not used in Orthodox worship, but it is sometimes printed (without the *filioque*) in the *Horologion* (Book of Hours).

(3) *Later Councils*

The formulation of Orthodox doctrine, as we have seen, did not cease with the Seventh Ecumenical Council. Since 787 there have been two chief ways whereby the Church has expressed its mind: (1) definitions by Local Councils (that is, councils attended by members of one or more national Churches, but not claiming to represent the Orthodox Catholic Church as a whole) and (2) letters or statements of faith put out by individual bishops. While the doctrinal decisions of General Councils are infallible, those of a Local Council or an individual bishop are always liable to error; but if such decisions are accepted by the rest of the Church, then they come to acquire Ecumenical authority (i.e. a universal authority similar to that possessed by the doctrinal statements of an Ecumenical Council). The doctrinal decisions of an Ecumenical

Council cannot be revised or corrected, but must be accepted *in toto*; but the Church has often been selective in its treatment of the acts of Local Councils: in the case of the seventeenth-century Councils, for example, their statements of faith have in part been received by the whole Orthodox Church, but in part set aside or corrected.

The following are the chief Orthodox doctrinal statements since 787:

i. The Encyclical Letter of Saint Photius (867).

ii. The First Letter of Michael Cerularius to Peter of Antioch (1054).

iii. The decisions of the Councils of Constantinople in 1341 and 1351 on the Hesychast Controversy.

iv. The Encyclical Letter of Saint Mark of Ephesus (1440–1).

v. The Confession of Faith by Gennadius, Patriarch of Constantinople (1455–6).

vi. The Replies of Jeremias II to the Lutherans (1573–81).

vii. The Confession of Faith by Metrophanes Kritopoulos (1625).

viii. The Orthodox Confession by Peter of Moghila, in its revised form (ratified by the Council of Jassy, 1642).

ix. The Confession of Dositheus (ratified by the Council of Jerusalem, 1672).

x. The Answers of the Orthodox Patriarchs to the Non-Jurors (1718, 1723).

xi. The Reply of the Orthodox Patriarchs to Pope Pius IX (1848).

xii. The Reply of the Synod of Constantinople to Pope Leo XIII (1895).

xiii. The Encyclical Letters by the Patriarchate of Constantinople on Christian unity and on the 'Ecumenical Movement' (1920, 1952).

These documents – particularly items v–ix – are sometimes called the 'Symbolical Books' of the Orthodox Church, but many Orthodox scholars today regard this title as misleading and do not use it.

(4) *The Fathers*

The definitions of the Councils must be studied in the wider context of the Fathers. But as with Local Councils, so with the Fathers, the judgement of the Church is selective: individual writers have at times fallen into error and at times contradict one another. Patristic wheat needs to be distinguished from Patristic chaff. An Orthodox must not simply know and quote the Fathers, he must enter into the spirit of the Fathers and acquire a 'Patristic mind'. He must treat the Fathers not merely as relics from the past, but as living witnesses and contemporaries.

The Orthodox Church has never attempted to define exactly who the Fathers are, still less to classify them in order of importance. But it has a particular reverence for the writers of the fourth century, and especially for those whom it terms 'the Three Great Hierarchs', Gregory of Nazianzus, Basil the Great, and John Chrysostom. In the eyes of Orthodoxy the 'Age of the Fathers' did not come to an end in the fifth century, for many later writers are also 'Fathers' – Maximus, John of Damascus, Theodore of Studium, Symeon the New Theologian, Gregory Palamas, Mark of Ephesus. Indeed, it is dangerous to look on 'the Fathers' as a closed cycle of writings belonging wholly to the past, for might not our own age produce a new Basil or Athanasius? To say that there can be no more Fathers is to suggest that the Holy Spirit has deserted the Church.

(5) *The Liturgy*

The Orthodox Church is not as much given to making formal dogmatic definitions as is the Roman Catholic Church. But it would be false to conclude that because some belief has never been specifically proclaimed as a dogma by Orthodoxy, it is therefore not a part of Orthodox Tradition, but merely a matter of private opinion. Certain doctrines, never formally defined, are yet held by the Church with an unmistakable inner conviction, an unruffled unanimity, which is just as binding as an explicit formulation. 'Some things we have from written teaching,' said Saint Basil, 'others we have received from the Apostolic Tradition handed down to us in a mystery; and both these things have the same force for piety.'[1]

This inner Tradition 'handed down to us in a mystery' is preserved above all in the Church's worship. *Lex orandi lex credendi*: men's faith is expressed in their prayer. Orthodoxy has made few explicit definitions about the Eucharist and the other Sacraments, about the next world, the Mother of God, the saints, and the faithful departed: Orthodox belief on these points is contained mainly in the prayers and hymns used at Orthodox services. Nor is it merely the *words* of the services which are a part of Tradition; the various *gestures* and *actions* – immersion in the waters of Baptism, the different anointings with oil, the sign of the Cross, and so on – all have a special meaning, and all express in symbolical or dramatic form the truths of the faith.

(6) *Canon Law*

Besides doctrinal definitions, the Ecumenical Councils drew up *Canons*, dealing with Church organization and discipline; other Canons were made by Local Councils and by individual bishops. Theodore Balsamon, Zonaras, and other Byzantine writers compiled collections of Canons, with explanations and commentaries. The standard modern Greek commentary, the *Pedalion* ('Rudder'), published in 1800, is the work of that indefatigable saint, Nicodemus of the Holy Mountain.

The Canon Law of the Orthodox Church has been very little studied in the west, and as a result western writers sometimes fall into the mistake of regarding Orthodoxy as an organization with virtually no outward regulations. On the contrary, the life of Orthodoxy has many rules, often of great strictness and rigour. It must be confessed, however, that at the present day many of the Canons are difficult or impossible to apply, and

1. *On the Holy Spirit*, xxvii (66).

have fallen widely into disuse. When and if a new General Council of the Church is assembled, one of its chief tasks may well be the revision and clarification of Canon Law.

The doctrinal definitions of the Councils possess an absolute and unalterable validity which Canons as such cannot claim; for doctrinal definitions deal with eternal truths, Canons with the earthly life of the Church, where conditions are constantly changing and individual situations are infinitely various. Yet between the Canons and the dogmas of the Church there exists an essential connexion: Canon Law is simply the attempt to apply dogma to practical situations in the daily life of each Christian. Thus in a relative sense the Canons form a part of Holy Tradition.

(7) *Icons*

The Tradition of the Church is expressed not only through words, not only through the actions and gestures used in worship, but also through art – through the line and colour of the Holy Icons. An icon is not simply a religious picture designed to arouse appropriate emotions in the beholder; it is one of the ways whereby God is revealed to man. Through icons the Orthodox Christian receives a vision of the spiritual world. Because the icon is a part of Tradition, the icon painter is not free to adapt or innovate as he pleases; for his work must reflect, not his own aesthetic sentiments, but the mind of the Church. Artistic inspiration is not excluded, but it is exercised within certain prescribed rules. It is important that an icon painter should be a good artist, but it is even more important that he should be a sincere Christian, living within the spirit of Tradition, preparing himself for his work by means of Confession and Holy Communion.

Such are the primary elements which from an outward point of view make up the Tradition of the Orthodox Church – Scripture, Councils, Fathers, Liturgy, Canons, Icons. These things are not to be separated and contrasted, for it is the same Holy Spirit which speaks through them all, and together they make up a single whole, each part being understood in the light of the rest.

It has sometimes been said that the underlying cause for the break-up of western Christendom in the sixteenth century was the separation between theology and mysticism, between liturgy and personal devotion, which existed in the later Middle Ages. Orthodoxy for its part has always tried to avoid any such division. All true Orthodox theology is mystical; just as mysticism divorced from theology becomes subjective and heretical, so theology, when it is not mystical, degenerates into an arid scholasticism, 'academic' in the bad sense of the word.

Theology, mysticism, spirituality, moral rules, worship, art: these things must not be kept in separate compartments. Doctrine cannot be understood unless it is prayed: a theologian, said Evagrius, is one who knows how to pray, and he who prays in spirit and in truth is by that very act a theologian.[1] And doctrine, if it is to be prayed, must also be lived: theology without action, as Saint Maximus put it, is the theology of demons.[2] The Creed belongs only to those who live it. Faith and love, theology and life, are inseparable. In the Byzantine Liturgy, the Creed is introduced with the words: 'Let us love one another, that with one mind we may confess Father, Son, and Holy Spirit, Trinity one in essence and undivided.' This exactly expresses the Orthodox attitude to Tradition. If we do not love one another, we cannot love God; and if we do not love God, we cannot make a true confession of faith and cannot enter into the inner spirit of Tradition, for there is no other way of knowing God than to love Him.

1. *On Prayer*, 60 (*P. G.* lxxix, 1180B).
2. *Letter* 20 (*P.G.* xci, 601C).

CHAPTER 11

God and Man

In His unbounded love, God became what we are
that He might make us what He is.
                              Saint Irenaeus (died 202)

GOD IN TRINITY

OUR social programme, said the Russian thinker Fedorov, is
the dogma of the Trinity. Orthodoxy believes most passion-
ately that the doctrine of the Holy Trinity is not a piece of 'high
theology' reserved for the professional scholar, but something
that has a living, *practical* importance for every Christian. Man,
so the Bible teaches, is made in the image of God, and to
Christians God means the Trinity: thus it is only in the light
of the dogma of the Trinity that man can understand who he
is and what God intends him to be. Our private lives, our personal relations, and all our plans of forming a Christian society
depend upon a right theology of the Trinity. 'Between the
Trinity and Hell there lies no other choice.'[1] As an Anglican
writer has put it: 'In this doctrine is summed up the new way
of thinking about God, in the power of which the fishermen
went out to convert the Greco-Roman world. It marks a saving
revolution in human thought.'[2]

The basic elements in the Orthodox doctrine of God have
already been mentioned in the first part of this book, so that
here they will only be summarized briefly:

(1) *God is absolutely transcendent.* 'No single thing of all that
is created has or ever will have even the slightest communion

1. V. Lossky, *The Mystical Theology of the Eastern Church*, p. 66.
2. D. J. Chitty, 'The Doctrine of the Holy Trinity told to the
Children', in *Sobornost*, series 4, no. 5, 1961, p. 241.

with the supreme nature or nearness to it.'[1] This absolute
transcendence Orthodoxy safeguards by its emphatic use of the
'way of negation', of 'apophatic' theology. Positive or 'cata-
phatic' theology – the 'way of affirmation' – must always be
balanced and corrected by the employment of negative language. Our positive statements about God – that He is good,
wise, just and so on – are true as far as they go, yet they cannot
adequately describe the inner nature of the deity. These positive statements, said John of Damascus, reveal 'not the nature,
but the things around the nature'. '*That* there is a God is clear;
but *what* He is by essence and nature, this is altogether beyond
our comprehension and knowledge.'[2]

(2) *God, although absolutely transcendent, is not cut off from the
world which He has made.* God is above and outside His
creation, yet He also exists within it. As a much used Orthodox prayer puts it: 'Thou art everywhere and fillest all things.'
Orthodoxy therefore distinguishes between God's essence and
His energies, thus safeguarding both divine transcendence and
divine immanence: God's essence remains unapproachable,
but His energies come down to us. God's energies, *which are
God Himself*, permeate all His creation, and we experience them
in the form of deifying grace and divine light. Truly our God
is a God who hides Himself, yet He is also a God who acts –
the God of history, intervening directly in concrete situations.

(3) *God is personal, that is to say, Trinitarian.* This God who
acts is not only a God of energies, but a personal God. When
man participates in the divine energies, he is not overwhelmed
by some vague and nameless power, but he is brought face to
face with a person. Nor is this all: God is not simply a single
person confined within his own being, but a Trinity of three
persons, Father, Son, and Holy Spirit, each of whom 'dwells'
in the other two, by virtue of a perpetual movement of love.
God is not only a unity but a union.

1. Gregory Palamas, *P.G.* cl, 1176c (quoted on p. 77).
2. *On the Orthodox Faith*, I, 4 (*P.G.* xciv, 800B, 797B).

(4) *Our God is an Incarnate God.* God has come down to man, not only through His energies, but in His own person. The Second Person of the Trinity, 'true God from true God', was made man: 'The Word became flesh and dwelt among us' (John i, 14). A closer union than this between God and His creation there could not be. God Himself became one of His creatures.[1]

Those brought up in other traditions have sometimes found it difficult to accept the Orthodox emphasis on apophatic theology and the distinction between essence and energies; but apart from these two matters, Orthodox agree in their doctrine of God with the overwhelming majority of all who call themselves Christians. Monophysites and Lutherans, Nestorians and Roman Catholics, Calvinists, Anglicans, and Orthodox: all alike worship One God in Three Persons and confess Christ as Incarnate Son of God.[2]

Yet there is one point in the doctrine of God the Trinity over which east and west part company – the *filioque*. We have already seen how decisive a part this one word played in the unhappy fragmentation of Christendom. But granted that the *filioque* is important historically, does it really matter from a theological point of view? Many people today – not excluding many Orthodox – find the whole dispute so technical and obscure that they are tempted to dismiss it as utterly trivial. From the viewpoint of traditional Orthodox theology there can be but one rejoinder to this: technical and obscure it undoubtedly is, like most questions of Trinitarian theology; but it is not trivial. Since belief in the Trinity lies at the very heart of the Christian faith, a tiny difference in Trinitarian theology is

1. For the first and second of these four points, see pp. 72–9; for the third and fourth points, see pp. 28–37.
2. In the past hundred years, under the influence of 'Modernism', many Protestants have virtually abandoned the doctrines of the Trinity and the Incarnation. Thus when I speak here of Calvinists, Lutherans, and Anglicans, I have in mind those who still respect the classical Protestant formularies of the sixteenth century.

bound to have repercussions upon every aspect of Christian life and thought. Let us try therefore to understand some of the issues involved in the *filioque* dispute.

One essence in three persons. God is one and God is three: the Holy Trinity is a mystery of unity in diversity, and of diversity in unity. Father, Son, and Spirit are 'one in essence' (*homoousios*), yet each is distinguished from the other two by personal characteristics. 'The divine is indivisible in its divisions',[1] for the persons are 'united yet not confused, distinct yet not divided';[2] 'both the distinction and the union alike are paradoxical'.[3]

But if each of the persons is distinct, what holds the Holy Trinity together? Here the Orthodox Church, following the Cappadocian Fathers, answers that there is one God because there is one Father. In the language of theology, the Father is the 'cause' or 'source' of Godhead, He is the principle (*arche*) of unity among the three; and it is in this sense that Orthodoxy talks of the 'monarchy' of the Father. The other two persons trace their origin to the Father and are defined in terms of their relation to Him. The Father is the source of Godhead, born of none and proceeding from none; the Son is born of the Father from all eternity ('before all ages', as the Creed says); the Spirit proceeds from the Father from all eternity.

It is at this point that Roman Catholic theology begins to disagree. According to Roman theology, the Spirit proceeds eternally from the Father *and the Son*; and this means that the Father ceases to be the unique source of Godhead, since the Son also is a source. Since the principle of unity in the Godhead can no longer be the person of the Father, Rome finds its principle of unity in the substance or essence which all three persons share. In Orthodoxy the principle of God's unity is personal, in Roman Catholicism it is not.

But what is meant by the term 'proceed'? Unless this is properly understood, nothing is understood. The Church

1. Gregory of Nazianzus, *Orations*, xxxi, 14.
2. John of Damascus, *On the Orthodox Faith*, I, 8 (*P.G.* xciv, 809A).
3. Gregory of Nazianzus, *Orations*, xxv, 17.

believes that Christ underwent two births, the one eternal, the other at a particular point in time: he was born of the Father 'before all ages', and born of the Virgin Mary in the days of Herod, King of Judaea, and of Augustus, Emperor of Rome. In the same way a firm distinction must be drawn between the *eternal procession* of the Holy Spirit, and the *temporal mission*, the sending of the Spirit to the world: the one concerns the relations existing from all eternity within the Godhead, the other concerns the relation of God to creation. Thus when the west says that the Spirit proceeds from the Father and the Son, and when Orthodoxy says that He proceeds from the Father alone, both sides are referring not to the outward action of the Trinity towards creation, but to certain eternal relations within the Godhead – relations which existed before ever the world was. But Orthodoxy, while disagreeing with the west over the eternal procession of the Spirit, agrees with the west in saying that, so far as the mission of the Spirit to the world is concerned, He is sent by the Son, and is indeed the 'Spirit of the Son'.

The Orthodox position is based on John xv, 26, where Christ says: 'When the Comforter has come, whom *I will send to you* from the Father – the Spirit of truth, who *proceeds from the Father* – he will bear witness to me.' Christ sends the Spirit, but the Spirit proceeds from the Father: so the Bible teaches, and so Orthodoxy believes. What Orthodoxy does not teach, and what the Bible never says, is that the Spirit proceeds from the Son.

An eternal procession from Father and Son: such is the western position. An eternal procession of the Spirit from the Father alone, a temporal mission from the Son: such was the position upheld by Saint Photius against the west. But Byzantine writers of the thirteenth and fourteenth centuries – most notably Gregory of Cyprus, Patriarch of Constantinople from 1283 to 1289, and Gregory Palamas – went somewhat further than Photius, in an attempt to bridge the gulf between east and west. They were willing to allow not only a temporal mission, but an *eternal manifestation* of the Holy Spirit by the Son. While Photius had spoken only of a temporal relation between Son and Spirit, they admitted an eternal relation. Yet on the essential point the two Gregories agreed with Photius: the Spirit is manifested by the Son, but does not proceed from the Son. The Father is the unique origin, source, and cause of Godhead.

Such in outline are the positions taken up by either side; let us now consider the Orthodox objections to the western position. The *filioque* leads either to ditheism or to semi-Sabellianism.[1] If the Son as well as the Father is an *arche*, a principle or source of Godhead, are there then (the Orthodox asked) two independent sources, two separate principles in the Trinity? Obviously not, since this would be tantamount to belief in two Gods; and so the Reunion Councils of Lyons (1274) and Florence (1438–9) were most careful to state that the Spirit proceeds from Father and Son 'as from *one* principle', *tanquam ex* (or *ab*) *uno principio*. From the Orthodox point of view, however, this is equally objectionable: ditheism is avoided, but the persons of Father and Son are merged and confused. The Cappadocians regarded the 'monarchy' as the distinctive characteristic of the Father: He alone is a principle or *arche* within the Trinity. But western theology ascribes the distinctive characteristic of the Father to the Son as well, thus fusing the two persons into one; and what else is this but 'Sabellius reborn, or rather some semi-Sabellian monster', as Saint Photius put it?[2]

Let us look more carefully at this charge of semi-Sabellianism. Orthodox Trinitarian theology has a personal principle of unity, but the west finds its unitary principle in the essence of God. In Latin Scholastic theology, so it seems to Orthodox, the persons are overshadowed by the common nature, and God is thought of not so much in concrete and personal terms, but as an essence in which various relations are distinguished. This way of thinking about God comes to full development in

1. Sabellius, a heretic of the second century, regarded Father, Son, and Spirit not as three distinct persons, but simply as varying 'modes' or 'aspects' of the deity.
2. *P.G.* cii, 289B.

Thomas Aquinas, who went so far as to identify the persons with the relations: *personae sunt ipsae relationes*.[1] Orthodox thinkers find this a very meagre idea of personality. The relations, they would say, are not the *persons* – they are the *personal characteristics* of Father, Son, and Holy Spirit; and (as Gregory Palamas put it) 'personal characteristics do not constitute the person, but they characterize the person'.[2] The relations, while designating the persons, in no way exhaust the mystery of each.

Latin Scholastic theology, emphasizing as it does the essence at the expense of the persons, comes near to turning God into an abstract idea. He becomes a remote and impersonal being, whose existence has to be proved by metaphysical arguments – a God of the philosophers, not the God of Abraham, Isaac, and Jacob. Orthodoxy, on the other hand, has been far less concerned than the Latin west to find philosophical proofs of God's existence: what is important is not that a man should argue about the deity, but that he should have a direct and living encounter with a concrete and personal God.

Such are some of the reasons why Orthodox regard the *filioque* as dangerous and heretical. Filioquism confuses the persons, and destroys the proper balance between unity and diversity in the Godhead. The oneness of the deity is emphasized at the expense of His threeness; God is regarded too much in terms of abstract essence and too little in terms of concrete personality.

But this is not all. Many Orthodox feel that, as a result of the *filioque*, the Holy Spirit in western thought has become subordinated to the Son – if not in theory, then at any rate in practice. The west pays insufficient attention to the work of the Spirit in the world, in the Church, in the daily life of each man.

Orthodox writers also argue that these two consequences of the *filioque* – subordination of the Holy Spirit, over-emphasis on the unity of God – have helped to bring about a distortion

1. *Summa Theologica*, 1, question 40, article 2.
2. Quoted in J. Meyendorff, *Introduction à l'étude de Grégoire Palamas*, Paris, 1959, p. 294.

in the Roman Catholic doctrine of the Church. Because the rôle of the Spirit has been neglected in the west, the Church has come to be regarded too much as an institution of this world, governed in terms of earthly power and jurisdiction. And just as in the western doctrine of God unity was stressed at the expense of diversity, so in the western conception of the Church unity has triumphed over diversity, and the result has been too great a centralization and too great an emphasis on Papal authority.

Such in outline is the Orthodox attitude to the *filioque*, although not all would state the case in such an uncompromising form. In particular, many of the criticisms given above apply only to a decadent form of Scholasticism, not to Latin theology as a whole.

MAN: HIS CREATION, HIS VOCATION, HIS FAILURE

'Thou hast made us for Thyself and our hearts are restless till they rest in Thee.'[1] Man was made for fellowship with God: this is the first and primary affirmation in the Christian doctrine of man. But man, made for fellowship with God, everywhere repudiates that fellowship: this is the second fact which all Christian anthropology takes into account. Man was made for fellowship with God: in the language of the Church, God created Adam according to His image and likeness, and set him in Paradise.[2] Man everywhere repudiates that fellowship: in the language of the Church, Adam fell, and his fall – his 'original sin' – has affected all mankind.

The Creation of Man. 'And God said, let us make man according to our image and likeness' (Genesis i, 26). God speaks in the plural: 'Let *us* make man.' The creation of man, so the Greek Fathers continually emphasized, was an act of all

1. Augustine, *Confessions*, I, i.
2. The opening chapters of Genesis are of course concerned with certain *religious* truths, and are not to be taken as literal history. Fifteen centuries before modern Biblical criticism, Greek Fathers were already interpreting the Creation and Paradise stories symbolically rather than literally.

three persons in the Trinity, and therefore the image and likeness of God must always be thought of as a *Trinitarian* image and likeness. We shall find that this is a point of vital importance.

Image and Likeness. According to most of the Greek Fathers, the terms *image* and *likeness* do not mean exactly the same thing. 'The expression *according to the image*,' wrote John of Damascus, 'indicates rationality and freedom, while the expression *according to the likeness* indicates assimilation to God through virtue.'[1] The image, or to use the Greek term the *icon*, of God signifies man's free will, his reason, his sense of moral responsibility – everything, in short, which marks man out from the animal creation and makes him a *person*. But the image means more than that. It means that we are God's 'offspring' (Acts xvii, 28), His kin; it means that between us and Him there is a point of contact, an essential similarity. The gulf between creature and Creator is not impassable, for because we are in God's image we can know God and have communion with Him. And if a man makes proper use of this faculty for communion with God, then he will become 'like' God, he will acquire the divine likeness; in the words of John Damascene, he will be 'assimilated to God through virtue'. To acquire the likeness is to be deified, it is to become a 'second god', a 'god by grace'. 'I said, *you are gods*, and all of you sons of the Most High' (Psalm lxxxi, 6).[2]

The image denotes the powers with which every man is endowed by God from the first moment of his existence; the likeness is not an endowment which man possesses from the start, but a goal at which he must aim, something which he can only acquire by degrees. However sinful a man may be, he never loses the image; but the likeness depends upon our moral choice, upon our 'virtue', and so it is destroyed by sin.

Man at his first creation was therefore perfect, not so much

1. *On the Orthodox Faith*, II, 12 (*P.G.* xciv, 920B).
2. In quotations from the Psalms, the numbering of the Septuagint is followed. Some versions of the Bible reckon this Psalm as lxxxii.

in an actual as in a potential sense. Endowed with the image from the start, he was called to acquire the likeness by his own efforts (assisted of course by the grace of God). Adam began in a state of innocence and simplicity. 'He was a child, not yet having his understanding perfected,' wrote Irenaeus. 'It was necessary that he should grow and so come to his perfection.'[1] God set Adam on the right path, but Adam had in front of him a long road to traverse in order to reach his final goal.

This picture of Adam before the fall is somewhat different from that presented by Saint Augustine and generally accepted in the west since his time. According to Augustine, man in Paradise was endowed from the start with all possible wisdom and knowledge: his was a realized, and in no sense potential, perfection. The dynamic conception of Irenaeus clearly fits more easily with modern theories of evolution than does the static conception of Augustine; but both were speaking as theologians, not as scientists, so that in neither case do their views stand or fall with any particular scientific hypothesis.

The west has often associated the image of God with man's intellect. While many Orthodox have done the same, others would say that since man is a single unified whole, the image of God embraces his entire person, body as well as soul. 'When God is said to have made man according to His image,' wrote Gregory Palamas, 'the word *man* means neither the soul by itself nor the body by itself, but the two together.'[2] The fact that man has a body, so Gregory argued, makes him not lower but higher than the angels. True, the angels are 'pure' spirit, whereas man's nature is 'mixed' – material as well as intellectual; but this means that his nature is more complete than the angelic and endowed with richer potentialities. Man is a microcosm, a bridge and point of meeting for the whole of God's creation.

Orthodox religious thought lays the utmost emphasis on the image of God in man. Man is a 'living theology', and because he is God's icon, he can find God by looking within his own

1. *Demonstration of the Apostolic Preaching*, 12.
2. *P.G.* cl, 1361c.

heart, by 'returning within himself': 'The Kingdom of God is within you' (Luke xvii, 21). 'Know yourselves,' said Saint Antony of Egypt. '. . . He who knows himself, knows God.'[1] 'If you are pure,' wrote Saint Isaac the Syrian (late seventh century), 'heaven is within you; within yourself you will see the angels and the Lord of the angels.'[2] And of Saint Pachomius it is recorded: 'In the purity of his heart he saw the invisible God as in a mirror.'[3]

Because he is an icon of God, each member of the human race, even the most sinful, is infinitely precious in God's sight. 'When you see your brother,' said Clement of Alexandria (died 215), 'you see God.'[4] And Evagrius taught: 'After God, we must count all men as God Himself.'[5] This respect for every human being is visibly expressed in Orthodox worship, when the priest censes not only the icons but the members of the congregation, saluting the image of God in each person. 'The best icon of God is man.'[6]

Grace and Free Will. As we have seen, the fact that man is in God's image means among other things that he possesses free will. God wanted a son, not a slave. The Orthodox Church rejects any doctrine of grace which might seem to infringe upon man's freedom. To describe the relation between the grace of God and free will of man, Orthodoxy uses the term cooperation or synergy (*synergeia*); in Paul's words: 'We are fellow-workers (*synergoi*) with God' (1 Corinthians iii, 9). If man is to achieve full fellowship with God, he cannot do so without God's help, yet he must also play his own part: man as well as God must make his contribution to the common work, although what God does is of immeasurably greater importance than what man does. 'The incorporation of man into Christ and his union with God require the cooperation of two unequal, but

1. *Letter* 3 (in the Greek and Latin collections, 6).
2. Quoted in P. Evdokimov, *L'Orthodoxie*, p. 88.
3. *First Greek Life*, 22.
4. *Stromateis*, I, xix (94, 5).
5. *On Prayer*, 123 (*P.G.* lxxix, 1193C).
6. P. Evdokimov, *L'Orthodoxie*, p. 218.

equally necessary forces: divine grace and human will.'[1] The supreme example of synergy is the Mother of God. [2]

The west, since the time of Augustine and the Pelagian controversy, has discussed this question of grace and free will in somewhat different terms; and many brought up in the Augustinian tradition – particularly Calvinists – have viewed the Orthodox idea of 'synergy' with some suspicion. Does it not ascribe too much to man's free will, and too little to God? Yet in reality the Orthodox teaching is very straightforward. 'Behold, I stand at the door and knock; if anyone hears my voice and opens the door, I will come in' (Revelation iii, 20). God knocks, but waits for man to open the door – He does not break it down. The grace of God invites all but compels none. In the words of John Chrysostom: 'God never draws anyone to Himself by force and violence. He wishes all men to be saved, but forces no one.'[3] 'It is for God to grant His grace,' said Saint Cyril of Jerusalem (died 386); 'your task is to accept that grace and to guard it.'[4] But it must not be imagined that because a man accepts and guards God's grace, he thereby earns 'merit'. God's gifts are always free gifts, and man can never have any claims upon his Maker. But man, while he cannot 'merit' salvation, must certainly work for it, since 'faith without works is dead' (James ii, 17).

The Fall: Original Sin. God gave Adam free will – the power to choose between good and evil – and it therefore rested with Adam either to accept the vocation set before him or to refuse it. He refused it. Instead of continuing along the path marked out for him by God, he turned aside and disobeyed God. Adam's fall consisted essentially in his disobedience of the will of God; he set up his own will against the divine will, and so by his own act he separated himself from God. As a result, a new form of existence appeared on earth – that of

1. A Monk of the Eastern Church, *Orthodox Spirituality*, p. 23.
2. See p. 263.
3. *Sermon on the words 'Saul, Saul . . .'*, 6 (*P.G.* li, 144).
4. *Catechetical Orations*, i, 4.

disease and death. By turning away from God, who is immortality and life, man put himself in a state that was contrary to nature, and this unnatural condition led to an inevitable disintegration of his being and eventually to physical death. The consequences of Adam's disobedience extended to all his descendants. We are members one of another, as Saint Paul never ceased to insist, and if one member suffers the whole body suffers. In virtue of this mysterious unity of the human race, not only Adam but all mankind became subject to mortality. Nor was the disintegration which followed from the fall merely physical. Cut off from God, Adam and his descendants passed under the domination of sin and of the devil. Each new human being is born into a world where sin prevails everywhere, a world in which it is easy to do evil and hard to do good. Man's will is weakened and enfeebled by what the Greeks call 'desire' and the Latins 'concupiscence'. We are all subject to these, the spiritual effects of original sin.

Thus far there is fairly close agreement between Orthodoxy, Roman Catholicism, and classic Protestantism; but beyond this point east and west do not entirely concur. Orthodoxy, holding as it does a less exalted idea of man's state before he fell, is also less severe than the west in its view of the consequences of the fall. Adam fell, not from a great height of knowledge and perfection, but from a state of undeveloped simplicity; hence he is not to be judged too harshly for his error. Certainly, as a result of the fall man's mind became so darkened, and his will-power was so impaired, that he could no longer hope to attain to the likeness of God. Orthodox, however, do not hold that the fall deprived man entirely of God's grace, though they would say that after the fall grace acts on man from the outside, not from within. Orthodox do not say, as Calvin said, that man after the fall was utterly depraved and incapable of good desires. They cannot agree with Augustine, when he writes that man is under 'a harsh necessity' of committing sin, and that 'man's nature was overcome by the fault into which it fell, *and so came to lack freedom*'.[1] The image of

1. *On the perfection of man's righteousness*, iv (9).

God is distorted by sin, but never destroyed; in the words of a hymn sung by Orthodox at the Funeral Service for the laity: 'I am the image of Thine inexpressible glory, even though I bear the wounds of sin.' And because he still retains the image of God, man still retains free will, although sin restricts its scope. Even after the fall, God 'takes not away from man the power to will – to will to obey or not to obey Him'.[1] Faithful to the idea of synergy, Orthodoxy repudiates any interpretation of the fall which allows no room for human freedom.

Most orthodox theologians reject the idea of 'original guilt', put forward by Augustine and still accepted (albeit in a mitigated form) by the Roman Catholic Church. Men (Orthodox usually teach) automatically inherit Adam's corruption and mortality, but not his guilt: they are only guilty in so far as by their own free choice they imitate Adam. Many western Christians believe that whatever a man does in his fallen and unredeemed state, since it is tainted by original guilt, cannot possibly be pleasing to God: 'Works before Justification,' says the thirteenth of the Thirty-nine Articles of the Church of England, ' ... are not pleasant to God ... but have the nature of sin.' Orthodox would hesitate to say this. And Orthodox have never held (as Augustine and many others in the west have done) that unbaptized babies, because tainted with original guilt, are consigned by the just God to the everlasting flames of Hell.[2] The Orthodox picture of fallen humanity is far less sombre than the Augustinian or Calvinist view.

But although Orthodox maintain that man after the fall still

1. Dositheus, *Confession*, Decree iii. Compare Decree xiv.
2. Thomas Aquinas, in his discussion of the fall, on the whole followed Augustine, and in particular retained the idea of original guilt; but as regards unbaptized babies, he maintained that they go not to Hell but to Limbo – a view now generally accepted by Roman theologians. So far as I can discover, Orthodox writers do not make use of the idea of Limbo.

It should be noted that an Augustinian view of the fall is found from time to time in Orthodox theological literature; but this is usually the result of western influence. The *Orthodox Confession* by Peter of Moghila is, as one might expect, strongly Augustinian; on the other hand the *Confession* of Dositheus is free from Augustinianism.

possessed free will and was still capable of good actions, yet they certainly agree with the west in believing that man's sin had set up between him and God a barrier, which man by his own efforts could never break down. Sin blocked the path to union with God. Since man could not come to God, God came to man.

JESUS CHRIST

The Incarnation is an act of God's *philanthropia*, of His loving-kindness towards mankind. Many eastern writers, looking at the Incarnation from this point of view, have argued that even if man had never fallen, God in His love for humanity would still have become man: the Incarnation must be seen as part of the eternal purpose of God, and not simply as an answer to the fall. Such was the view of Maximus the Confessor and of Isaac the Syrian; such has also been the view of certain western writers, most notably Duns Scotus (1265–1308).

But because man fell, the Incarnation is not only an act of love but an act of salvation. Jesus Christ, by uniting man and God in His own person, reopened for man the path to union with God. In His own person Christ showed what the true 'likeness of God' is, and through His redeeming and victorious sacrifice He set that likeness once again within man's reach. Christ, the Second Adam, came to earth and reversed the effects of the first Adam's disobedience.

The essential elements in the Orthodox doctrine of Christ have already been outlined in Chapter 2: true God and true man, one person in two natures, without separation and without confusion: a single person, but endowed with two wills and two energies.

True God and true man; as Bishop Theophan the Recluse put it: 'Behind the veil of Christ's flesh, Christians behold the Triune God.' These words bring us face to face with what is perhaps the most striking feature in the Orthodox approach to the Incarnate Christ: an overwhelming sense of His *divine glory*. There are two moments in Christ's life when this divine glory was made especially manifest: the Transfiguration, when on Mount Thabor the uncreated light of His Godhead shone visibly through the garments of His flesh; and the Resurrection, when the tomb burst open under the pressure of divine life, and Christ returned triumphant from the dead. In Orthodox worship and spirituality tremendous emphasis is placed on both these events. In the Byzantine calendar the Transfiguration is reckoned as one of the Twelve Great Feasts, and enjoys a far greater prominence in the Church's year than it possesses in the west; and we have already seen the central place which the uncreated light of Thabor holds in the Orthodox doctrine of mystical prayer. As for the Resurrection, its spirit fills the whole life of the Orthodox Church:

Through all the vicissitudes of her history the Greek Church has been enabled to preserve something of the very spirit of the first age of Christianity. Her liturgy still enshrines that element of sheer joy in the Resurrection of the Lord that we find in so many of the early Christian writings.[1]

The theme of the Resurrection of Christ binds together all theological concepts and realities in eastern Christianity and unites them in a harmonious whole.[2]

Yet it would be wrong to think of Orthodoxy simply as the cult of Christ's divine glory, of His Transfiguration and Resurrection, and nothing more. However great their devotion to the divine glory of Our Lord, Orthodox do not overlook His humanity. Consider for example the Orthodox love of the Holy Land: nothing could exceed the vivid reverence of Russian peasants for the exact places where the Incarnate Christ lived as a man, where as a man He ate, taught, suffered, and died. Nor does the sense of Resurrection joy lead Orthodoxy to minimize the importance of the Cross. Representations of the Crucifixion are no less prominent in Orthodox than in non-Orthodox churches, while the veneration of the Cross is more developed in Byzantine than in Latin worship.

1. P. Hammond, *The Waters of Marah*, p. 20.
2. O. Rousseau, 'Incarnation et anthropologie en orient et en occident', in *Irénikon*, vol. XXVI (1953), p. 373.

One must therefore reject as misleading the common assertion that the east concentrates on the Risen Christ, the west on Christ Crucified. If we are going to draw a contrast, it would be more exact to say that east and west think of the Crucifixion in slightly different ways. The Orthodox attitude to the Crucifixion is best seen in the hymns sung on Good Friday, such as the following:

> He who clothes himself with light as with a garment,
>   Stood naked at the judgement.
> On his cheek he received blows
>   From the hands which he had formed.
> The lawless multitude nailed to the Cross
>   The Lord of glory.

The Orthodox Church on Good Friday thinks not simply of Christ's human pain and suffering by itself, but rather of the contrast between His outward humiliation and His inward glory. Orthodox see not just the *suffering humanity* of Christ, but a *suffering God*:

> Today is hanged upon the tree
>   He who hanged the earth in the midst of the waters.
> A crown of thorns crowns him
>   Who is the king of the angels.
> He is wrapped about with the purple of mockery
>   Who wraps the heaven in clouds.

Behind the veil of Christ's bleeding and broken flesh, Orthodox still discern the Triune God. Even Golgotha is a theophany; even on Good Friday the Church sounds a note of Resurrection joy:

> We worship thy Passion, O Christ:
> Show us also thy glorious Resurrection!

> I magnify thy sufferings,
> I praise thy burial and thy Resurrection,
>   Shouting, Lord, glory to thee!

The Crucifixion is not separated from the Resurrection, for both are but a single action. Calvary is seen always in the light of the empty tomb; the Cross is an emblem of victory. When Orthodox think of Christ Crucified, they think not only of His suffering and desolation; they think of Him as Christ the Victor, Christ the King, reigning in triumph from the Tree:

The Lord came into the world and dwelt among men, that he might destroy the tyranny of the Devil and set men free. On the Tree he triumphed over the powers which opposed him, when the sun was darkened and the earth was shaken, when the graves were opened and the bodies of the saints arose. By death he destroyed death, and brought to nought him who had the power of death.[1]

Christ is our victorious king, not in spite of the Crucifixion, but because of it: 'I call Him king, because I see Him crucified.'[2]

Such is the spirit in which Orthodox Christians regard Christ's death upon the Cross. Between this approach to the Crucifixion and that of the medieval and post-medieval west, there are of course many points of contact; yet in the western approach there are also certain things which make Orthodox feel uneasy. The west, so it seems to them, tends to think of the Crucifixion in isolation, separating it too sharply from the Resurrection. As a result the vision of Christ as a suffering God is in practice replaced by the picture of Christ's suffering humanity: the western worshipper, when he meditates upon the Cross, is encouraged all too often to feel a morbid sympathy with the Man of Sorrows, rather than to adore the victorious and triumphant king. Orthodox feel thoroughly at home in the language of the great Latin hymn by Venantius Fortunatus (530–609), *Pange lingua*, which hails the Cross as an emblem of victory:

> Sing, my tongue, the glorious battle,
>   Sing the ending of the fray;
> Now above the Cross, our trophy,
>   Sound the loud triumphal lay:
> Tell how Christ, the world's redeemer,
>   As a victim won the day.

1. From the First Exorcism before Holy Baptism.
2. John Chrysostom, *Second Sermon on the Cross and the Robber*, 3 (*P.G.* xlix, 413).

They feel equally at home in that other hymn by Fortunatus, *Vexilla regis*:

> Fulfilled is all that David told
> In true prophetic song of old:
> Among the nations God, said he,
> Hath reigned and triumphed from the Tree.

But Orthodox feel less happy about compositions of the later Middle Ages such as *Stabat Mater*:

> For his people's sins, in anguish,
> There she saw the victim languish,
>   Bleed in torments, bleed and die:
> Saw the Lord's anointed taken;
> Saw her Child in death forsaken;
>   Heard his last expiring cry.

It is significant that *Stabat Mater*, in the course of its sixty lines, makes not a single reference to the Resurrection.

Where Orthodoxy sees chiefly Christ the Victor, the late medieval and post-medieval west sees chiefly Christ the Victim. While Orthodoxy interprets the Crucifixion primarily as an act of triumphant victory over the powers of evil, the west – particularly since the time of Anselm of Canterbury (?1033–1109) – has tended rather to think of the Cross in penal and juridical terms, as an act of satisfaction or substitution designed to propitiate the wrath of an angry Father.

Yet these contrasts must not be pressed too far. Eastern writers, as well as western, have applied juridical and penal language to the Crucifixion; western writers, as well as eastern, have never ceased to think of Good Friday as a moment of victory. In the west during recent years there has been a revival of the Patristic idea of *Christus Victor*, alike in theology, in spirituality, and in art; and Orthodox are naturally very happy that this should be so.

THE HOLY SPIRIT

In their activity among men the second and the third persons of the Trinity are complementary and reciprocal. Christ's work of redemption cannot be considered apart from the Holy Spirit's work of sanctification. The Word took flesh, said Athanasius, that we might receive the Spirit:[1] from one point of view, the whole 'aim' of the Incarnation is the sending of the Spirit at Pentecost.

The Orthodox Church lays great stress upon the work of the Holy Spirit. As we have seen, one of the reasons why Orthodox object to the *filioque* is because they see in it a tendency to subordinate and neglect the Spirit. Saint Seraphim of Sarov briefly described the whole purpose of the Christian life as nothing else than the acquisition of the Holy Spirit, saying at the beginning of his conversation with Motovilov:

> Prayer, fasting, vigils, and all other Christian practices, however good they may be in themselves, certainly do not constitute the aim of our Christian life: they are but the indispensable means of attaining that aim. *For the true aim of the Christian life is the acquisition of the Holy Spirit of God.* As for fasts, vigils, prayer, and almsgiving, and other good works done in the name of Christ, they are only the means of acquiring the Holy Spirit of God. Note well that it is only good works done in the name of Christ that bring us the fruits of the Spirit.

'This definition,' Vladimir Lossky has commented, 'while it may at first sight appear oversimplified, sums up the whole spiritual tradition of the Orthodox Church.'[2] As Saint Pachomius' disciple Theodore said: 'What is greater than to possess the Holy Spirit?'[3]

In the next chapter we shall have occasion to note the place of the Spirit in the Orthodox doctrine of the Church; and in later chapters something will be said of the Holy Spirit in Orthodox worship. In every sacramental action of the Church, and most notably at the climax of the Eucharistic Prayer, the Spirit is solemnly invoked. In his private prayers at the start of each day, an Orthodox Christian places himself under the protection of the Spirit, saying these words:

1. *On the Incarnation and against the Arians*, 8 (*P.G.* xxvi, 996c).
2. *The Mystical Theology of the Eastern Church*, p. 196.
3. *First Greek Life* of Pachomius, 135.

O heavenly king, O Comforter, the Spirit of Truth, who art everywhere and fillest all things, the treasury of blessings and giver of life, come and abide in us. Cleanse us from all impurity, and of thy goodness save our souls.[1]

'PARTAKERS OF THE DIVINE NATURE'

The aim of the Christian life, which Seraphim described as the acquisition of the Holy Spirit of God, can equally well be defined in terms of *deification*. Basil described man as a creature who has received the order to become a god; and Athanasius, as we know, said that God became man that man might become god. 'In my kingdom, said Christ, I shall be God with you as gods.'[2] Such, according to the teaching of the Orthodox Church, is the final goal at which every Christian must aim: to become god, to attain *theosis*, 'deification' or 'divinization'. For Orthodoxy man's salvation and redemption mean his deification.

Behind the doctrine of deification there lies the idea of man made according to the image and likeness of God the Holy Trinity. 'May they all be one,' Christ prayed at the Last Supper; 'as Thou, Father, art in me and I in Thee, so also may they be in us' (John xvii, 21). Just as the three persons of the Trinity 'dwell' in one another in an unceasing movement of love, so man, made in the image of the Trinity, is called to 'dwell' in the Trinitarian God. Christ prays that we may share in the life of the Trinity, in the movement of love which passes between the divine persons; He prays that we may be taken up into the Godhead. The saints, as Maximus the Confessor put it, are those who express the Holy Trinity in themselves. This idea of a personal and organic union between God and man – God dwelling in us, and we in Him – is a constant theme in Saint John's Gospel; it is also a constant theme in the Epistles of Saint Paul, who sees the Christian life above all else as a life 'in Christ'. The same idea recurs in the famous text of 2 Peter:

1. This same prayer is used at the beginning of most liturgical services.

2. Canon for Matins of Holy Thursday, Ode 4, Troparion 3.

'Through these promises you may become partakers of the divine nature' (i, 4). It is important to keep this New Testament background in mind. The Orthodox doctrine of deification, so far from being unscriptural (as is sometimes thought), has a solid Biblical basis, not only in 2 Peter, but in Paul and the Fourth Gospel.

The idea of deification must always be understood in the light of the distinction between God's essence and His energies. Union with God means union with the divine energies, not the divine essence: the Orthodox Church, while speaking of deification and union, rejects all forms of pantheism.

Closely related to this is another point of equal importance. The mystical union between God and man is a true union, yet in this union Creator and creature do not become fused into a single being. Unlike the eastern religions which teach that man is swallowed up in the deity, Orthodox mystical theology has always insisted that man, however closely linked to God, retains his full personal integrity. Man, when deified, remains distinct (though not separate) from God. The mystery of the Trinity is a mystery of unity *in diversity*, and those who express the Trinity in themselves do not sacrifice their personal characteristics. When Saint Maximus wrote 'God and those who are worthy of God have one and the same energy',[1] he did not mean that the saints lose their free will, but that when deified they voluntarily and in love conform their will to the will of God. Nor does man, when he 'becomes god', cease to be human: 'We remain creatures while becoming god by grace, as Christ remained God when becoming man by the Incarnation.'[2] Man does not become God *by nature*, but is merely a 'created god', a god *by grace* or *by status*.

Deification is something that involves the body. Since man is a unity of body and soul, and since the Incarnate Christ has saved and redeemed the whole man, it follows that 'man's body is deified at the same time as his soul'.[3] In that divine likeness

1. *Ambigua, P.G.* xci, 1076C.
2. V. Lossky, *The Mystical Theology of the Eastern Church*, p. 87.
3. Maximus, *Gnostic Centuries*, 11, 88 (*P.G.* xc, 1168A).

which man is called to realize in himself, the body has its place. 'Your body is a temple of the Holy Spirit,' wrote Saint Paul (1 Corinthians vi, 19). 'Therefore, my brothers, I beseech you by God's mercy to offer your bodies as a living sacrifice to God' (Romans xii, 1). The full deification of the body must wait, however, until the Last Day, for in this present life the glory of the saints is as a rule an inward splendour, a splendour of the soul alone; but when the righteous rise from the dead and are clothed with a spiritual body, then their sanctity will be outwardly manifest. 'At the day of Resurrection the glory of the Holy Spirit *comes out from within*, decking and covering the bodies of the saints – the glory which they had before, but hidden within their souls. What a man has now, the same then comes forth externally *in the body*.'[1] The bodies of the saints will be outwardly transfigured by divine light, as Christ's body was transfigured on Mount Thabor. 'We must look forward also to the springtime of the body.'[2]

But even in this present life some saints have experienced the firstfruits of this visible and bodily glorification. Saint Seraphim is the best known, but by no means the only instance of this. When Arsenius the Great was praying, his disciples saw him 'just like a fire';[3] and of another Desert Father it is recorded: 'Just as Moses received the image of the glory of Adam, when his face was glorified, so the face of Abba Pambo shone like lightning, and he was as a king seated on his throne.'[4]

1. *Homilies of Macarius*, v, 9. It is this transfigured 'Resurrection body' which the icon painter attempts symbolically to depict. Hence, while preserving the distinctive personal traits in a saint's physiognomy he deliberately avoids making a realistic and 'photographic' portrait. To paint men exactly as they now appear is to paint them still in their fallen state, in their 'earthy', not their 'heavenly' body.

2. Minucius Felix (? late second century), *Octavius*, 34.

3. *Apophthegmata* (*P.G.* lxv), Arsenius 27.

4. *Apophthegmata* (*P.G.* lxv), Pambo 12. Compare *Apophthegmata*, Sisoes 14 and Silvanus 12. Epiphanius, in his Life of Sergius of Radonezh, states that the saint's body shone with glory after death.

It is sometimes said, and with a certain truth, that bodily transfiguration by divine light corresponds, among Orthodox saints, to the receiving of the stigmata among western saints. We must not, how-

In the words of Gregory Palamas: 'If in the age to come the body will share with the soul in unspeakable blessings, it is certain that it must share in them, so far as possible, even now.'[1]

Because Orthodox are convinced that the body is sanctified and transfigured together with the soul, they have an immense reverence for the relics of the saints. Like Roman Catholics, they believe that the grace of God present in the saints' bodies during life remains active in their relics when they have died, and that God uses these relics as a channel of divine power and an instrument of healing. In some cases the bodies of saints have been miraculously preserved from corruption, but even where this has not happened, Orthodox show just as great a veneration towards their bones. This reverence for relics is not the fruit of ignorance and superstition, but springs from a highly developed theology of the body.

Not only man's body but the whole of the material creation will eventually be transfigured: 'Then I saw a new heaven *and a new earth*; for the first heaven and the first earth had passed away' (Revelation xxi, 1). Redeemed man is not to be snatched away from the rest of creation, but creation is to be saved and glorified along with him (icons, as we have seen, are the first-fruits of this redemption of matter).[2] 'The created universe waits with eager expectation for God's sons to be revealed ... for the universe itself will be set free from its bondage to corruption and will enter into the liberty and splendour of the children of God. We know that until now the whole created

---

ever, draw too absolute a contrast in this matter. Instances of bodily glorification are found in the west, for example, in the case of an Englishwoman, Evelyn Underhill (1875–1941): a friend records how on one occasion her face could be seen transfigured with light (the whole account recalls Saint Seraphim: see *The Letters of Evelyn Underhill*, edited by Charles Williams, London, 1943, p. 37). Similarly, in the east stigmatization is not unknown: in the Coptic life of Saint Macarius of Egypt, it is said that a cherub appeared to him, 'took the measure of his chest', and 'crucified him on the earth'.

1. *The Tome of the Holy Mountain* (*P.G.* cl, 1233c).
2. See p. 42.

universe has been groaning in the pangs of childbirth' (Romans viii, 19–22). This idea of *cosmic redemption* is based, like the Orthodox doctrine of the human body and the Orthodox doctrine of icons, upon a right understanding of the Incarnation: Christ took flesh – something from the material order – and so has made possible the redemption and metamorphosis of *all* creation – not merely the immaterial, but the physical.

This talk of deification and union, of the transfiguration of the body and of cosmic redemption, may sound very remote from the experience of ordinary Christians; but anyone who draws such a conclusion has entirely misunderstood the Orthodox conception of *theosis*. To prevent any such misinterpretation, six points must be made.

First, deification is not something reserved for a few select initiates, but something intended for all alike. The Orthodox Church believes that it is the normal goal for *every* Christian without exception. Certainly, we shall only be fully deified at the Last Day; but for each of us the process of divinization must begin here and now in this present life. It is true that in this present life very few indeed attain full mystical union with God. But every true Christian tries to love God and to fulfil His commandments; and so long as a man sincerely seeks to do that, then however weak his attempts may be and however often he may fall, he is already in some degree deified.

Secondly, the fact that a man is being deified does not mean that he ceases to be conscious of sin. On the contrary, deification always presupposes a continued act of repentance. A saint may be well advanced in the way of holiness, yet he does not therefore cease to employ the words of the Jesus Prayer 'Lord Jesus Christ, Son of God, *have mercy on me a sinner*'. Father Silvan of Mount Athos used to say to himself 'Keep your mind in Hell and despair not'; other Orthodox saints have repeated the words 'All will be saved, and I alone will be condemned'. Eastern spiritual writers attach great importance to the 'gift of tears'. Orthodox mystical theology is a theology of glory and of transfiguration, but it is also a theology of penitence.

In the third place, there is nothing esoteric or extraordinary about the methods which we must follow in order to be deified. If a man asks 'How can I become god?' the answer is very simple: go to church, receive the sacraments regularly, pray to God 'in spirit and in truth', read the Gospels, follow the commandments. The last of these items – 'follow the commandments' – must never be forgotten. Orthodoxy, no less than western Christianity, firmly rejects the kind of mysticism that seeks to dispense with moral rules.

Fourthly, deification is not a solitary but a 'social' process. We have said that deification means 'following the commandments'; and these commandments were briefly described by Christ as love of God and love of neighbour. The two forms of love are inseparable. A man can love his neighbour as himself only if he loves God above all; and a man cannot love God if he does not love his fellow men (1 John iv, 20). Thus there is nothing selfish about deification; for only if he loves his neighbour can a man be deified. 'From our neighbour is life and from our neighbour is death,' said Antony of Egypt. 'If we win our neighbour we win God, but if we cause our neighbour to stumble we sin against Christ.'[1] Man, made in the image of the Trinity, can only realize the divine likeness if he lives a common life such as the Blessed Trinity lives: as the three persons of the Godhead 'dwell' in one another, so a man must 'dwell' in his fellow men, living not for himself alone, but in and for others. 'If it were possible for me to find a leper,' said one of the Desert Fathers, 'and to give him my body and to take his, I would gladly do it. For this is perfect love.'[2] Such is the true nature of *theosis*.

Fifthly, love of God and of other men must be practical: Orthodoxy rejects all forms of Quietism, all types of love which do not issue in action. Deification, while it includes the heights of mystical experience, has also a very prosaic and down-to-earth aspect. When we think of deification, we must think of the Hesychasts praying in silence and of Saint Seraphim with his face transfigured; but we must think also of Saint Basil

1. *Apophthegmata (P.G.* lxv), Antony 9.
2. ibid., Agatho 26.

caring for the sick in the hospital at Caesarea, of Saint John the Almsgiver helping the poor at Alexandria, of Saint Sergius in his filthy clothing, working as a peasant in the kitchen garden to provide the guests of the monastery with food. These are not two different ways, but one.

Finally, deification presupposes life in the Church, life in the sacraments. *Theosis* according to the likeness of the Trinity involves a common life, but only within the fellowship of the Church can this common life of coinherence be properly realized. Church and sacraments are the means appointed by God whereby man may acquire the sanctifying Spirit and be transformed into the divine likeness.

CHAPTER 12

The Church of God

> Christ loved the Church, and gave himself up for it.
> *Ephesians v, 25*
> The Church is one and the same with the Lord – His
> Body, of His flesh and of His bones. The Church is the
> living vine, nourished by Him and growing in Him.
> Never think of the Church apart from the Lord
> Jesus Christ, from the Father and the Holy Spirit.
> *Father John of Kronstadt*

GOD AND HIS CHURCH

AN Orthodox Christian is vividly conscious of belonging to
a community. 'We know that when any one of us falls,' wrote
Khomiakov, 'he falls alone; but no one is saved alone. He is
saved in the Church, as a member of it and in union with all
its other members.'[1]

Some of the differences between the Orthodox doctrine of
the Church and those of western Christians will have become
apparent in the first part of this book. Unlike Protestantism,
Orthodoxy insists upon the hierarchical structure of the
Church, upon the Apostolic Succession, the episcopate, and
the priesthood; it prays to the saints and intercedes for the departed. Thus far Rome and Orthodoxy agree – but where
Rome thinks in terms of the supremacy and the universal
jurisdiction of the Pope, Orthodoxy thinks in terms of the
college of bishops and of the Ecumenical Council; where Rome
stresses Papal infallibility, Orthodox stress the infallibility of the
Church as a whole. Doubtless neither side is entirely fair to
the other, but to Orthodox it often seems that Rome envisages
the Church too much in terms of earthly power and organization, while to Roman Catholics it often seems that the more

1. *The Church is One*, section 9.

spiritual and mystical doctrine of the Church held by Orthodoxy is vague, incoherent, and incomplete. Orthodox would answer that they do not neglect the earthly organization of the Church, but have many strict and minute rules, as anyone who reads the Canons can quickly discover.

Yet the Orthodox idea of the Church is certainly spiritual and mystical in this sense, that Orthodox theology never treats the earthly aspect of the Church in isolation, but thinks always of the Church in Christ and the Holy Spirit. All Orthodox thinking about the Church starts with the special relationship which exists between the Church and God. Three phrases can be used to describe this relation: the Church is (1) the Image of the Holy Trinity, (2) the Body of Christ, (3) a continued Pentecost. The Orthodox doctrine of the Church is Trinitarian, Christological, and 'pneumatological'.

(1) *The Image of the Holy Trinity.* Just as each man is made according to the image of the Trinitarian God, so the Church as a whole is an icon of God the Trinity, reproducing on earth the mystery of unity in diversity. In the Trinity the three are one God, yet each is fully personal; in the Church a multitude of human persons are united in one, yet each preserves his personal diversity unimpaired. The mutual indwelling of the persons of the Trinity is paralleled by the coinherence of the members of the Church. In the Church there is no conflict between freedom and authority; in the Church there is unity, but no totalitarianism. When Orthodox apply the word 'Catholic' to the Church, they have in mind (among other things) this living miracle of the unity of many persons in one.

This conception of the Church as an icon of the Trinity has many further applications. 'Unity in diversity' – just as each person of the Trinity is autonomous, so the Church is made up of a number of independent Autocephalous Churches; and just as in the Trinity the three persons are equal, so in the Church no one bishop can claim to wield an absolute power over all the rest.

This idea of the Church as an icon of the Trinity also helps us to understand the Orthodox emphasis upon Councils. A council is an expression of the Trinitarian nature of the Church. The mystery of unity in diversity according to the image of the Trinity can be seen in action, as the many bishops assembled in council freely reach a common mind under the guidance of the Spirit.

The unity of the Church is linked more particularly with the person of Christ, its diversity with the person of the Holy Spirit.

(2) *The Body of Christ*: 'We, who are many, are one body in Christ' (Romans xii, 5). Between Christ and the Church there is the closest possible bond: in the famous phrase of Ignatius, 'where Christ is, there is the Catholic Church'.[1] The Church is the extension of the Incarnation, the place where the Incarnation perpetuates itself. The Church, the Greek theologian Chrestos Androutsos has written, is 'the centre and organ of Christ's redeeming work; ... it is nothing else than the continuation and extension of His prophetic, priestly, and kingly power.... The Church and its Founder are inextricably bound together.... The Church is Christ with us.'[2] Christ did not leave the Church when He ascended into heaven: 'Lo! I am with you always, even to the end of the world,' He promised (Matthew xxviii, 20), 'for where two or three are gathered together in my name, there am I in the midst of them' (Matthew xviii, 20). It is only too easy to fall into the mistake of speaking of Christ as absent:

> And still the Holy Church is here
> Although her Lord is gone.[3]

But how can we say that Christ 'is gone', when He has promised us His perpetual presence?

The unity between Christ and His Church is effected above

1. *To the Smyrnaeans*, viii, 2.
2. *Dogmatic Theology*, Athens, 1907, pp. 262–5 (in Greek).
3. From a hymn by J. M. Neale.

all through the sacraments. At Baptism, the new Christian is buried and raised with Christ; at the Eucharist the members of Christ's Body the Church receive His Body in the sacraments. The Eucharist, by uniting the members of the Church to Christ, at the same time unites them to one another: 'We, who are many, are one bread, one body; for we all partake of the one bread' (1 Corinthians x, 17). The Eucharist creates the unity of the Church. The Church (as Ignatius saw) is a Eucharistic society, a sacramental organism which exists – and exists in its fullness – wherever the Eucharist is celebrated. It is no coincidence that the term 'Body of Christ' should mean both the Church and the sacrament; and that the phrase *communio sanctorum* in the Apostles' Creed should mean both 'the communion of the holy people' (communion of saints) and 'the communion of the holy things' (communion in the sacraments).

The Church must be thought of primarily in sacramental terms. Its outward organization, however important, is secondary to its sacramental life.

(3) *A continued Pentecost.* It is easy to lay such emphasis on the Church as the Body of Christ that the rôle of the Holy Spirit is forgotten. But, as we have said, in their work among men Son and Spirit are complementary to one another, and this is as true in the doctrine of the Church as it is elsewhere. While Ignatius said 'where Christ is, there is the Catholic Church', Irenaeus wrote with equal truth 'where the Church is, there is the Spirit, and where the Spirit is, there is the Church'.[1] The Church, precisely because it is the Body of Christ, is also the temple and dwelling place of the Spirit.

The Holy Spirit is a Spirit of freedom. While Christ unites us, the Holy Spirit ensures our infinite diversity in the Church: at Pentecost the tongues of fire were 'cloven' or divided, descending *separately* upon each one of those present. The gift of the Spirit is a gift to the Church, but it is at the same time a personal gift, appropriated by each in his own way. 'There

1. *Against the Heresies* III, xxiv, 1.

246

are diversities of gifts, but the same Spirit' (1 Corinthians xii, 4). Life in the Church does not mean the ironing out of human variety, nor the imposition of a rigid and uniform pattern upon all alike, but the exact opposite. The saints, so far from displaying a drab monotony, have developed the most vivid and distinctive personalities. It is not holiness but evil which is dull.

Such in brief is the relation between the Church and God. This Church – the icon of the Trinity, the Body of Christ, the fullness of the Spirit – is both *visible* and *invisible*, both *divine* and *human*. It is visible, for it is composed of concrete congregations, worshipping here on earth; it is invisible, for it also includes the saints and the angels. It is human, for its earthly members are sinners; it is divine, for it is the Body of Christ. There is no separation between the visible and the invisible, between (to use western terminology) the Church militant and the Church triumphant, for the two make up a single and continuous reality. 'The Church visible, or upon earth, lives in complete communion and unity with the whole body of the Church, of which Christ is the Head.'[1] It stands at a point of intersection between the Present Age and the Age to Come, and it lives in both Ages at once.

Orthodoxy, therefore, while using the phrase 'the Church visible and invisible', insists always that there are not two Churches, but one. As Khomiakov said:

It is only in relation to man that it is possible to recognize a division of the Church into visible and invisible; its unity is, in reality, true and absolute. Those who are alive on earth, those who have finished their earthly course, those who, like the angels, were not created for a life on earth, those in future generations who have not yet begun their earthly course, are all united together in one Church, in one and the same grace of God. . . . The Church, the Body of Christ, manifests forth and fulfils itself in time, without changing its essential unity or inward life of grace. And therefore, when we speak of 'the Church visible and invisible', we so speak only in relation to man.[2]

1. Khomiakov, *The Church is One*, section 9.
2. ibid., section 1.

The Church, according to Khomiakov, *is accomplished on earth without losing its essential characteristics*; it is, in Georges Florovsky's words, 'the living image of eternity within time'.[1] This is a cardinal point in Orthodox teaching. Orthodoxy does not believe merely in an ideal Church, invisible and heavenly. This 'ideal Church' exists visibly on earth as a concrete reality.

Yet Orthodoxy does not forget that there is a human element in the Church as well as a divine. The dogma of Chalcedon must be applied to the Church as well as to Christ. Just as Christ the God–Man has two natures, divine and human, so in the Church there is a synergy or cooperation between the divine and the human. Yet between Christ's humanity and that of the Church there is this obvious difference, that the one is perfect and sinless, while the other is not yet fully so. Only a part of the humanity of the Church – the saints in heaven – has attained perfection, while here on earth the Church's members often misuse their human freedom. The Church on earth exists in a state of tension: it is already the Body of Christ, and thus perfect and sinless, and yet, since its members are imperfect and sinful, it must continually become what it is.[2]

But the sin of man cannot affect the essential nature of the Church. We must not say that because Christians on earth sin and are imperfect, therefore the Church sins and is imperfect; for the Church, even on earth, is a thing of heaven, and cannot sin.[3] Saint Ephraim of Syria rightly spoke of 'the Church of the penitents, the Church of those who perish', but this Church is at the same time the icon of the Trinity. How is it that the members of the Church are sinners, and yet they belong to the communion of saints? 'The mystery of the Church consists in the very fact that *together* sinners become *something different*

1. 'Sobornost: the Catholicity of the Church', in *The Church of God*, edited by E. L. Mascall, p. 63.

2. 'This idea of "becoming what you are" is the key to the whole eschatological teaching of the New Testament' (Gregory Dix, *The Shape of the Liturgy*, p. 247).

3. See the *Declaration on Faith and Order* made by the Orthodox Delegates at Evanston in 1954, where this point is put very clearly.

from what they are as individuals; this "something different" is the Body of Christ.'[1]

Such is the way in which Orthodoxy approaches the mystery of the Church. The Church is integrally linked with God. It is a new life according to the image of the Holy Trinity, a life in Christ and in the Holy Spirit, a life realized by participation in the sacraments. The Church is a single reality, earthly and heavenly, visible and invisible, human and divine.

THE UNITY AND INFALLIBILITY OF THE CHURCH

'The Church is one. Its unity follows of necessity from the unity of God.'[2] So wrote Khomiakov in the opening words of his famous essay. If we take seriously the bond between God and His Church, then we must inevitably think of the Church as one, even as God is one: there is only one Christ, and so there can be only one Body of Christ. Nor is this unity merely ideal and invisible; Orthodox theology refuses to separate the 'invisible' and the 'visible Church', and therefore it refuses to say that the Church is invisibly one but visibly divided. No: the Church is one, in the sense that here on earth there is a single, visible community which alone can claim to be the one true Church. The 'undivided Church' is not merely something that existed in the past, and which we hope will exist again in the future: it is something that exists here and now. Unity is one of the essential characteristics of the Church, and since the Church on earth, despite the sinfulness of its members, retains its essential characteristics, it remains and always will remain visibly one. There can be schisms *from* the Church, but no schisms *within* the Church. And while it is undeniably true that, on a purely human level, the Church's life is grievously impoverished as a result of schisms, yet such schisms cannot affect the essential nature of the Church.

In its teaching upon the visible unity of the Church,

1. J. Meyendorff, 'What Holds the Church Together?', in the *Ecumenical Review*, vol. XII (1960), p. 298.
2. *The Church is One*, section 1.

Orthodoxy stands far closer to Roman Catholicism than to the Protestant world. But if we ask how this visible unity is maintained, Rome and the east give somewhat different answers. For Rome the unifying principle in the Church is the Pope whose jurisdiction extends over the whole body, whereas Orthodox do not believe any bishop to be endowed with universal jurisdiction. What then holds the Church together? Orthodox answer, the act of communion in the sacraments. The Orthodox theology of the Church is above all else a *theology of communion*. Each local Church is constituted, as Ignatius saw, by the congregation of the faithful, gathered round their bishop and celebrating the Eucharist; the Church universal is constituted by the communion of the heads of the local Churches, the bishops, with one another. Unity is not maintained from without by the authority of a Supreme Pontiff, but created from within by the celebration of the Eucharist. The Church is not monarchical in structure, centred round a single hierarch; it is collegial, formed by the communion of many hierarchs with one another, and of each hierarch with the members of his flock. The act of communion therefore forms the criterion for membership of the Church. An individual ceases to be a member of the Church if he severs communion with his bishop; a bishop ceases to be a member of the Church if he severs communion with his fellow bishops.

Orthodoxy, believing that the Church on earth has remained and must remain visibly one, naturally also believes itself to be that one visible Church. This is a bold claim, and to many it will seem an arrogant one; but this is to misunderstand the spirit in which it is made. Orthodox believe that they are the true Church, not on account of any personal merit, but by the grace of God. They say with Saint Paul: 'We are no better than pots of earthenware to contain this treasure; the sovereign power comes from God and not from us' (2 Corinthians iv, 7). But while claiming no credit for themselves, Orthodox are in all humility convinced that they have received a precious and unique gift from God; and if they pretended to men that they did not possess this gift, they would be guilty of an act of betrayal in the sight of heaven.

Orthodox writers sometimes speak as if they accepted the 'Branch Theory', once popular among High Church Anglicans. (According to this theory, the Catholic Church is divided in several 'branches'; usually three such branches are posited, the Roman Catholic, the Anglican, and the Orthodox.) But such a view cannot be reconciled with traditional Orthodox theology. If we are going to speak in terms of 'branches', then from the Orthodox point of view the only branches which the Catholic Church can have are the local Autocephalous Churches of the Orthodox communion.

Claiming as it does to be the one true Church, the Orthodox Church also believes that, if it so desired, it could by itself convene and hold another Ecumenical Council, equal in authority to the first seven. Since the separation of east and west the Orthodox (unlike the west) have never in fact chosen to summon such a Council; but this does not mean that they believe themselves to lack the power to do so.

So much for the Orthodox idea of the unity of the Church. Orthodoxy also teaches that *outside the Church there is no salvation.* This belief has the same basis as the Orthodox belief in the unbreakable unity of the Church: it follows from the close relation between God and His Church. 'A man cannot have God as his Father if he does not have the Church as his Mother.'[1] So wrote Saint Cyprian; and to him this seemed an evident truth, because he could not think of God and the Church apart from one another. God is salvation, and God's saving power is mediated to man in His Body, the Church. *'Extra Ecclesiam nulla salus.* All the categorical strength and point of this aphorism lies in its tautology. Outside the Church there is no salvation, because *salvation is the Church.'*[2] Does it therefore follow that anyone who is not visibly within the

1. *On the Unity of the Catholic Church*, 6.
2. G. Florovsky, 'Sobornost: the Catholicity of the Church', in *The Church of God*, p. 53.

Church is necessarily damned? Of course not; still less does it follow that everyone who is visibly within the Church is necessarily saved. As Augustine wisely remarked: 'How many sheep there are without, how many wolves within!'[1] While there is no division between a 'visible' and an 'invisible Church', yet there may be members of the Church who are not visibly such, but whose membership is known to God alone. If anyone is saved, he must *in some sense* be a member of the Church; *in what sense*, we cannot always say.[2]

The Church is infallible. This again follows from the indissoluble unity between God and His Church. Christ and the Holy Spirit cannot err, and since the Church is Christ's body, since it is a continued Pentecost, it is therefore infallible. It is 'the pillar and the ground of truth' (1 Timothy iii, 15). 'When he, the Spirit of truth, has come, he will guide you into all truth' (John xvi, 13). So Christ promised at the Last Supper; and Orthodoxy believes that Christ's promise cannot fail. In the words of Dositheus: 'We believe the Catholic Church to be taught by the Holy Spirit . . . and therefore we both believe and profess as true and undoubtedly certain, that it is impossible for the Catholic Church to err, or to be at all deceived, or ever to choose falsehood instead of truth.'[3]

The Church's infallibility is expressed chiefly through Ecumenical Councils. But before we can understand what makes a Council Ecumenical, we must consider the place of bishops and of the laity in the Orthodox communion.

BISHOPS: LAITY: COUNCILS

The Orthodox Church is a hierarchical Church. An essential element in its structure is the Apostolic Succession of bishops. 'The dignity of the bishop is so necessary in the Church,' wrote Dositheus, 'that without him neither the Church nor the name

1. *Homilies on John*, xlv, 12.
2. On this question, see pp. 315–17.
3. *Confession*, Decree xii.

Christian could exist or be spoken of at all. .... He is a living image of God upon earth ... and a fountain of all the sacraments of the Catholic Church, through which we obtain salvation.'[1] 'If any are not with the bishop,' said Cyprian, 'they are not in the Church.'[2]

At his election and consecration an Orthodox bishop is endowed with the threefold power of (1) ruling, (2) teaching, and (3) celebrating the sacraments.

(1) A bishop is appointed by God to guide and to rule the flock committed to his charge; he is a 'monarch' in his own diocese.

(2) At his consecration a bishop receives a special gift or *charisma* from the Holy Spirit, in virtue of which he acts as a teacher of the faith. This ministry of teaching the bishop performs above all at the Eucharist, when he preaches the sermon to the people; when other members of the Church – priests or laymen – preach sermons, strictly speaking they act as the bishop's delegates. But although the bishop has a special *charisma*, it is always possible that he may fall into error and give false teaching: here as elsewhere the principle of synergy applies, and the divine element does not expel the human. The bishop remains a man, and as such he may make mistakes. The Church is infallible, but there is no such thing as personal infallibility.

(3) The bishop, as Dositheus put it, is 'the fountain of all the sacraments'. In the primitive Church the celebrant at the Eucharist was normally the bishop, and even today a priest, when he celebrates Mass, is really acting as the bishop's deputy.

But the Church is not only hierarchical, it is charismatic and Pentecostal. 'Quench not the Spirit. Despise not prophesyings' (1 Thessalonians v, 19–20). The Holy Spirit is poured out upon *all* God's people. There is a special ordained ministry of bishops, priests, and deacons; yet at the same time the whole people of God are prophets and priests. In the Apostolic Church, besides the institutional ministry conferred by the lay-

1. *Confession*, Decree x.   2. *Letter* lxvi, 8.

ing on of hands, there were other *charismata* or gifts conferred directly by the Spirit: Paul mentions 'gifts of healing', the working of miracles, 'speaking with tongues', and the like (1 Corinthians xii, 28–30). In the Church of later days, these charismatic ministries have been less in evidence, but they have never been wholly extinguished. One thinks, for example, of the ministry of 'eldership', so prominent in nineteenth-century Russia; this is not imparted by a special act of ordination, but can be exercised by the layman as well as by priest or bishop. Seraphim of Sarov and the *startsi* of Optino exercised an influence far greater than any hierarch.

This 'spiritual', non-institutional aspect of the Church's life has been particularly emphasized by certain recent theologians in the Russian emigration; but it is also stressed by Byzantine writers, most notably Symeon the New Theologian. More than once in Orthodox history the 'charismatics' have come into conflict with the hierarchy, but in the end there is no contradiction between the two elements in the Church's life: it is the same Spirit who is active in both.

We have called the bishop a ruler and monarch, but these terms are not to be understood in a harsh and impersonal sense; for in exercising his powers the bishop is guided by the Christian law of love. He is not a tyrant but a father to his flock. The Orthodox attitude to the episcopal office is well expressed in the prayer used at a consecration:

Grant, O Christ, that this man, who has been appointed a steward of the episcopal grace, may become an imitator of thee, the True Shepherd, by laying down his life for thy sheep. Make him a guide to the blind, a light to those in darkness, a teacher to the unreasonable, an instructor to the foolish, a flaming torch in the world; so that having brought to perfection the souls entrusted to him in this present life, he may stand without confusion before thy judgement seat, and receive the great reward which thou hast prepared for those who have suffered for the preaching of thy Gospel.

The authority of the bishop is fundamentally the authority of the Church. However great the prerogatives of the bishop may be, he is not someone set up *over* the Church, but the holder of an office *in* the Church. Bishop and people are joined in an organic unity, and neither can properly be thought of apart from the other. Without bishops there can be no Orthodox people, but without Orthodox people there can be no true bishop. 'The Church,' said Cyprian, 'is the people united to the bishop, the flock clinging to its shepherd. The bishop is in the Church and the Church in the bishop.'[1]

The relation between the bishop and his flock is a mutual one. The bishop is the divinely appointed *teacher* of the faith, but the *guardian* of the faith is not the episcopate alone, but the whole people of God, bishops, clergy, and laity together. The proclamation of the truth is not the same as the possession of the truth: all the people possess the truth, but it is the bishop's particular office to proclaim it. Infallibility belongs to the whole Church, not just to the episcopate in isolation. As the Orthodox Patriarchs said in their Letter of 1848 to Pope Pius IX:

Among us, neither Patriarchs nor Councils could ever introduce new teaching, for the guardian of religion is the very body of the Church, that is, the people (*laos*) itself.

Commenting on this statement, Khomiakov wrote:

The Pope is greatly mistaken in supposing that we consider the ecclesiastical hierarchy to be the guardian of dogma. The case is quite different. The unvarying constancy and the unerring truth of Christian dogma does not depend upon any hierarchical order; it is guarded by the totality, by the whole people of the Church, which is the Body of Christ.[2]

This conception of the laity and their place in the Church must be kept in mind when considering the nature of an Ecumenical Council. The laity are guardians and not teachers; therefore, although they may attend a council and take an active part in the proceedings (as Constantine and other Byzantine Emperors did), yet when the moment comes for the

1. *Letter* lxvi, 8.
2. Letter in W. J. Birkbeck, *Russia and the English Church*, p. 94.

council to make a formal proclamation of the faith, it is the bishops alone who, in virtue of their teaching *charisma*, take the final decision.

But councils of bishops can err and be deceived. How then can one be certain that a particular gathering is truly an Ecumenical Council and therefore that its decrees are infallible? Many councils have considered themselves ecumenical and have claimed to speak in the name of the whole Church, and yet the Church has rejected them as heretical: Ephesus in 449, for example, or the Iconoclast Council of Hieria in 754, or Florence in 1438-9. Yet these councils seem in no way different in outward appearance from the Ecumenical Councils. What, then, is the criterion for determining whether a council is ecumenical?

This is a more difficult question to answer than might at first appear, and though it has been much discussed by Orthodox during the past hundred years, it cannot be said that the solutions suggested are entirely satisfactory. All Orthodox know which are the seven Councils that their Church accepts as ecumenical, but precisely what it is that makes a council ecumenical is not so clear. There are, so it must be admitted, certain points in the Orthodox theology of Councils which remain obscure and which call for further thinking on the part of theologians. With this caution in mind, let us briefly consider the present trend of Orthodox thought on this subject.

To the question how one can know whether a council is ecumenical, Khomiakov and his school gave an answer which at first sight appears clear and straightforward: a council cannot be considered ecumenical unless its decrees are accepted by the whole Church. Florence, Hieria, and the rest, while ecumenical in outward appearance, are not truly so, precisely because they failed to secure this acceptance by the Church at large. (One might object: What about Chalcedon? It was rejected by Syria and Egypt – can we say, then, that it was 'accepted by the Church at large'?) The bishops, so Khomiakov argued, because they are the teachers of the faith, define and proclaim the truth in council; but these definitions must then be acclaimed by the whole people of God, including the laity, because it is the whole people of God that constitutes the guardian of Tradition. This emphasis on the need for councils to be received by the Church at large has been viewed with suspicion by some Orthodox theologians, both Greek and Russian, who fear that Khomiakov and his followers have endangered the prerogatives of the episcopate and 'democratized' the idea of the Church. But in a qualified and carefully guarded form, Khomiakov's view is now fairly widely accepted in contemporary Orthodox thought.

This act of acceptance, this reception of councils by the Church as a whole, must not be understood in a juridical sense:

It does not mean that the decisions of the councils should be confirmed by a general plebiscite and that without such a plebiscite they have no force. There is no such plebiscite. But from historical experience it clearly appears that the voice of a given council has truly been the voice of the Church or that it has not: that is all.[1]

At a true Ecumenical Council the bishops recognize what the truth is and proclaim it; this proclamation is then verified by the assent of the whole Christian people, an assent which is not, as a rule, expressed formally and explicitly, but *lived*.

It is not merely the numbers or the distribution of its members which determines the ecumenicity of a council:

An 'Ecumenical' Council is such, not because accredited representatives of all the Autocephalous Churches have taken part in it, but because it has borne witness to the faith of the Ecumenical Church.[2]

The ecumenicity of a council cannot be decided by outward criteria alone: 'Truth can have no external criterion, for it is manifest of itself and made inwardly plain.'[3] The infallibility of the Church must not be 'exteriorized', nor understood in too 'material' a sense:

1. S. Bulgakov, *The Orthodox Church*, p. 89.
2. Metropolitan Seraphim, *L'Église orthodoxe*, p. 51.
3. V. Lossky, *The Mystical Theology of the Eastern Church*, p. 188.

It is not the 'ecumenicity' but the truth of the councils which makes their decisions obligatory for us. We touch here upon the fundamental mystery of the Orthodox doctrine of the Church: the Church is the miracle of the presence of God among men, beyond all formal 'criteria', all formal 'infallibility'. It is not enough to summon an 'Ecumenical Council' . . . it is also necessary that in the midst of those so assembled there should be present He who said: 'I am the Way, the Truth, the Life.' Without this presence, however numerous and representative the assembly may be, it will not be in the truth. Protestants and Catholics usually fail to understand this fundamental truth of Orthodoxy: both materialize the presence of God in the Church – the one party in the *letter* of Scripture, the other in the *person* of the Pope – though they do not thereby avoid the miracle, but clothe it in a concrete form. For Orthodoxy, the sole 'criterion of truth' remains God Himself, living mysteriously in the Church, leading it in the way of the Truth.[1]

THE LIVING AND THE DEAD:
THE MOTHER OF GOD

In God and in His Church there is no division between the living and the departed, but all are one in the love of the Father. Whether we are alive or whether we are dead, as members of the Church we still belong to the same family, and still have a duty to bear one another's burdens. Therefore just as Orthodox Christians here on earth pray for one another and ask for one another's prayers, so they pray also for the faithful departed and ask the faithful departed to pray for them. Death cannot sever the bond of mutual love which links the members of the Church together.

Prayers for the Departed. 'With the saints give rest, O Christ, to the souls of thy servants, where there is neither sickness, nor sorrow, nor sighing, but life everlasting.' So the Orthodox Church prays for the faithful departed; and again:

1. J. Meyendorff, quoted by M. J. le Guillou, *Mission et unité*, Paris, 1960, vol. 11, p. 313.

O God of spirits and of all flesh, who hast trampled down death and overthrown the Devil, and given life unto Thy world: Do thou, the same Lord, give rest to the souls of Thy departed servants, in a place of light, refreshment, and repose, whence all pain, sorrow, and sighing have fled away. Pardon every transgression which they have committed, whether by word or deed or thought.

Orthodox are convinced that Christians here on earth have a duty to pray for the departed, and they are confident that the dead are helped by such prayers. But precisely in what way do our prayers help the dead? What exactly is the condition of souls in the period between death and the Resurrection of the Body at the Last Day? Here Orthodox teaching is not entirely clear, and has varied somewhat at different times. In the seventeenth century a number of Orthodox writers – most notably Peter of Moghila and Dositheus in his *Confession* – upheld the Roman Catholic doctrine of Purgatory, or something very close to it.[1] (According to the normal Roman teaching, souls in Purgatory undergo expiatory suffering, and so render 'satisfaction' or 'atonement' for their sins.) Today most if not all Orthodox theologians reject the idea of Purgatory, at any rate in this form. The majority would be inclined to say that the faithful departed do not suffer at all. Another school holds that perhaps they suffer, but, if so, their suffering is of a purificatory but not an expiatory character; for when a man dies in the grace of God, then God freely forgives him all his sins and demands no expiatory penalties: Christ, the Lamb of God who takes away the sin of the world, is our *only* atonement and satisfaction. Yet a third group would prefer to leave the whole question entirely open: let us avoid detailed formulation about the life after death, they say, and preserve instead a reverent and agnostic

1. It should be remarked, however, that even in the seventeenth century there were many Orthodox who rejected the Roman teaching on Purgatory. The statements on the departed in Moghila's *Orthodox Confession* were carefully changed by Meletius Syrigos, while in later life Dositheus specifically retracted what he had written on the subject in his *Confession*.

reticence. When Saint Antony of Egypt was once worrying about divine providence, a voice came to him, saying: 'Antony, attend to yourself; for these are the judgements of God, and it is not for you to know them.'[1]

The Saints. Symeon the New Theologian describes the saints as forming a golden chain:

> The Holy Trinity, pervading all men from first to last, from head to foot, binds them all together. . . . The saints in each generation, joined to those who have gone before, and filled like them with light, become a golden chain, in which each saint is a separate link, united to the next by faith, works, and love. So in the One God they form a single chain which cannot quickly be broken.[2]

Such is the Orthodox idea of the communion of saints. This chain is a chain of mutual love and prayer; and in this loving prayer the members of the Church on earth, 'called to be saints', have their place.

In private an Orthodox Christian is free to ask for the prayers of any member of the Church, whether canonized or not. It would be perfectly normal for an Orthodox child, if orphaned, to end his evening prayers by asking for the intercessions not only of the Mother of God and the saints, but of his own mother and father. In its public worship, however, the Church usually prays only to those whom it has officially proclaimed as saints; but in exceptional circumstances a public cult may become established without any formal act of canonization. The Greek Church under the Ottoman Empire soon began to commemorate the New Martyrs in its worship, but to avoid the notice of the Turks there was usually no official act of proclamation: the cult of the New Martyrs was in most cases something that arose spontaneously under popular initiative. The same thing has happened in recent years with the New Martyrs of Russia: in certain places, both within and outside the Soviet Union, they have begun to be honoured as saints in the Church's worship, but present

1. *Apophthegmata* (*P.G.* lxv), Antony, 2.
2. *Centuries*, III, 2–4.

conditions in the Russian Church make a formal canonization impossible.

Reverence for the saints is closely bound up with the veneration of icons. These are placed by Orthodox not only in their churches, but in each room of their homes, and even in cars and buses. These ever-present icons act as a point of meeting between the living members of the Church and those who have gone before. Icons help Orthodox to look on the saints not as remote and legendary figures from the past, but as contemporaries and personal friends.

At Baptism an Orthodox is given the name of a saint, 'as a symbol of his entry into the unity of the Church which is not only the earthly Church, but also the Church in heaven'.[1] An Orthodox has a special devotion to the saint whose name he bears; he usually keeps an icon of his patron saint in his room, and prays daily to him. The festival of his patron saint he keeps as his *Name Day*, and to most Orthodox (as to most Roman Catholics in continental Europe) this is a date far more important than one's actual birthday.

An Orthodox Christian prays not only to the saints but to the angels, and in particular to his guardian angel. The angels 'fence us around with their intercessions and shelter us under their protecting wings of immaterial glory'.[2]

The Mother of God. Among the saints a special position belongs to the Blessed Virgin Mary, whom Orthodox reverence as the most exalted among God's creatures, 'more honourable than the cherubim and incomparably more glorious than the seraphim'.[3] Note that we have termed her 'most exalted *among God's creatures*': Orthodox, like Roman Catholics, *venerate* or *honour* the Mother of God, but in no sense do the members of

1. P. Kovalevsky, *Exposé de la foi catholique orthodoxe*, Paris, 1957, p. 16.
2. From the Dismissal Hymn for the Feast of the Archangels (8 November).
3. From the hymn *Meet it is*, sung at the Liturgy of Saint John Chrysostom.

either Church regard her as a fourth person of the Trinity, nor do they assign to her the *worship* due to God alone. In Greek theology the distinction is very clearly marked: there is a special word, *latreia*, reserved for the worship of God, while for the veneration of the Virgin entirely different terms are employed (*duleia, hyperduleia, proskynesis*).

In Orthodox services Mary is often mentioned, and on each occasion she is usually given her full title: 'Our All-Holy, immaculate, most blessed and glorified Lady, Mother of God and Ever-Virgin Mary.' Here are included the three chief epithets applied to Our Lady by the Orthodox Church: *Theotokos* (Mother of God), *Aeiparthenos* (Ever-Virgin), and *Panagia* (All-Holy). The first of these titles was assigned to her by the third Ecumenical Council (Ephesus, 431), the second by the fifth Ecumenical Council (Constantinople, 553).[1] The title *Panagia*, although never a subject of dogmatic definition, is accepted and used by all Orthodox.

The appellation *Theotokos* is of particular importance, for it provides the key to the Orthodox cult of the Virgin. We honour Mary because she is the Mother of our God. We do not venerate her in isolation, but because of her relation to Christ. Thus the reverence shown to Mary, so far from eclipsing the worship of God, has exactly the opposite effect: the more we esteem Mary, the more vivid is our awareness of the majesty of her Son, for it is precisely on account of the Son that we venerate the Mother.

We honour the Mother on account of the Son: Mariology is simply an extension of Christology. The Fathers of the Council of Ephesus insisted on calling Mary *Theotokos*, not because they desired to glorify her as an end in herself, apart from her Son, but because only by honouring Mary could they safeguard a right doctrine of Christ's person. Anyone who thinks out the implications of that great phrase, *The Word was made flesh*, can-

---

1. Belief in the Perpetual Virginity of Mary may seem at first sight contrary to Scripture, since Mark iii, 31 mentions the 'brothers' of Christ. But the word used here in Greek can mean half-brother, cousin, or near relative, as well as brother in the strict sense.

not but feel a certain awe for her who was chosen as the instrument of so surpassing a mystery. When men refuse to honour Mary, only too often it is because they do not really believe in the Incarnation.

But Orthodox honour Mary, not only because she is *Theotokos*, but because she is *Panagia*, All-Holy. Among all God's creatures, she is the supreme example of synergy or cooperation between the purpose of the deity and the free will of man. God, who always respects human liberty, did not wish to become incarnate without the free consent of His Mother. He waited for her voluntary response: 'Behold the handmaid of the Lord; be it unto me according to your word' (Luke i, 38). Mary could have refused; she was not merely passive, but an active participant in the mystery. As Nicholas Cabasilas said:

> The Incarnation was not only the work of the Father, of His Power and His Spirit . . . but it was also the work of the will and faith of the Virgin. . . . Just as God became incarnate voluntarily, so He wished that His Mother should bear Him freely and with her full consent.[1]

If Christ is the New Adam, Mary is the New Eve, whose obedient submission to the will of God counterbalanced Eve's disobedience in Paradise. 'So the knot of Eve's disobedience was loosed through the obedience of Mary; for what Eve, a virgin, bound by her unbelief, that Mary, a virgin, unloosed by her faith.'[2] 'Death by Eve, life by Mary.'[3]

The Orthodox Church calls Mary 'All-Holy'; it calls her 'immaculate' or 'spotless' (in Greek, *achrantos*); and all Orthodox are agreed in believing that Our Lady was free from *actual* sin. But was she also free from *original* sin? In other words, does Orthodoxy agree with the Roman Catholic doctrine of the Immaculate Conception, proclaimed as a dogma by Pope Pius IX in 1854, according to which Mary, from the moment she was conceived by her mother Saint Anne, was by

1. *On the Annunciation*, 4–5 (*Patrologia Orientalis*, vol. XIX, Paris, 1926, p. 488).
2. Irenaeus, *Against the Heresies*, III, xxii, 4.
3. Jerome, *Letter* xxii, 21.

God's special decree delivered from 'all stain of original sin'? The Orthodox Church has never in fact made any formal and definitive pronouncement on the matter. In the past individual Orthodox have made statements which, if not definitely affirming the doctrine of the Immaculate Conception, at any rate approach close to it; but since 1854 the great majority of Orthodox have rejected the doctrine, for several reasons. They feel it to be unnecessary; they feel that, at any rate as defined by the Roman Catholic Church, it implies a false understanding of original sin; they suspect the doctrine because it seems to separate Mary from the rest of the descendants of Adam, putting her in a completely different class from all the other righteous men and women of the Old Testament. From the Orthodox point of view, however, the whole question belongs to the realm of theological opinion; and if an individual Orthodox today felt impelled to believe in the Immaculate Conception, he could not be termed a heretic for so doing.

But Orthodoxy, while for the most part denying the doctrine of the Immaculate Conception of Mary, firmly believes in her Bodily Assumption.[1] Like the rest of mankind, Our Lady underwent physical death, but in her case the Resurrection of the Body has been anticipated: after death her body was taken up or 'assumed' into heaven and her tomb was found to be empty. She has passed beyond death and judgement, and lives already in the Age to Come. Yet she is not thereby utterly separated from the rest of humanity, for that same bodily glory which Mary enjoys now, all of us hope one day to share.

Belief in the Assumption of the Mother of God is clearly and unambiguously affirmed in the hymns sung by the Church on 15 August, the Feast of the 'Dormition' or 'Falling Asleep'. But Orthodoxy, unlike Rome, has never proclaimed the Assumption as a dogma, nor would it ever wish to do so. The

1. Immediately after the Pope proclaimed the Assumption as a dogma in 1950, a few Orthodox (by way of reaction against the Roman Catholic Church) began to express doubts about the Bodily Assumption and even explicitly to deny it; but they are certainly *not* representative of the Orthodox Church as a whole.

doctrines of the Trinity and the Incarnation have been proclaimed as dogmas, for they belong to the public preaching of
the Church; but the glorification of Our Lady belongs to the
Church's inner Tradition:

It is hard to speak and not less hard to think about the mysteries which the Church keeps in the hidden depths of her inner
consciousness. . . . The Mother of God was never a theme of the
public preaching of the Apostles; while Christ was preached on
the housetops, and proclaimed for all to know in an initiatory
teaching addressed to the whole world, the mystery of his
Mother was revealed only to those who were within the Church.
. . . It is not so much an object of faith as a foundation of our
hope, a fruit of faith, ripened in Tradition. Let us therefore keep
silence, and let us not try to dogmatize about the supreme glory
of the Mother of God.[1]

THE LAST THINGS

For the Christian there exist but two ultimate alternatives,
Heaven and Hell. The Church awaits the final consummation
of the end, which in Greek theology is termed the *apocatastasis*
or 'restoration', when Christ will return in great glory to judge
both the living and the dead. This final *apocatastasis* involves,
as we have seen, the redemption and the glorification of matter:
at the Last Day the righteous will rise from the grave and be
united once more to a body – not such a body as we now
possess, but one that is transfigured and 'spiritual', in which
inward sanctity is made outwardly manifest. And not only
man's body but the whole material order will be transformed:
God will create a New Heaven and a New Earth.

But Hell exists as well as Heaven. In recent years many
Christians – not only in the west, but at times also in the
Orthodox Church – have come to feel that the idea of Hell is
inconsistent with belief in a loving God. But to argue thus is to
display a sad and perilous confusion of thought. While it is
true that God loves us with an infinite love, it is also true that

1. V. Lossky, *'Panagia'*, in *The Mother of God*, edited by E. L.
Mascall, p. 35.

He has given us free will; and since we have free will, it is possible for us to reject God. Since free will exists, Hell exists; for Hell is nothing else than the rejection of God. If we deny Hell, we deny free will. 'No one is so good and full of pity as God,' wrote Mark the Monk or Hermit (early fifth century); 'but even He does not forgive those who do not repent.'[1] God will not force us to love Him, for love is no longer love if it is not free; how then can God reconcile to Himself those who refuse all reconciliation?

The Orthodox attitude towards the Last Judgement and Hell is clearly expressed in the choice of Gospel readings at the Liturgy on three successive Sundays shortly before Lent. On the first Sunday is read the parable of the Publican and Pharisee, on the second the parable of the Prodigal Son, stories which illustrate the immense forgiveness and mercy of God towards all sinners who repent. But in the Gospel for the third Sunday – the parable of the Sheep and the Goats – we are reminded of the other truth: that it is possible to reject God and to turn away from Him to Hell. 'Then shall He say to those on the left hand, The curse of God is upon you, go from my sight into everlasting fire' (Matthew xxv, 41).

There is no terrorism in the Orthodox doctrine of God. Orthodox Christians do not cringe before Him in abject fear, but think of Him as *philanthropos*, the 'lover of men'. Yet they keep in mind that Christ at His Second Coming will come as *judge*.

Hell is not so much a place where God imprisons man, as a place where man, by misusing his free will, chooses to imprison himself. And even in Hell the wicked are not deprived of the love of God, but by their own choice they experience as suffering what the saints experience as joy. 'The love of God will be an intolerable torment for those who have not acquired it within themselves.'[2]

Hell exists as a final possibility, but several of the Fathers have none the less believed that in the end all will be reconciled

1. *On those who think to be justified from works*, 71 (*P.G.* lxv, 940D).
2. V. Lossky, *The Mystical Theology of the Eastern Church*, p. 234.

to God. It is heretical to say that all *must* be saved, for this is to deny free will; but it is legitimate to hope that all *may* be saved. Until the Last Day comes, we must not despair of anyone's salvation, but must long and pray for the reconciliation of all without exception. No one must be excluded from our loving intercession. 'What is a merciful heart?' asked Isaac the Syrian. 'It is a heart that burns with love for the whole of creation, for men, for the birds, for the beasts, *for the demons*, for all creatures.'[1] Gregory of Nyssa said that Christians may legitimately hope even for the redemption of the Devil.

The Bible ends upon a note of keen expectation: 'Surely I am coming quickly. Amen. Even so, come, Lord Jesus' (Revelation xxii, 20). In the same spirit of eager hope the primitive Christians used to pray: 'Let grace come and let this world pass away.'[2] From one point of view the first Christians were wrong: they imagined that the end of the world would occur almost immediately, whereas in fact two millennia have passed and still the end has not yet come. It is not for us to know the times and the seasons, and perhaps this present order will last for many millennia more. Yet from another point of view the primitive Church was right. For whether the end comes early or late, it is always *imminent*, always spiritually close at hand, even though it may not be temporally close. The Day of the Lord will come 'as a thief in the night' (1 Thessalonians v, 2) at an hour when men expect it not. Christians, therefore, as in Apostolic times, so today must always be prepared, waiting in constant expectation. One of the most encouraging signs of revival in contemporary Orthodoxy is the renewed awareness among many Orthodox of the Second Coming and its relevance. 'When a pastor on a visit to Russia asked what is the burning problem of the Russian Church, a priest replied without hesitation: the *Parousia*.'[3]

1. *Mystic Treatises*, edited by A. J. Wensinck, Amsterdam, 1923, p. 341.
2. *Didache*, x. 6.
3. P. Evdokimov, *L'Orthodoxie*, p. 9 (*Parousia*: the Greek term for the Second Coming).

Yet the Second Coming is not simply an event in the future, for in the life of the Church, the Age to Come has already begun to break through into this present age. For members of God's Church, the 'Last Times' are already inaugurated, since here and now Christians enjoy the firstfruits of God's Kingdom. *Even so, come, Lord Jesus.* He comes already – in the Holy Liturgy and the worship of the Church.

CHAPTER 13

Orthodox Worship, I:
The Earthly Heaven

The church is the earthly heaven in which the
heavenly God dwells and moves.
Germanus, Patriarch of Constantinople (died 733)

DOCTRINE AND WORSHIP

THERE is a story in the *Russian Primary Chronicle* of how
Vladimir, Prince of Kiev, while still a pagan, desired to know
which was the true religion, and therefore sent his followers to
visit the various countries of the world in turn. They went first
to the Moslem Bulgars of the Volga, but observing that these
when they prayed gazed around them like men possessed,
the Russians continued on their way dissatisfied. 'There is no
joy among them,' they reported to Vladimir, 'but mournfulness
and a great smell; and there is nothing good about their
system.' Travelling next to Germany and Rome, they found
the worship more satisfactory, but complained that here too it
was without beauty. Finally they journeyed to Constantinople,
and here at last, as they attended the Divine Liturgy in the
great Church of the Holy Wisdom, they discovered what they
desired. 'We knew not whether we were in heaven or on earth,
for surely there is no such splendour or beauty anywhere upon
earth. We cannot describe it to you: only this we know, that
God dwells there among men, and that their service surpasses
the worship of all other places. For we cannot forget that
beauty.'

In this story can be seen several features characteristic of
Orthodox Christianity. There is first the emphasis upon divine
beauty: *we cannot forget that beauty*. It has seemed to many
that the peculiar gift of Orthodox peoples – and especially of

Byzantium and Russia – is this power of perceiving the beauty of the spiritual world, and expressing this celestial beauty in their worship.

In the second place it is characteristic that the Russians should have said, *we knew not whether we were in heaven or on earth*. Worship, for the Orthodox Church, is nothing else than 'heaven on earth'. The Holy Liturgy is something that embraces two worlds at once, for both in heaven and on earth the Liturgy is one and the same – one altar, one sacrifice, one presence. In every place of worship, however humble its outward appearance, as the faithful gather to perform the Eucharist, they are taken up into the 'heavenly places'; in every place of worship when the Holy Sacrifice is offered, not merely the local congregation are present, but the Church universal – the saints, the angels, the Mother of God, and Christ himself. 'Now the celestial powers are present with us, and worship invisibly.'[1] *This we know, that God dwells there among men.*

Orthodox, inspired by this vision of 'heaven on earth', have striven to make their worship in outward splendour and beauty an icon of the great Liturgy in heaven. In the year 612, on the staff of the Church of the Holy Wisdom, there were 80 priests, 150 deacons, 40 deaconesses, 70 subdeacons, 160 readers, 25 cantors, and 100 doorkeepers: this gives some faint idea of the magnificence of the service which Vladimir's envoys attended. But many who have experienced Orthodox worship under very different outward surroundings have felt, no less than those Russians from Kiev, a sense of God's presence among men. Turn, for example, from the *Russian Primary Chronicle* to the letter of an Englishwoman, written in 1935:

This morning was so queer. A very grimy and sordid Presbyterian mission hall in a mews over a garage, where the Russians are allowed once a fortnight to have the Liturgy. A very stage property iconostasis and a few modern icons. A dirty floor to kneel on and a form along the wall . . . And in this two superb

1. Words sung at the Great Entrance in the Liturgy of the Presanctified.

old priests and a deacon, clouds of incense and, at the Anaphora, an overwhelming supernatural impression.[1]

There is yet a third characteristic of Orthodoxy which the story of Vladimir's envoys illustrates. When they wanted to discover the true faith, the Russians did not ask about moral rules nor demand a reasoned statement of doctrine, but watched the different nations at prayer. The Orthodox approach to religion is fundamentally a liturgical approach, which understands doctrine in the context of divine worship: it is no coincidence that the word 'Orthodoxy' should signify alike right belief and right worship, for the two things are inseparable. It has been truly said of the Byzantines: 'Dogma with them is not only an intellectual system apprehended by the clergy and expounded to the laity, but a field of vision wherein all things on earth are seen in their relation to things in heaven, first and foremost through liturgical celebration.'[2] In the words of Georges Florovsky: 'Christianity is a liturgical religion. The Church is first of all a worshipping community. Worship comes first, doctrine and discipline second.'[3] Those who wish to know about Orthodoxy should not so much read books as follow the example of Vladimir's retinue and attend the Liturgy. As Philip said to Nathanael: 'Come and see' (John i, 46).

Because they approach religion in this liturgical way, Orthodox often attribute to minute points of ritual an importance which astonishes western Christians. But once we have understood the central place of worship in the life of Orthodoxy, an incident such as the schism of the Old Believers will no longer appear entirely unintelligible: if worship is the faith in action, then liturgical changes cannot be lightly regarded. It is typical that a Russian writer of the fifteenth century, when attacking the Council of Florence, should find fault with the Latins, not for any errors in doctrine, but for their behaviour in worship:

1. *The Letters of Evelyn Underhill*, p. 248.
2. G. Every, *The Byzantine Patriarchate*, first edition, p. ix.
3. 'The Elements of Liturgy in the Orthodox Catholic Church', in the periodical *One Church*, vol. XIII (New York, 1959), nos. 1–2, p. 24.

What have you seen of worth among the Latins? They do not even know how to venerate the church of God. They raise their voices as the fools, and their singing is a discordant wail. They have no idea of beauty and reverence in worship, for they strike trombones, blow horns, use organs, wave their hands, trample with their feet, and do many other irreverent and disorderly things which bring joy to the devil.[1]

Orthodoxy sees man above all else as a liturgical creature who is most truly himself when he glorifies God, and who finds his perfection and self-fulfilment in worship. Into the Holy Liturgy which expresses their faith, the Orthodox peoples have poured their whole religious experience. It is the Liturgy which has inspired their best poetry, art, and music. Among Orthodox, the Liturgy has never become the preserve of the learned and the clergy, as it tended to be in the medieval west, but it has remained *popular* – the common possession of the whole Christian people:

The normal Orthodox lay worshipper, through familiarity from earliest childhood, is entirely at home in church, thoroughly conversant with the audible parts of the Holy Liturgy, and takes part with unconscious and unstudied ease in the action of the rite, to an extent only shared in by the hyper-devout and ecclesiastically minded in the west.[2]

In the dark days of their history – under the Mongols, the Turks, or the communists – it is to the Holy Liturgy that the Orthodox peoples have always turned for inspiration and new hope; nor have they turned in vain.

THE OUTWARD SETTING OF THE SERVICES:
PRIEST AND PEOPLE

The basic pattern of services is the same in the Orthodox as in the Roman Catholic Church: there is, first, the *Holy Liturgy*

1. Quoted in N. Zernov, *Moscow the Third Rome*, p. 37; I cite this passage simply as an example of the liturgical approach of Orthodoxy, without necessarily endorsing the strictures on western worship which it contains!

2. Austin Oakley, *The Orthodox Liturgy*, London, 1958, p. 12.

(the Eucharist or Mass); secondly, the *Divine Office* (i.e. the two chief offices of Matins and Vespers, together with the six 'Lesser Hours' of Nocturns, Prime, Terce, Sext, None, and Compline);[1] and thirdly, the *Occasional Offices* – i.e. services intended for special occasions, such as Baptism, Marriage, Monastic Profession, Royal Coronation, Consecration of a Church, Burial of the Dead. (In addition to these, the Orthodox Church makes use of a great variety of lesser blessings.)

While in many Anglican and almost all Roman Catholic parish churches, the Eucharist is celebrated daily, in the Orthodox Church today a daily Liturgy is not usual except in cathedrals and large monasteries; in a normal parish church it is celebrated only on Sundays and feasts. But in contemporary Russia, where places of worship are few and many Christians are obliged to work on Sundays, a daily Liturgy has become the practice in many town parishes.

The Divine Office is recited daily in monasteries, large and small, and in some cathedrals; also in a number of town parishes in Russia. But in an ordinary Orthodox parish church it is sung only at week-ends and on feasts. Greek churches hold Vespers on Saturday night, and Matins on Sunday morning before the Liturgy; in Russian parishes Matins is usually 'anticipated' and sung immediately after Vespers on Saturday night, so that Vespers and Matins, followed by Prime, together constitute what is termed the 'Vigil Service' or the 'All-Night Vigil'. Thus while western Christians, if they worship in the evening, tend to do so on Sundays, Orthodox Christians worship on the evening of Saturdays.

In its services the Orthodox Church uses the language of the people: Arabic at Antioch, Finnish at Helsinki, Japanese at Tokyo, English (when required) at New York. One of the first tasks of Orthodox missionaries – from Cyril and Methodius in the ninth century, to Innocent Veniaminov and Nicholas Kassatkin in the nineteenth – has always been to translate the

1. In the Roman rite Nocturns is a part of Matins, but in the Byzantine rite Nocturns is a separate service. Byzantine Matins is equivalent to Matins and Lauds in the Roman rite.

service books into native tongues. In practice, however, there are partial exceptions to this general principle of using the vernacular: the Greek-speaking Churches employ, not modern Greek, but the Greek of New Testament and Byzantine times, while the Russian Church still uses the ninth-century translations in Church Slavonic. Yet in both cases the difference between the liturgical language and the contemporary vernacular is not so great as to make the service unintelligible to the congregation. In 1906 many Russian bishops in fact recommended that Church Slavonic be replaced more or less generally by modern Russian, but the Bolshevik Revolution occurred before this scheme could be carried into effect.

In the Orthodox Church today, as in the early Church, all services are sung or chanted. There is no Orthodox equivalent to the Roman 'Low Mass' or to the Anglican 'Said Celebration'. At every Liturgy, as at every Matins and Vespers, incense is used and the service is sung, even though there may be no choir or congregation, but the priest and a single reader alone. In their Church music the Greek-speaking Orthodox continue to use the ancient Byzantine plain-chant, with its eight 'tones'. This plain-chant the Byzantine missionaries took with them into the Slavonic lands, but over the centuries it has become extensively modified, and the various Slavonic Churches have each developed their own style and tradition of ecclesiastical music. Of these traditions the Russian is the best known and the most immediately attractive to western ears; many consider Russian Church music the finest in all Christendom, and alike in the Soviet Union and in the emigration there are justly celebrated Russian choirs. Until very recent times all singing in Orthodox churches was usually done by the choir; today, a small but increasing number of parishes in Greece, Russia, Romania, and the diaspora are beginning to revive congregational singing – if not throughout the service, then at any rate at special moments such as the Creed and the Lord's Prayer.

In the Orthodox Church today, as in the early Church, singing is unaccompanied and instrumental music is not found, except among certain Orthodox in America – particularly the Greeks – who are now showing a *penchant* for the organ or the harmonium. Most Orthodox do not use hand or sanctuary bells inside the church; but they have outside belfries, and take great delight in ringing the bells not only before but at various moments during the service itself. Russian bell-ringing used to be particularly famous. 'Nothing,' wrote Paul of Aleppo during his visit to Moscow in 1655, 'nothing affected me so much as the united clang of all the bells on the eves of Sundays and great festivals, and at midnight before the festivals. The earth shook with their vibrations, and like thunder the drone of their voices went up to the skies.' 'They rang the brazen bells after their custom. May God not be startled at the noisy pleasantness of their sounds!'[1]

An Orthodox Church is usually more or less square in plan, with a wide central space covered by a dome. (In Russia the church dome has assumed that striking onion shape which forms so characteristic a feature of every Russian landscape.) The elongated naves and chancels, common in cathedrals and larger parish churches of the Gothic style, are not found in eastern church architecture. There are as a rule no chairs or pews in the central part of the church, although there may be benches or stalls along the walls. An Orthodox normally stands during Church services (non-Orthodox visitors are often astonished to see old women remaining on their feet for several hours without apparent signs of fatigue); but there are moments when the congregation can sit or kneel. Canon XX of the first Ecumenical Council forbids all kneeling on Sundays or on any of the fifty days between Easter and Pentecost; but today this rule is unfortunately not always strictly observed.

It is a remarkable thing how great a difference the presence or absence of pews can make to the whole spirit of Christian worship. There is in Orthodox worship a flexibility, an unself-conscious informality, not found among western congregations, at any rate north of the Alps. Western worshippers, ranged in their neat rows, each in his proper place, cannot move about

1. *The Travels of Macarius*, edited Ridding, p. 27 and p. 6.

during the service without causing a disturbance; a western congregation is generally expected to arrive at the beginning and to stay to the end. But in Orthodox worship people can come and go far more freely, and nobody is greatly surprised if one moves about during the service. The same informality and freedom also characterizes the behaviour of the clergy: ceremonial movements are not so minutely prescribed as in the west, priestly gestures are less stylized and more natural. This informality, while it can lead at times to irreverence, is in the end a precious quality which Orthodox would be most sorry to lose. They are at home in their church – not troops on a parade ground, but children in their Father's house. Orthodox worship is often termed 'otherworldly', but could more truly be described as 'homely': it is a *family* affair. Yet behind this homeliness and informality there lies a deep sense of mystery.

In every Orthodox Church the sanctuary is divided from the rest of the interior by the *iconostasis*, a solid screen, usually of wood, covered with panel icons. In early days the chancel was separated merely by a low screen three or four feet high. Sometimes this screen was surmounted by an open series of columns supporting a horizontal beam or architrave: a screen of this kind can still be seen at Saint Mark's, Venice. Only in comparatively recent times – in many places not until the fifteenth or sixteenth century – was the space between these columns filled up, and the iconostasis given its present solid form. Many Orthodox liturgists today would be glad to follow Father John of Kronstadt's example, and revert to a more open type of iconostasis; in a few places this has actually been done.

The iconostasis is pierced by three doors. The large door in the centre – the *Holy Door* – when opened affords a view through to the altar. This doorway is closed by double gates, behind which hangs a curtain. Outside service time, except during Easter week, the gates are kept closed and the curtain drawn. During services, at particular moments the gates are sometimes open, sometimes closed, while occasionally when the gates are closed the curtain is drawn across as well. Many Greek parishes, however, now no longer close the gates or draw the curtain at any point in the Liturgy; in a number of churches the gates have been removed altogether, while other churches have followed a course which is liturgically far more correct – keeping the gates, but removing the curtain. Of the two other doors, that on the left leads into the 'chapel' of the *Prothesis* or Preparation (here the sacred vessels are kept, and here the priest prepares the bread and the wine at the beginning of the Liturgy); that on the right leads into the *Diakonikon* (now generally used as a vestry, but originally the place where the sacred books, particularly the Book of the Gospels, were kept together with the relics). Laymen are not allowed to go behind the iconostasis, except for a special reason such as serving at the Liturgy. The altar in an Orthodox Church – the Holy Table or Throne, as it is called – stands free of the east wall, in the centre of the sanctuary; behind the altar and against the wall is set the bishop's throne.

Orthodox Churches are full of icons – on the screen, on the walls, in special shrines, or on a kind of desk where they can be venerated by the faithful. When an Orthodox enters church, his first action will be to buy a candle, go up to an icon, cross himself, kiss the icon, and light the candle in front of it. 'They be great offerers of candles,' commented the English merchant Richard Chancellor, visiting Russia in the reign of Elizabeth I. In the decoration of the church, the various iconographical scenes and figures are not arranged fortuitously, but according to a definite theological scheme, so that the whole edifice forms one great icon or image of the Kingdom of God. In Orthodox religious art, as in the religious art of the medieval west, there is an elaborate system of symbols, involving every part of the church building and its decoration. Icons, frescoes, and mosaics are not mere ornaments, designed to make the church 'look nice', but have a theological and liturgical function to fulfil.

The icons which fill the church serve as a point of meeting between heaven and earth. As each local congregation prays Sunday by Sunday, surrounded by the figures of Christ, the angels, and the saints, these visible images remind the faithful unceasingly of the invisible presence of the whole company of heaven at the Liturgy. The faithful can feel that the walls of the church open out upon eternity, and they are helped to realize that their Liturgy on earth is one and the same with the great Liturgy of heaven. The multitudinous icons express visibly the sense of 'heaven on earth'.

The worship of the Orthodox Church is communal and popular. Any non-Orthodox who attends Orthodox services with some frequency will quickly realize how closely the whole worshipping community, priest and people alike, are bound together into one; among other things, the absence of pews helps to create a sense of unity. Although most Orthodox congregations do not join in the singing, it should not therefore be imagined that they are taking no real part in the service; nor does the iconostasis – even in its present solid form – make the people feel cut off from the priest in the sanctuary. In any case, many of the ceremonies take place in front of the screen, in full view of the congregation.

Orthodox laity do not use the phrase 'to *hear* Mass', for in the Orthodox Church the Mass has never become something done by the clergy for the laity, but is something which clergy and laity perform *together*. In the medieval west, where the Eucharist was performed in a learned language not understood by the people, men came to church to adore the Host at the Elevation, but otherwise treated the Mass mainly as a convenient occasion for saying their private prayers.[1] In the Orthodox Church, where the Liturgy has never ceased to be a common action performed by priest and people together, the congregation do not come to church to say their private prayers, but to pray the public prayers of the Liturgy and to take part in the action of the rite itself. Orthodoxy has never undergone that separation between liturgy and personal devotion from which the medieval and post-medieval west has suffered so much.

Certainly the Orthodox Church, as well as the west, stands

1. All this, of course, has now been changed in the west by the Liturgical Movement.

in need of a Liturgical Movement; indeed, some such movement has already begun in a small way in several parts of the Orthodox world (revival of congregational singing; gates of the Holy Door left open in the Liturgy; more open form of iconostasis, and so on). Yet in Orthodoxy the scope of this Liturgical Movement will be far more restricted, since the changes required are very much less drastic. That sense of corporate worship which it is the primary aim of liturgical reform in the west to restore has never ceased to be a living reality in the Orthodox Church.

There is in most Orthodox worship an unhurried and timeless quality, an effect produced in part by the constant repetition of *Litanies*. Either in a longer or a shorter form, the Litany recurs several times in every service of the Byzantine rite. In these Litanies, the deacon (if there is no deacon, the priest) calls the people to pray for the various needs of the Church and the world, and to each petition the choir or the people replies *Lord, have mercy – Kyrie eleison* in Greek, *Gospodi pomilui* in Russian – probably the first words in an Orthodox service which the visitor grasps. (In some Litanies the response is changed to *Grant this, O Lord*.) The congregation associate themselves with the different intercessions by making the sign of the Cross and bowing. In general the sign of the Cross is employed far more frequently by Orthodox than by western worshippers, and there is a far greater freedom about the times when it is used: different worshippers cross themselves at different moments, each as he wishes, although there are of course occasions in the service when almost all sign themselves at the same time.

We have described Orthodox worship as timeless and unhurried. Most western people have the idea that Byzantine services, even if not literally timeless, are at any rate of an extreme and intolerable length. Certainly Orthodox functions tend to be more prolonged than their western counterparts, but we must not exaggerate. It is perfectly possible to celebrate the Byzantine Liturgy, and to preach a short sermon, in an hour and a quarter; and in 1943 the Patriarch of Constantinople laid down that in parishes under his jurisdiction the Sunday Liturgy should not last over an hour and a half. Russians on the whole take longer than Greeks over services, but in a normal Russian parish of the emigration, the Vigil Service on Saturday nights lasts no more than two hours, and often less. Monastic offices of course are more extended, and on Mount Athos at great festivals the service sometimes goes on for twelve or even fifteen hours without a break, but this is altogether exceptional.

Non-Orthodox may take heart from the fact that Orthodox are often as alarmed as they by the length of services. 'And now we are entered on our travail and anguish,' writes Paul of Aleppo in his diary as he enters Russia. 'For all their churches are empty of seats. There is not one, even for the bishop; you see the people all through the service standing like rocks, motionless or incessantly bending with their devotions. God help us for the length of their prayers and chants and Masses, for we suffered great pain, so that our very souls were tortured with fatigue and anguish.' And in the middle of Holy Week he exclaims: 'God grant us His special aid to get through the whole of this present week! As for the Muscovites, their feet must surely be of iron.'[1]

1. *The Travels of Macarius*, edited Ridding, p. 14 and p. 46.

CHAPTER 14

Orthodox Worship, II:
The Sacraments

> He who was visible as our Redeemer has now passed
> into the sacraments.
>
> *Saint Leo the Great*

THE chief place in Christian worship belongs to the sacraments or, as they are called in Greek, the *mysteries*. 'It is called
a mystery,' writes Saint John Chrysostom of the Eucharist,
'because what we believe is not the same as what we see, but
we see one thing and believe another.... When I hear the Body
of Christ mentioned, I understand what is said in one sense,
the unbeliever in another.'[1] This double character, at once outward and inward, is the distinctive feature of a sacrament: the
sacraments, like the Church, are both visible and invisible; in
every sacrament there is the combination of an outward visible
sign with an inward spiritual grace. At Baptism the Christian
undergoes an outward washing in water, and he is at the same
time cleansed inwardly from his sins; at the Eucharist he receives what appears from the visible point of view to be bread
and wine, but in reality he eats the Body and Blood of Christ.

In most of the sacraments the Church takes material things –
water, bread, wine, oil – and makes them a vehicle of the Spirit.
In this way the sacraments look back to the Incarnation, when
Christ took material flesh and made it a vehicle of the Spirit;
and they look forward to, or rather they anticipate, the *apocatastasis* and the final redemption of matter at the Last Day.

The Orthodox Church speaks customarily of seven sacraments, basically the same seven as in Roman Catholic theology:

1. *Homilies on 1 Corinthians*, vii, 1 (*P.G.* lxi, 55).

   (i)   Baptism;
  (ii)   Chrismation (equivalent to Confirmation in the west);
 (iii)   The Eucharist;
 (iv)   Repentance or Confession;
  (v)   Holy Orders;
 (vi)   Marriage or Holy Matrimony;
(vii)   The Anointing of the Sick (corresponding to Extreme
       Unction in the Roman Catholic Church).

Only in the seventeenth century, when Latin influence was at its height, did this list become fixed and definite. Before that date Orthodox writers vary considerably as to the number of sacraments: John of Damascus speaks of two; Dionysius the Areopagite of six; Joasaph, Metropolitan of Ephesus (fifteenth century), of ten; and those Byzantine theologians who in fact speak of seven sacraments differ as to the items which they include in their list. Even today the number seven has no absolute dogmatic significance for Orthodox theology, but is used primarily as a convenience in teaching.

Those who think in terms of 'seven sacraments' must be careful to guard against two misconceptions. In the first place, while all seven are true sacraments, they are not all of equal importance, but there is a certain 'hierarchy' among them. The Eucharist, for example, stands at the heart of all Christian life and experience in a way that the Anointing of the Sick does not. Among the seven, Baptism and the Eucharist occupy a special position: to use a phrase adopted by the Joint Committee of Romanian and Anglican theologians at Bucharest in 1935, these two sacraments are 'pre-eminent among the divine mysteries'.

In the second place, when we talk of 'seven sacraments', we must never isolate these seven from the many other actions in the Church which also possess a sacramental character, and which are conveniently termed *sacramentals*. Included among these sacramentals are the rites for a monastic profession, the great blessing of waters at Epiphany, the service for the burial of the dead, and the anointing of a monarch. In all these there is a combination of outward visible sign and inward spiritual grace. The Orthodox Church also employs a great number of minor blessings, and these, too, are of a sacramental nature: blessings of corn, wine, and oil; of fruits, fields, and homes; of any object or element. These lesser blessings and services are often very practical and prosaic: there are prayers for blessing a car or a railway engine, or for clearing a place of vermin.[1] Between the wider and the narrower sense of the term 'sacrament' there is no rigid division: the whole Christian life must be seen as a unity, as a single mystery or one great sacrament, whose different aspects are expressed in a great variety of acts, some performed but once in a man's life, others perhaps daily.

The sacraments are *personal*: they are the means whereby God's grace is appropriated to every Christian *individually*. For this reason, in most of the sacraments of the Orthodox Church, the priest mentions the Christian name of each person as he administers the sacrament. When giving Holy Communion, for example, he says: 'The servant of God . . . [name] partakes of the holy, precious Body and Blood of Our Lord'; at the Anointing of the Sick he says: 'O Father, heal Thy servant [name] from his sickness both of body and soul.'

BAPTISM[2]

In the Orthodox Church today, as in the Church of the early centuries, the three sacraments of Christian initiation – Baptism, Confirmation, First Communion – are linked closely together. An Orthodox who becomes a member of Christ is admitted at once to the full privileges of such membership.

1. 'The popular religion of Eastern Europe is liturgical and ritualistic, but not wholly otherworldly. A religion that continues to propagate new forms for cursing caterpillars and for removing dead rats from the bottoms of wells can hardly be dismissed as pure mysticism' (G. Every, *The Byzantine Patriarchate*, first edition, p. 198).

2. In this and the following sections, the sacraments are described according to the present practice in the Byzantine rite; but we must not, of course, forget the possibility, or rather the fact, of a western rite in Orthodoxy (see pp. 192–3).

Orthodox children are not only baptized in infancy, but confirmed in infancy, and given communion in infancy. 'Suffer the little children to come to me, and forbid them not; for of such is the Kingdom of Heaven' (Matthew xix, 14).

There are two essential elements in the act of Baptism: the invocation of the Name of the Trinity, and the threefold immersion in water. The priest says: 'The servant of God [name] is baptized into the Name of the Father, Amen. And of the Son, Amen. And of the Holy Spirit, Amen.' As the name of each person in the Trinity is mentioned, the priest immerses the child in the font, either plunging it entirely under the water, or at any rate pouring water over the whole of its body. If the person to be baptized is so ill that immersion would endanger his life, then it is sufficient to pour water over his forehead; but otherwise immersion must not be omitted.

Orthodox are greatly distressed by the fact that western Christendom, abandoning the primitive practice of Baptism by immersion, is now content merely to pour a little water over the candidate's forehead. Orthodoxy regards immersion as essential (except in emergencies), for if there is no immersion the correspondence between outward sign and inward meaning is lost, and the symbolism of the sacrament is overthrown. Baptism signifies a mystical burial and resurrection with Christ (Romans vi, 4–5 and Colossians ii, 12); and the outward sign of this is the plunging of the candidate into the font, followed by his emergence from the water. Sacramental symbolism therefore requires that he shall be immersed or 'buried' in the waters of Baptism, and then 'rise' out of them once more.

Through Baptism we receive a full forgiveness of all sin, whether original or actual; we 'put on Christ', becoming members of His Body the Church. To remind them of their Baptism, Orthodox Christians usually wear throughout life a small Cross, hung round the neck on a chain.

Baptism must normally be performed by a bishop or a priest. In cases of emergency, it can be performed by a deacon, or by any man or woman, provided they are Christian. But whereas Roman Catholic theologians hold that if necessary even a non-

Christian can administer Baptism, Orthodoxy holds that this is not possible. The person who baptizes must himself have been baptized.

CHRISMATION

Immediately after Baptism, an Orthodox child is 'chrismated' or 'confirmed'. The priest takes a special ointment, the Chrism (in Greek, *myron*), and with this he anoints various parts of the child's body, marking them with the sign of the Cross: first the forehead, then the eyes, nostrils, mouth, and ears, the breast, the hands, and the feet. As he marks each he says: 'The seal of the gift of the Holy Spirit.' The child, who has been incorporated into Christ at Baptism, now receives in Chrismation the gift of the Spirit, thereby becoming a *laïkos* (layman), a full member of the people (*laos*) of God. Chrismation is an extension of Pentecost: the same Spirit who descended visibly on the Apostles in tongues of fire now descends invisibly on the newly baptized. Through Chrismation every member of the Church becomes a prophet, and receives a share in the royal priesthood of Christ; all Christians alike, because they are chrismated, are called to act as conscious witnesses to the Truth. 'You have an anointing (*chrisma*) from the Holy One, and know all things' (1 John ii, 20).

In the west, it is normally the bishop in person who confers Confirmation; in the east, Chrismation is administered by a priest, but the Chrism which he uses must first have been blessed by a bishop. (In modern Orthodox practice, only a bishop who is head of an autocephalous Church enjoys the right to bless the Chrism.) Thus both in east and west the bishop is involved in the second sacrament of Christian initiation: in the west directly, in the east indirectly.

Chrismation is also used as a sacrament of reconciliation. If an Orthodox apostatizes to Islam and then returns to the Church, when he is accepted back he is chrismated. Similarly if Roman Catholics become Orthodox, the Patriarchate of Constantinople and the Church of Greece usually receive them by Chrismation; but the Russian Church commonly receives them after a simple profession of faith, without chrismating them. Anglicans and other Protestants are always received by Chrismation. Sometimes converts are received by Baptism.

As soon as possible after Chrismation an Orthodox child is brought to communion. His earliest memories of the Church will centre on the act of receiving the Holy Gifts of Christ's Body and Blood. Communion is not something to which he comes at the age of six or seven (as in the Roman Catholic Church) or in adolescence (as in Anglicanism), but something from which he has never been excluded.

THE EUCHARIST

Today the Eucharist is celebrated in the eastern Church according to one of four different services:

(1) *The Liturgy of Saint John Chrysostom* (the normal Liturgy on Sundays and weekdays).

(2) *The Liturgy of Saint Basil the Great* (used ten times a year; outwardly it is very little different from the Liturgy of Saint John Chrysostom, but the prayers said privately by the priest are far longer).

(3) *The Liturgy of Saint James, the Brother of the Lord* (used once a year, on Saint James's Day, 23 October, in certain places only).[1]

(4) *The Liturgy of the Presanctified* (used on Wednesdays and Fridays in Lent, and on the first three days of Holy Week. There is no consecration in this Liturgy, but communion is given from elements consecrated on the previous Sunday.)

In general structure the Liturgies of Saint John Chrysostom and Saint Basil are as follows:

I. THE OFFICE OF PREPARATION – the *Prothesis* or *Pros-komidia*: the preparation of the bread and wine to be used at the Eucharist.

1. Until recently, used only at Jerusalem and on the Greek island of Zante; now revived elsewhere (e.g. the Patriarch's church at Constantinople; the Greek Cathedral in London; the Russian monastery at Jordanville, U.S.A.).

II. THE LITURGY OF THE WORD – the *Synaxis*

A. *The Opening of the Service – the Enarxis*[1]

The Litany of Peace

Psalm 102 (103)

The Little Litany

Psalm 145 (146), followed by the hymn *Only-begotten Son and Word of God*

The Little Litany

The Beatitudes (with special hymns or *Troparia* appointed for the day)

B. *The Little Entrance*, followed by the Entrance Hymn or Introit for the day

The *Trisagion* – 'Holy God, Holy and Strong, Holy and Immortal, have mercy upon us' – sung three or more times

C. *Readings from Scripture*

The *Prokimenon* – verses, usually from the Psalms

The Epistle

Alleluia – sung nine or sometimes three times, with verses from Scripture intercalated

The Gospel

The Sermon (often transferred to the end of the service)

D. *Intercession for the Church*

The Litany of Fervent Supplication

The Litany of the Departed

The Litany of the Catechumens, and the dismissal of the Catechumens

III. THE EUCHARIST

A. Two short Litanies of the Faithful lead up to the *Great Entrance*, which is then followed by the Litany of Supplication

B. *The Kiss of Peace* and *the Creed*

1. Strictly speaking the *Synaxis* only begins with the Little Entrance; the *Enarxis* is now added at the start, but was originally a separate service.

c. *The Eucharistic Prayer*
   Opening Dialogue
   Thanksgiving – culminating in the narrative of the Last
      Supper, and the words of Christ: 'This is my Body
      ... This is my Blood ... '
   Anamnesis – the act of 'calling to mind' and offering.
      The priest 'calls to mind' Christ's death, burial,
      Resurrection, Ascension, and Second Coming, and
      he 'offers' the Holy Gifts to God
   Epiclesis – the Invocation or 'calling down' of the Spirit
      on the Holy Gifts
   A great Commemoration of all the members of the
      Church: the Mother of God, the saints, the departed,
      the living
   The Litany of Supplication, followed by the Lord's
      Prayer
D. The *Elevation* and *Fraction* ('breaking') of the Conse-
      crated Gifts
E. *Communion* of the clergy and people
F. *Conclusion* of the service: Thanksgiving and final
      Blessing; distribution of the *Antidoron*

The first part of the Liturgy, the Office of Preparation, is
performed privately by the priest and deacon in the chapel of
the *Prothesis*. Thus the public portion of the service falls into
two sections, the Synaxis (a service of hymns, prayers, and
readings from Scripture) and the Eucharist proper: originally
the Synaxis and the Eucharist were often held separately, but
since the fourth century the two have virtually become fused
into one service. Both Synaxis and Eucharist contain a procession, known respectively as the Little and the Great Entrance. At the Little Entrance the Book of the Gospels is
carried in procession round the church, at the Great Entrance
the bread and wine (prepared before the beginning of the
Synaxis) are brought processionally from the *Prothesis* chapel
to the altar. The Little Entrance corresponds to the Introit in
the western rite (originally the Little Entrance marked the

beginning of the public part of the service, but at present it is preceded by various Litanies and Psalms); the Great Entrance is in essence an Offertory Procession. Synaxis and Eucharist alike have a clearly marked climax: in the Synaxis, the reading of the Gospel; in the Eucharist, the *Epiclesis* of the Holy Spirit.

The belief of the Orthodox Church concerning the Eucharist is made quite clear during the course of the Eucharistic Prayer. The priest reads the opening part of the Thanksgiving in a low voice, until he comes to the words of Christ at the Last Supper: 'Take, eat, This is my Body . . .' 'Drink of it, all of you, This is my Blood . . . '; these words are always read in a loud voice, in the full hearing of the congregation. In a low voice once more, the priest recites the *Anamnesis*:

Commemorating the Cross, the Grave, the Resurrection after three days, the Ascension into Heaven, the Enthronement at the right hand of the Father, and the second and glorious Coming again.

He continues aloud:

Thine of Thine own we offer to Thee, in all and for all.

Then comes the *Epiclesis*, as a rule read secretly, but sometimes in full hearing of the congregation:

Send down Thy Holy Spirit upon us and upon these gifts here set forth:
And make this bread the Precious Body of Thy Christ,
And that which is in this cup, the Precious Blood of Thy Christ,
Changing them by Thy Holy Spirit. Amen, Amen, Amen.[1]

Priest and deacon immediately prostrate themselves before the Holy Gifts, which have now been consecrated.

It will be evident that the 'moment of consecration' is under-

1. The *Anamnesis* and *Epiclesis*, as quoted here, are from the Liturgy of Saint John Chrysostom. In the Liturgy of Saint Basil they are slightly different.

stood somewhat differently by the Orthodox and the Roman Catholic Churches. According to Latin theology, the consecration is effected by the Words of Institution: 'This is my Body ...' 'This is my Blood ...'. According to Orthodox theology, the act of consecration is not complete until the end of the *Epiclesis*, and worship of the Holy Gifts before this point is condemned by the Orthodox Church as 'artolatry' (bread worship). Orthodox, however, do not teach that consecration is effected *solely* by the *Epiclesis*, nor do they regard the Words of Institution as incidental and unimportant. On the contrary, they look upon the entire Eucharistic Prayer as forming a single and indivisible whole, so that the three main sections of the prayer – Thanksgiving, *Anamnesis*, *Epiclesis* – all form an integral part of the one act of consecration.[1] But this of course means that if we are to single out a 'moment of consecration', such a moment cannot come until the *Amen* of the *Epiclesis*.[2]

The Presence of Christ in the Eucharist. As the words of the *Epiclesis* make abundantly plain, the Orthodox Church believes that after consecration the bread and wine become in very truth the Body and Blood of Christ: they are not mere symbols, but the reality. But while Orthodoxy has always insisted on the *reality* of the change, it has never attempted to explain the *manner* of the change: the Eucharistic Prayer in the Liturgy simply uses the neutral term *metaballo*, to 'turn about', 'change', or 'alter'. It is true that in the seventeenth century not only individual Orthodox writers, but Orthodox Councils such as that of Jerusalem in 1672, made use of the Latin term

1. Some Orthodox writers go even further than this, and maintain that the consecration is brought about by the whole process of the Liturgy, starting with the *Prothesis* and including the *Synaxis*! Such a view, however, presents many difficulties, and has little or no support in Patristic tradition.

2. Before Vatican II the Roman Canon to all appearances had no *Epiclesis*; but many Orthodox liturgists, most notably Nicholas Cabasilas, regard the paragraph *Supplices te* as constituting in effect an *Epiclesis*, although Roman Catholics today, with a few notable exceptions, do not understand it as such.

'transubstantiation' (in Greek, *metousiosis*), together with the
Scholastic distinction between Substance and Accidents.[1] But
at the same time the Fathers of Jerusalem were careful to add
that the use of these terms does not constitute an explanation
of the manner of the change, since this is a mystery and must
always remain incomprehensible.[2] Yet despite this disclaimer,
many Orthodox felt that Jerusalem had committed itself too
unreservedly to the terminology of Latin Scholasticism, and it
is significant that when in 1838 the Russian Church issued a
translation of the Acts of Jerusalem, while retaining the word
transubstantiation, it carefully paraphrased the rest of the
passage in such a way that the technical terms Substance and
Accidents were not employed.[3]

Today Orthodox writers still use the word transubstantiation, but they insist on two points: first, there are many other
words which can with equal legitimacy be used to describe the
consecration, and, among them all, the term transubstantiation
enjoys no unique or decisive authority; secondly, its use does
not commit theologians to the acceptance of Aristotelian philosophical concepts. The general position of Orthodoxy in the
whole matter is clearly summed up in the *Longer Catechism*,

1. In medieval philosophy a distinction is drawn between the
substance or essence (i.e. that which constitutes a thing, which makes
it what it is), and the accidents or qualities that belong to a substance
(i.e. everything that can be perceived by the senses – size, weight,
shape, colour, taste, smell, and so on). A substance is something
existing by itself (*ens per se*), an accident can only exist by inhering
in something else (*ens in alio*).

Applying this distinction to the Eucharist, we arrive at the doctrine
of Transubstantiation. According to this doctrine, at the moment of
consecration in the Mass there is a change of substance, but the
accidents continue to exist as before: the substances of bread and wine
are changed into those of the Body and Blood of Christ, but the
accidents of bread and wine – i.e. the qualities of colour, taste, smell,
and so forth – continue miraculously to exist and to be perceptible to
the senses.

2. Doubtless many Roman Catholics would say the same.

3. This is an interesting example of the way in which the Church
is 'selective' in its acceptance of the decrees of Local Councils (see
above, p. 211).

written by Philaret, Metropolitan of Moscow (1782–1867), and authorized by the Russian Church in 1839:

QUESTION: How are we to understand the word transubstantiation?

ANSWER: ... The word transubstantiation is not to be taken to define the manner in which the bread and wine are changed into the Body and Blood of the Lord; for this none can understand but God; but only thus much is signified, that the bread truly, really, and substantially becomes the very true Body of the Lord, and the wine the very Blood of the Lord.[1]

And the Catechism continues with a quotation from John of Damascus:

If you enquire how this happens, it is enough for you to learn that it is through the Holy Spirit ... we know nothing more than this, that the word of God is true, active, and omnipotent, but in its manner of operation unsearchable.[2]

In every Orthodox parish church, the Blessed Sacrament is normally reserved, most often in a tabernacle on the altar, although there is no strict rule as to the place of reservation. Orthodox, however, do not hold services of public devotion before the reserved sacrament, nor do they have any equivalent to the Roman Catholic functions of Exposition and Benediction, although there seems to be no theological (as distinct from liturgical) reason why they should not do so. The priest blesses the people with the sacrament during the course of the Liturgy, but never outside it.

The Eucharist as a sacrifice. The Orthodox Church believes the Eucharist to be a sacrifice; and here again the basic Orthodox teaching is set forth clearly in the text of the Liturgy itself. 'Thine of Thine own we offer to Thee, in all and for all.' (1) We offer *Thine of Thine own.* At the Eucharist, the sacrifice offered is Christ himself, and it is Christ himself who in the

1. English translation in R. W. Blackmore, *The Doctrine of the Russian Church*, London, 1845, p. 92.
2. *On the Orthodox Faith*, IV, 13 (*P.G.* xciv, 1145A).

Church performs the act of offering: he is both priest and victim. 'Thou thyself art He who offers and He who is offered.'[1] (2) We offer *to Thee*. The Eucharist is offered to God the Trinity – not just to the Father but also to the Holy Spirit and to Christ himself.[2] Thus if we ask, *what* is the sacrifice of the Eucharist? *By whom* is it offered? *To whom* is it offered? – in each case the answer is *Christ*. (3) We offer *for all*: according to Orthodox theology, the Eucharist is a propitiatory sacrifice (in Greek, *thusia hilastirios*), offered on behalf of both the living and the dead.

In the Eucharist, then, the sacrifice which we offer is the sacrifice of Christ. But what does this mean? Theologians have held and continue to hold many different theories on this subject. Some of these theories the Church has rejected as inadequate, but it has never formally committed itself to any particular explanation of the Eucharistic sacrifice. Nicholas Cabasilas sums up the standard Orthodox position as follows:

> First, the sacrifice is not a mere figure or symbol but a true sacrifice; secondly, it is not the bread that is sacrificed, but the very Body of Christ; thirdly, the Lamb of God was sacrificed once only, for all time. . . . The sacrifice at the Eucharist consists, not in the real and bloody immolation of the Lamb, but in the transformation of the bread into the sacrificed Lamb.[3]

The Eucharist is not a bare commemoration nor an imaginary representation of Christ's sacrifice, but the true sacrifice itself; yet on the other hand it is not a new sacrifice, nor a repetition of the sacrifice on Calvary, since the Lamb was sacrificed 'once only, for all time'. The events of Christ's sacrifice – the Incarnation, the Last Supper, the Crucifixion, the Resurrection, the Ascension[4] – are not repeated in the Eucharist, but they are

1. From the Priest's prayer before the Great Entrance.
2. This was stated with great 'emphasis by a Council of Constantinople in 1156 (see *P.G.* cxl, 176–7).
3. *Commentary on the Divine Liturgy*, 32.
4. Note that Christ's sacrifice includes many things besides His death: this is a most important point in Patristic and Orthodox teaching.

made present. 'During the Liturgy, through its divine power, we are projected to the point where eternity cuts across time, and at this point we become true *contemporaries* with the events which we commemorate.'[1] 'All the holy suppers of the Church are nothing else than one eternal and unique Supper, that of Christ in the Upper Room. The same divine act both takes place at a specific moment in history, and is offered always in the sacrament.'[2]

Holy Communion. In the Orthodox Church the laity as well as the clergy always receive communion 'under both kinds'. Communion is given to the laity in a spoon, containing a small piece of the Holy Bread together with a portion of the Wine; it is received standing. Orthodoxy insists on a strict fast before communion, and nothing can be eaten or drunk after waking in the morning.[3] Many Orthodox at the present day receive communion infrequently – perhaps only five or six times a year – not from any disrespect towards the sacrament, but because that is the way in which they have been brought up. But during recent years a few parishes in Greece and in the Russian diaspora have restored the primitive practice of weekly communion, and it appears that communion is also becoming more frequent in Orthodox Churches behind the Iron Curtain. There seems every hope that this movement towards frequent communion will continue to gain ground slowly but surely in the years to come.

After the final blessing with which the Liturgy ends, the people come up to kiss a Cross which the priest holds in his hand, and to receive a little piece of bread, called the *Antidoron*,

1. P. Evdokimov, *L'Orthodoxie*, p. 241.
2. ibid., p. 208.
3. 'You know that those who invite the Emperor to their house, first clean their home. So you, if you want to bring God into your bodily home for the illumination of your life, must first sanctify your body by fasting' (from the *Hundred Chapters* of Gennadius). In cases of sickness or genuine necessity, a confessor can grant dispensations from this communion fast.

which is blessed but not consecrated, although taken from the same loaf as the bread used in the consecration. In most Orthodox parishes non-Orthodox present at the Liturgy are permitted (and indeed, encouraged) to receive the *Antidoron*, as an expression of Christian fellowship and love.

REPENTANCE

An Orthodox child receives communion from infancy. Once he is old enough to know the difference between right and wrong and to understand what sin is – probably when he is six or seven – he may be taken to receive another sacrament: Repentance, Penitence, or Confession (in Greek, *metanoia* or *exomologisis*). Through this sacrament sins committed after Baptism are forgiven and the sinner is reconciled to the Church: hence it is often called a 'Second Baptism'. The sacrament acts at the same time as a cure for the healing of the soul, since the priest gives not only absolution but spiritual advice. Since all sin is sin not only against God but against our neighbour, against the community, confession and penitential discipline in the early Church were a public affair; but for many centuries alike in eastern and western Christendom confession has taken the form of a private 'conference' between priest and penitent alone. The priest is strictly forbidden to reveal to any third party what he has learnt in confession.

In Orthodoxy confessions are heard, not in a closed confessional with a grille separating confessor and penitent, but in any convenient part of the church, usually in the open immediately in front of the iconostasis; sometimes priest and penitent stand behind a screen, or there may be a special room in the church set apart for confessions. Whereas in the west the priest sits and the penitent kneels, in the Orthodox Church they both stand (or sometimes they both sit). The penitent faces a desk on which are placed the Cross and an icon of the Saviour or the Book of the Gospels; the priest stands slightly to one side. This outward arrangement emphasizes, more clearly than does the western system, that in confession it is not the priest but God who is the judge, while the priest is only a witness and God's minister. This point is also stressed in words which the priest says immediately before the confession proper:

Behold, my child, *Christ stands here invisibly and receives your confession.* Therefore be not ashamed nor afraid; conceal nothing from me, but tell me without hesitation everything that you have done, and so you shall have pardon from Our Lord Jesus Christ. See, His holy icon is before us: and *I am but a witness,* bearing testimony before Him of all the things which you have to say to me. But if you conceal anything from me, you shall have the greater sin. Take heed, therefore, lest having come to a physician you depart unhealed.[1]

After this the priest questions the penitent about his sins and gives him advice. When the penitent has confessed everything, he kneels or bows his head, and the priest, placing his stole (*epitrachilion*) on the penitent's head and then laying his hand upon the stole, says the prayer of absolution. In the Greek books the formula of absolution is deprecative (i.e. in the third person, 'May God forgive . . .'), in the Slavonic books it is indicative (i.e. in the first person, 'I forgive . . .'). The Greek formula runs:

Whatever you have said to my humble person, and whatever you have failed to say, whether through ignorance or forgetfulness, whatever it may be, may God forgive you in this world and the next. . . . Have no further anxiety; go in peace.

In Slavonic there is this formula:

May Our Lord and God, Jesus Christ, through the grace and bounties of His love towards mankind, forgive you, my child [name], all your transgressions. And I, an unworthy priest, through the power given me by Him, forgive and absolve you from all your sins.

This form, using the first person 'I', was originally introduced into Orthodox service books under Latin influence by

1. This exhortation is found in the Slavonic but not in the Greek books.

Peter of Moghila in the Ukraine, and was adopted by the Russian Church in the eighteenth century.

The priest may, if he thinks it advisable, impose a penance (*epitimion*), but this is not an essential part of the sacrament and is very often omitted. Many Orthodox have a special 'spiritual father', not necessarily their parish priest, to whom they go regularly for confession and spiritual advice.[1] There is in Orthodoxy no strict rule laying down how often one should go to confession; the Russians tend to go more often than the Greeks do. Where infrequent communion prevails – for example, four or five times a year – the faithful may be expected to go to confession before each communion; but in circles where frequent communion has been re-established, the priest does not necessarily expect a confession to be made before every communion.

HOLY ORDERS

There are three 'Major Orders' in the Orthodox Church, Bishop, Priest, and Deacon; and two 'Minor Orders', Subdeacon and Reader (once there were other Minor Orders, but at present all except these two have fallen largely into disuse). Ordinations to the Major Orders always occur during the course of the Liturgy, and must always be done individually (the Byzantine rite, unlike the Roman, lays down that no more than one deacon, one priest, and one bishop can be ordained at any single Liturgy). Only a bishop has power to ordain,[2] and the consecration of a new bishop must be performed by three or at least two bishops, never by one alone: since the episcopate is 'collegial' in character, an episcopal consecration is carried out by a 'college' of bishops. An ordination, while performed

1. In the Orthodox Church it is not entirely unknown for a layman to act as a spiritual father; but in that case, while he hears the confession, gives advice, and assures the penitent of God's forgiveness, he does not pronounce the prayer of sacramental absolution, but sends the penitent to a priest.

2. In cases of necessity an Archimandrite or Archpriest, acting as the bishop's delegate, can ordain a Reader.

by the bishop, also requires the consent of the *whole* people of God; and so at a particular point in the service the assembled congregation acclaim the ordination by shouting '*Axios!*' ('He is worthy!').[1]

Orthodox priests are divided into two distinct groups, the 'white' or married clergy, and the 'black' or monastic. Ordinands must make up their mind before ordination to which group they wish to belong, for it is a strict rule that no one can marry after he has been ordained to a Major Order. Those who wish to marry must therefore do so before they are made deacon. Those who do not wish to marry are normally expected to become monks prior to their ordination; but in the Orthodox Church today there are now a number of celibate clergy who have not taken formal monastic vows. These celibate priests, however, cannot afterwards change their minds and decide to get married. If a priest's wife dies, he cannot marry again.

As a rule the parochial clergy of the Orthodox Church are married, and a monk is only appointed to have charge of a parish for exceptional reasons.[2] Bishops are drawn exclusively from the monastic clergy,[3] although a widower can be made a bishop if he takes monastic vows. Such is the state of monasticism in many parts of the Orthodox Church today that it is not always easy to find suitable candidates for the episcopate, and a few Orthodox have even begun to argue that the limitation of bishops to the monastic clergy is no longer desirable under modern conditions. Yet surely the true solution

1. What happens if they shout '*Anaxios!*' ('He is unworthy!')? This is not very clear. On several occasions in Constantinople or Greece during the present century the congregation has in fact expressed its disapproval in this way, although without effect. But some would claim that, at any rate in theory, if the laity expresses its dissent, the ordination or consecration cannot take place.

2. In fact at the present day, particularly in the diaspora, monks are frequently put in charge of parishes. Many Orthodox regret this departure from the traditional practice.

3. This has been the rule since at least the sixth century; but in primitive times there are many instances of married bishops – for example, Saint Peter himself.

is not to change the present rule that bishops must be monks, but to reinvigorate the monastic life itself.

In the early Church the bishop was elected by the people of the diocese, clergy and laity together. In Orthodoxy today it is usually the Governing Synod in each autocephalous Church which appoints bishops to vacant sees; but in some Churches – Antioch, for example, and Cyprus – a modified system of election still exists. The Moscow Council of 1917–18 laid down that henceforward bishops in the Russian Church should be elected by the clergy and laity; this ruling is followed by the Paris group of Russians and the OCA, but conditions have made its application impossible within the Soviet Union itself.

The order of deacons is far more prominent in the Orthodox Church than in western communions. In Roman Catholicism prior to Vatican II the diaconate had become simply a preliminary stage on the way to the priesthood, but in Orthodoxy it has remained a permanent office, and many deacons have no intention of ever becoming priests. In the west today the deacon's part at High Mass is usually carried out by a priest, but in the Orthodox Liturgy none but a real deacon can perform the diaconal functions.

Canon Law lays down that no one may become a priest before the age of thirty nor a deacon before the age of twenty-five, but in practice this ruling is relaxed.

A Note on Ecclesiastical Titles

Patriarch. The title borne by the heads of certain autocephalous Churches. The heads of other Churches are called Archbishop or Metropolitan.

Metropolitan, Archbishop. Originally a Metropolitan was the bishop of the capital of a province, while Archbishop was a more general title of honour, given to bishops of special eminence. The Russians still use the titles more or less in the original way; but the Greeks (except at Jerusalem) now give the name Metropolitan to *every* diocesan bishop, and call by the title Archbishop those who in ancient times would have been styled Metropolitan. Thus among the Greeks an Archbishop now ranks above a Metropolitan, but among the Russians the Metropolitan is the higher position.

Archimandrite. Originally a monk charged with the spiritual supervision of several monasteries, or the superior of a monastery of special importance. Now used simply as a title of honour for priest-monks of distinction.

Higumenos. Among the Greeks, the Abbot of a monastery. Among the Russians, a title of honour for priest-monks (not necessarily Abbots). A Russian *Higumenos* ranks below an Archimandrite.

Archpriest or *Protopope.* A title of honour given to non-monastic priests; equivalent to Archimandrite.

Hieromonk. A priest-monk.

Hierodeacon. A monk who is a deacon.

Archdeacon. A title of honour given to monastic deacons. (In the west the Archdeacon is now a priest, but in the Orthodox Church he is still, as in primitive times, a deacon.)

Protodeacon. A title of honour given to deacons who are not monks.

MARRIAGE

The Trinitarian mystery of unity in diversity applies not only to the doctrine of the Church but to the doctrine of marriage. Man is made in the image of the Trinity, and except in special cases he is not intended by God to live alone, but in a family. And just as God blessed the first family, commanding Adam and Eve to be fruitful and multiply, so the Church today gives its blessing to the union of man and woman. Marriage is not only a state of nature but a state of grace. Married life, no less than the life of a monk, is a special vocation, requiring a particular gift or *charisma* from the Holy Spirit; and this gift is conferred in the sacrament of Holy Matrimony.

The Marriage Service is divided into two parts, formerly held separately but now celebrated in immediate succession: the preliminary *Office of Betrothal*, and the *Office of Crowning*, which constitutes the sacrament proper. At the Betrothal service the chief ceremony is the blessing and exchange of rings; this is an outward token that the two partners join in marriage of their own free will and consent, for without free consent on both sides there can be no sacrament of Christian marriage. The second part of the service culminates in the ceremony of coronation: on the heads of the bridegroom and bride the priest places crowns, made among the Greeks of leaves and flowers, but among the Russians of silver or gold. This, the outward and visible sign of the sacrament, signifies the special grace which the couple receive from the Holy Spirit, before they set out to found a new family or domestic Church. The crowns are crowns of joy, but they are also crowns of martyrdom, since every true marriage involves an immeasurable self-sacrifice on both sides. At the end of the service the newly married couple drink from the same cup of wine, which recalls the miracle at the marriage feast of Cana in Galilee: this common cup is a symbol of the fact that henceforward they will share a common life with one another.

The Orthodox Church permits divorce and remarriage, quoting as its authority the text of Matthew xix, 9, where Our Lord says: 'If a man divorces his wife, *for any cause other than unchastity*, and marries another, he commits adultery.' Since Christ allowed an exception to His general ruling about the indissolubility of marriage, the Orthodox Church also is willing to allow an exception. Certainly Orthodoxy regards the marriage bond as in principle lifelong and indissoluble, and it condemns the breakdown of marriage as a sin and an evil. But while condemning the sin, the Church still desires to help the sinners and to allow them a second chance. When, therefore, a marriage has entirely ceased to be a reality, the Orthodox Church does not insist on the preservation of a legal fiction. Divorce is seen as an exceptional but necessary concession to human sin; it is an act of *oikonomia* ('economy' or dispensation) and of *philanthropia* (loving kindness). Yet although assisting men and women to rise again after a fall, the Orthodox Church knows that a second alliance can never be the same as the first; and so in the service for a second marriage several of the joyful ceremonies are omitted, and replaced by penitential prayers.

Orthodox Canon Law, while permitting a second or even a third marriage, absolutely forbids a fourth. In theory the Canons only permit divorce in cases of adultery, but in practice it is sometimes granted for other reasons as well.

One point must be clearly understood: from the point of view of Orthodox theology a divorce granted by the State in the civil courts is not sufficient. Remarriage in church is only possible if the Church authorities have themselves granted a divorce.

The use of contraceptives and other devices for birth control is on the whole strongly discouraged in the Orthodox Church. Some bishops and theologians altogether condemn the employment of such methods. Others, however, have recently begun to adopt a less strict position, and urge that the question is best left to the discretion of each individual couple, in consultation with the spiritual father.

THE ANOINTING OF THE SICK

This sacrament – known in Greek as *evchelaion*, 'the oil of prayer' – is described by Saint James: 'Is any sick among you? Let him send for the presbyters of the Church, and let them pray over him. The prayer offered in faith will save the sick man and the Lord will raise him from his bed; and he will be forgiven any sins he has committed' (James v, 14–15). The sacrament, as this passage indicates, has a double purpose: not only bodily healing but the forgiveness of sins. The two things go together, for man is a unity of body and soul and there can therefore be no sharp and rigid distinction between bodily and spiritual ills. Orthodoxy does not of course believe that the

Anointing is invariably followed by a recovery of health. Some-times, indeed, the sacrament serves as an instrument of heal-ing, and the patient recovers; but at other times he does not recover, in which case the sacrament helps him in a different way, by giving him the spiritual strength to prepare for death.[1] In the Roman Catholic Church the sacrament has become 'Extreme' Unction, intended only for the dying;[2] thus the first aspect of the sacrament – healing – has become forgotten. But in the Orthodox Church Unction can be conferred on any who are sick, whether in danger of death or not.

1. 'This sacrament has two faces: one turns towards healing, the other towards the liberation from illness by death' (S. Bulgakov, *The Orthodox Church*, p. 135).

2. A change has now been made here by the second Vatican Council.

CHAPTER 15

Orthodox Worship, III:
Feasts, Fasts, and Private Prayer

> The true aim of prayer is to enter into conversation
> with God. It is not restricted to certain hours of the
> day. A Christian has to feel himself personally in
> the presence of God. The goal of prayer is precisely
> to be with God always.
>
> *Georges Florovsky*

THE CHRISTIAN YEAR

IF anyone wishes to recite or to follow the public services of
the Church of England, then (in theory, at any rate) two volumes will be sufficient – the Bible and the Book of Common
Prayer; similarly in the Roman Catholic Church he requires
only two books – the Missal and the Breviary; but in the Orthodox Church, such is the complexity of the services that he
will need a small library of some nineteen or twenty substantial
tomes. 'On a moderate computation,' remarked J. M. Neale of
the Orthodox Service Books, 'these volumes together comprise
5,000 closely printed quarto pages, in double columns.'[1] Yet
these books, at first sight so unwieldy, are one of the greatest
treasures of the Orthodox Church.

In these twenty volumes are contained the services for the
Christian year – that annual sequence of feasts and fasts which
commemorates the Incarnation and its fulfilment in the
Church. The ecclesiastical calendar begins on 1 September.
Pre-eminent among all festivals is Easter, the Feast of Feasts,
which stands in a class by itself. Next in importance come the
Twelve Great Feasts:

1. *Hymns of the Eastern Church*, third edition, London, 1866, p. 52.

The Nativity of the Mother of God (8 September)

The Exaltation (or Raising Up) of the Honourable and Life-giving Cross (14 September)

The Presentation of the Mother of God in the Temple (21 November)

The Nativity of Christ (Christmas) (25 December)

The Baptism of Christ in the Jordan (Epiphany) (6 January)

The Presentation of Our Lord in the Temple (western 'Candlemas') (2 February)

The Annunciation of the Mother of God (western 'Lady Day') (25 March)

The Entry of Our Lord into Jerusalem (Palm Sunday) (one week before Easter)

The Ascension of Our Lord Jesus Christ (40 days after Easter)

Pentecost (known in the west as Whit Sunday, but in the east as Trinity Sunday) (50 days after Easter)

The Transfiguration of Our Saviour Jesus Christ (6 August)

The Falling Asleep of the Mother of God (the Assumption) (15 August)

Thus three of the Twelve Great Feasts depend on the date of Easter and are 'movable'; the rest are 'fixed'. Eight are feasts of the Saviour, and four are feasts of the Mother of God.

There are also a large number of other festivals, of varying importance. Among the more prominent are:

The Circumcision of Christ (1 January)
The Three Great Hierarchs (30 January)
The Nativity of Saint John the Baptist (24 June)
Saint Peter and Saint Paul (29 June)
The Beheading of Saint John the Baptist (29 August)
The Protecting Veil of the Mother of God (1 October)
Saint Nicholas the Wonderworker (6 December)
All Saints (First Sunday after Pentecost)

But besides feasts there are fasts. The Orthodox Church, regarding man as a unity of soul and body, has always insisted
that the body must be trained and disciplined as well as the
soul. 'Fasting and self-control are the first virtue, the mother,
root, source, and foundation of all good.'[1] There are four main
periods of fasting during the year:

(i) *The Great Fast* (Lent) – begins seven weeks before
Easter.

(ii) *The Fast of the Apostles* – starts on the Monday eight
days after Pentecost, and ends on 28 June, the eve of
the Feast of Saints Peter and Paul; in length varies
between one and six weeks.

(iii) *The Assumption Fast* – lasts two weeks, from 1 to
14 August.

(iv) *The Christmas Fast* – lasts forty days, from 15 November to 24 December.

In addition to these four chief periods, all Wednesdays and
Fridays – and in some monasteries Mondays as well – are fast
days (except between Christmas and Epiphany, during Easter
week, and during the week after Pentecost). The Exaltation of
the Cross, the Beheading of Saint John the Baptist, and the eve
of Epiphany are also fasts.

The rules of fasting in the Orthodox Church are of a rigour
which will astonish and appal many western Christians. On
most days in Great Lent and Holy Week, for example, not only
is meat forbidden, but also fish and all animal products (lard,
eggs, butter, milk, cheese), together with wine and oil. In practice, however, many Orthodox – particularly in the diaspora –
find that under the conditions of modern life it is no longer
practicable to follow exactly the traditional rules, devised with
a very different outward situation in mind; and so certain dispensations are granted. Yet even so the Great Lent – especially
the first week and Holy Week itself – is still, for devout Orthodox, a period of genuine austerity and serious physical hard-

1. Callistos and Ignatios Xanthopoulos, in the *Philokalia*, Athens,
1961, vol. IV, p. 232.

ship. When all relaxations and dispensations are taken into account, it remains true that Orthodox Christians in the twentieth century – laymen as well as monks – fast with a severity for which there is no parallel in western Christendom, except perhaps in the strictest Religious Orders.

The Church's year, with its sequence of feasts and fasts, is something of overwhelming importance in the religious experience of the Orthodox Christian:

Nobody who has lived and worshipped amongst Greek Christians for any length of time but has sensed in some measure the extraordinary hold which the recurring cycle of the Church's liturgy has upon the piety of the common people. Nobody who has kept the Great Lent with the Greek Church, who has shared in the fast which lies heavy upon the whole nation for forty days; who has stood for long hours, one of an innumerable multitude who crowd the tiny Byzantine churches of Athens and overflow into the streets, while the familiar pattern of God's saving economy towards man is re-presented in psalm and prophecy, in lections from the Gospel, and the matchless poetry of the canons; who has known the desolation of the holy and great Friday, when every bell in Greece tolls its lament and the body of the Saviour lies shrouded in flowers in all the village churches throughout the land; who has been present at the kindling of the new fire and tasted of the joy of a world released from the bondage of sin and death – none can have lived through all this and not have realized that for the Greek Christian the Gospel is inseparably linked with the liturgy that is unfolded week by week in his parish church. Not among the Greeks only but throughout Orthodox Christendom the liturgy has remained at the very heart of the Church's life.[1]

Different moments in the year are marked by special ceremonies: the great blessing of waters at Epiphany (often performed out of doors, beside a river or on the sea shore); the blessing of fruits at the Transfiguration; the solemn exaltation and adoration of the Cross on 14 September; the service of forgiveness on the Sunday immediately before Lent, when clergy and people kneel one by one before each other, and ask

1. P. Hammond, *The Waters of Marah*, pp. 51–2.

one another's forgiveness. But naturally it is during Holy Week that the most moving and impressive moments in Orthodox worship occur, as day by day and hour by hour the Church enters into the Passion of the Lord. Holy Week reaches its climax, first in the procession of the *Epitaphion* (the figure of the Dead Christ laid out for burial) on the evening of Good Friday; and then in the exultant Matins of the Resurrection at Easter midnight.

None can be present at this midnight service without being caught up in the sense of universal joy. Christ has released the world from its ancient bondage and its former terrors, and the whole Church rejoices triumphantly in His victory over darkness and death:

The roaring of the bells overhead, answered by the 1,600 bells from the illuminated belfries of all the churches of Moscow, the guns bellowing from the slopes of the Kremlin over the river, and the processions in their gorgeous cloth of gold vestments and with crosses, icons, and banners, pouring forth amidst clouds of incense from all the other churches in the Kremlin, and slowly wending their way through the crowd, all combined to produce an effect which none who have witnessed it can ever forget.[1]

So W. J. Birkbeck wrote of Easter in pre-Revolutionary Russia. Today the churches of the Kremlin are museums, no more guns are fired in honour of the Resurrection, and though bells are rung, their number has sadly dwindled from the 1,600 of former days; but the vast and silent crowds which still gather at Easter midnight in thousands and tens of thousands around the churches of Moscow are in their way a more impressive testimony to the victory of Christ over the powers of evil.

Before we leave the subject of the Church's year, something must be said about the vexed question of the *calendar* – always, for some reason, an explosive topic among eastern Christians. Up to the end of the First World War, all Orthodox still used the Old Style or Julian Calendar, which is at present thirteen

1. A. Riley, *Birkbeck and the Russian Church*, p. 142.

days behind the New or Gregorian Calendar, followed in the west. In 1923 the Ecumenical Patriarch convened an 'Inter-Orthodox Congress' at Constantinople, attended by delegates from Serbia, Romania, Greece, and Cyprus (the Patriarchs of Antioch and Jerusalem refused to send delegates; the Patriarch of Alexandria did not even reply to the invitation; the Church of Bulgaria was not invited). Various proposals were put forward – married bishops; permission for a priest to remarry after his wife's death; the adoption of the Gregorian Calendar. The first two proposals have so far remained a dead letter, but the third was carried into effect by certain autocephalous Churches. In March 1924 Constantinople introduced the New Calendar; and in the same year, or shortly after, it was also adopted by Alexandria, Antioch, Greece, Cyprus, Romania, and Poland.[1] But the Churches of Jerusalem, Russia, and Serbia, together with the monasteries on the Holy Mountain of Athos, continue to this day to follow the Julian reckoning. This results in a difficult and confusing situation which one hopes will shortly be brought to an end. At present the Greeks (outside Athos and Jerusalem) keep Christmas at the same time as the west, on 25 December (New Style), while the Russians keep it thirteen days later, on 7 January (New Style); the Greeks keep Epiphany on 6 January, the Russians on 19 January; and so on. But practically the whole Orthodox Church observes Easter at the same time, reckoning it by the Julian (Old Style) Calendar: this means that the Orthodox date of Easter sometimes coincides with the western, but at other times it is one, four, or five weeks later.[2] The Church of Finland and a very few parishes in the diaspora always keep Easter on the western date.

The reform in the calendar aroused lively opposition, particularly in Greece, where groups of 'Old Calendarists' or *Palaioimerologitai* (including more than one bishop) continued to follow the old reckoning: they claimed that as the

1. The Church of Bulgaria adopted the New Calendar in 1968.
2. The discrepancy between Orthodox and western Easter is caused also by two different systems of calculating the 'epacts' which determine the lunar months.

calendar and the date of Easter depended on Canons of ecumenical authority, they could only be altered by a joint decision of the *whole* Orthodox Church – not by separate autocephalous Churches acting independently. While rejecting the New Calendar, the monasteries of Mount Athos have (all except one) maintained communion with the Patriarch of Constantinople and the Church of Greece, but the *Palaioimerologitai* on the Greek mainland were excommunicated by the official Church. They are usually treated by the Greek civil authorities as an illegal organization and have undergone persecution (many of their leaders suffered imprisonment); but they continue to exist in many areas and have their own bishops, monasteries, and parishes.

PRIVATE PRAYER

When an Orthodox thinks of prayer, he thinks primarily of public liturgical prayer. The corporate worship of the Church plays a far larger part in his religious experience than in that of the average western Christian. Of course this does not mean that Orthodox never pray except when in church: on the contrary, there exist special Manuals with daily prayers to be said by all Orthodox, morning and evening, before the icons in their own homes. But the prayers in these Manuals are taken for the most part directly from the Service Books used in public worship, so that even in his own home an Orthodox is still praying *with the Church*; even in his own home he is still joined in fellowship with all the other Orthodox Christians who are praying in the same words as he. 'Personal prayer is possible only in the context of the community. Nobody is a Christian by himself, but only as a member of the body. Even in solitude, "in the chamber", a Christian prays as a member of the redeemed community, of the Church. And it is in the Church that he learns his devotional practice.'[1] And just as there is in Orthodox spirituality no separation between liturgy and private devotion, so there is no separation between monks and those living in the world; the

1. G. Florovsky, *Prayer Private and Corporate* ('Ologos' publications, Saint Louis), p. 3.

prayers in the Manuals used by the laity are the very prayers which the monastic communities recite daily in church as part of the Divine Office. Husbands and wives are following the same Christian way as monks and nuns, and so all alike use the same prayers. Naturally the Manuals are only intended as a guide and a framework of prayer, and each Christian is also free to pray spontaneously and in his own words.

The directions at the start and conclusion of the morning prayers emphasize the need for recollection, for a *living* prayer to the Living God. At the beginning it is said:

When you wake up, before you begin the day, stand with reverence before the All-Seeing God. Make the sign of the Cross and say: *In the Name of the Father, and of the Son, and of the Holy Spirit. Amen.* Having invoked the Holy Trinity, keep silence for a little, so that your thoughts and feelings may be freed from worldly cares. Then recite the following prayers without haste, and with your whole heart.

And at the conclusion of the morning prayers a note states:

If the time at disposal is short, and the need to begin work is pressing, it is better to say only a few of the prayers suggested, with attention and devotion, rather than to recite them all in haste and without due concentration.

There is also a note in the morning prayers, encouraging everyone to read the Epistle and Gospel appointed daily for the Liturgy.

By way of example let us take two prayers from the Manual, the first a prayer for the beginning of the day, written by Philaret, Metropolitan of Moscow:

O Lord, grant me to greet the coming day in peace. Help me in all things to rely upon Thy holy will. In every hour of the day reveal Thy will to me. Bless my dealings with all who surround me. Teach me to treat all that comes to me throughout the day with peace of soul, and with firm conviction that Thy will governs all. In all my deeds and words guide my thoughts and feelings. In unforeseen events let me not forget that all are sent by Thee. Teach me to act firmly and wisely, without embittering and embarrassing others. Give me strength to bear the fatigue of the coming day with all that it shall bring. Direct my will, teach me to pray, pray Thou Thyself in me. Amen.

And these are a few clauses from the general intercession with which the night prayers close:

Forgive, O Lord, lover of men, those who hate and wrong us. Reward our benefactors. Grant to our brethren and friends all that they ask for their salvation and eternal life. Visit and heal the sick. Free the prisoners. Guide those at sea. Travel with those who travel. . . . On those who charge us in our unworthiness to pray for them, have mercy according to Thy great mercy. Remember, O Lord, our departed parents and brethren and give them rest where shines the light of Thy face. . . .

There is one type of private prayer, widely used in the west since the time of the Counter-Reformation, which has never been a feature of Orthodox spirituality – the formal 'Meditation', made according to a 'Method' – the Ignatian, the Sulpician, the Salesian, or some other. Orthodox are encouraged to read the Bible or the Fathers slowly and thoughtfully; but such an exercise, while regarded as altogether excellent, is not considered to constitute *prayer*, nor has it been systematized and reduced to a 'Method'. Each is urged to read in the way that he finds most helpful.

But while Orthodox do not practise discursive Meditation, there is another type of personal prayer which has for many centuries played an extraordinarily important part in the life of Orthodoxy – the Jesus Prayer: *Lord Jesus Christ, Son of God, have mercy on me a sinner*. Since it is sometimes said that Orthodox do not pay sufficient attention to the person of the Incarnate Christ, it is worth pointing out that this – surely the most classic of all Orthodox prayers – is essentially a Christocentric prayer, a prayer addressed to and concentrated upon the Lord Jesus. Those brought up in the tradition of the Jesus Prayer are never allowed for one moment to forget the Incarnate Christ.

As a help in reciting this prayer many Orthodox use a rosary, differing somewhat in structure from the western rosary; an

Orthodox rosary is often made of wool, so that unlike a string of beads it makes no noise.

The Jesus Prayer is a prayer of marvellous versatility. It is a prayer for beginners, but equally a prayer that leads to the deepest mysteries of the contemplative life. It can be used by anyone, at any time, in any place: standing in queues, walking, travelling on buses or trains; when at work; when unable to sleep at night; at times of special anxiety when it is impossible to concentrate upon other kinds of prayer. But while of course every Christian can use the Prayer at odd moments in this way, it is a different matter to recite it more or less continually and to use the physical exercises which have become associated with it. Orthodox spiritual writers insist that those who use the Jesus Prayer systematically should, if possible, place themselves under the guidance of an experienced director and do nothing on their own initiative.

For some there comes a time when the Jesus Prayer 'enters into the heart', so that it is no longer recited by a deliberate effort, but recites itself spontaneously, continuing even when a man talks or writes, present in his dreams, waking him up in the morning. In the words of Saint Isaac the Syrian:

When the Spirit takes its dwelling-place in a man he does not cease to pray, because the Spirit will constantly pray in him. Then, neither when he sleeps, nor when he is awake, will prayer be cut off from his soul; but when he eats and when he drinks, when he lies down or when he does any work, even when he is immersed in sleep, the perfumes of prayer will breathe in his heart spontaneously.[1]

Orthodox believe that the power of God is present in the Name of Jesus, so that the invocation of this Divine Name acts 'as an effective sign of God's action, as a sort of sacrament'.[2] 'The Name of Jesus, present in the human heart, communicates to it the power of deification. . . . Shining through the heart, the light of the Name of Jesus illuminates all the universe.'[3]

1. *Mystic Treatises*, edited by Wensinck, p. 174.
2. Un Moine de l'Église d'Orient, *La Prière de Jésus*, Chevetogne, 1952, p. 87.
3. S. Bulgakov, *The Orthodox Church*, pp. 170-1.

Alike to those who recite it continually and to those who only employ it occasionally, the Jesus Prayer proves a great source of reassurance and joy. To quote the Pilgrim:

And that is how I go about now, and ceaselessly repeat the Prayer of Jesus, which is more precious and sweet to me than anything in the world. At times I do as much as 43 or 44 miles a day, and do not feel that I am walking at all. I am aware only of the fact that I am saying my Prayer. When the bitter cold pierces me, I begin to say my Prayer more earnestly, and I quickly become warm all over. When hunger begins to overcome me, I call more often on the Name of Jesus, and I forget my wish for food. When I fall ill and get rheumatism in my back and legs, I fix my thoughts on the Prayer, and do not notice the pain. If anyone harms me I have only to think, 'How sweet is the Prayer of Jesus!' and the injury and the anger alike pass away and I forget it all. . . . I thank God that I now understand the meaning of those words I heard in the Epistle – *Pray without ceasing* (1 Thessalonians v, 17).[1]

1. *The Way of a Pilgrim*, p. 17–18.

CHAPTER 16

The Orthodox Church and the Reunion of Christians

> The greatest misfortune that befell mankind was, without doubt, the schism between Rome and the Ecumenical Church. The greatest blessing for which mankind can hope would be the reunion of east and west, the reconstitution of the great Christian unity.
> *General Alexander Kireev (1832–1910)*

'ONE HOLY CATHOLIC CHURCH': WHAT DO WE MEAN?

THE Orthodox Church in all humility believes itself to be the 'one, holy, Catholic, and Apostolic Church', of which the Creed speaks: such is the fundamental conviction which guides Orthodox in their relations with other Christians. There are divisions among Christians, but the Church itself is not divided nor can it ever be.

Christians of the Reformation traditions will perhaps protest, 'This is a hard saying; who can hear it?' It may seem to them that this exclusive claim on the Orthodox side precludes any serious 'ecumenical dialogue' with the Orthodox, and any constructive work for reunion. And yet they would be utterly wrong to draw such a conclusion: for, paradoxically enough, over the past half century there have been a large number of encouraging and fruitful contacts between Orthodox and other Christians. Although enormous obstacles still remain, there has also been great progress towards a reconciliation.

If Orthodox claim to be the one true Church, what then do they consider to be the status of those Christians who do not belong to their communion? Different Orthodox would answer in slightly different ways, for although all loyal Orthodox are agreed in their fundamental teaching concerning the Church, they do not entirely agree concerning the practical consequences which follow from this teaching. There is first a more moderate group, which includes most of those Orthodox who have had close personal contact with other Christians. This group holds that, while it is true to say that Orthodoxy is the Church, it is false to conclude from this that those who are not Orthodox cannot possibly belong to the Church. Many people may be members of the Church who are not visibly so; invisible bonds may exist despite an outward separation. The Spirit of God blows where it will, and, as Irenaeus said, where the Spirit is, there is the Church. We know where the Church is but we cannot be sure where it is not; and so we must refrain from passing judgement on non-Orthodox Christians. In the eloquent words of Khomiakov:

Inasmuch as the earthly and visible Church is not the fullness and completeness of the whole Church which the Lord has appointed to appear at the final judgement of all creation, she acts and knows only within her own limits; and ... does not judge the rest of mankind, and only looks upon those as excluded, that is to say, not belonging to her, who exclude themselves. The rest of mankind, whether alien from the Church, *or united to her by ties which God has not willed to reveal to her*, she leaves to the judgement of the great day.[1]

There is only one Church, but there are many different ways of being related to this one Church, and many different ways of being separated from it. Some non-Orthodox are very close indeed to Orthodoxy, others less so; some are friendly to the Orthodox Church, others indifferent or hostile. By God's grace the Orthodox Church possesses the fullness of truth (so its members are bound to believe), but there are other Christian communions which possess to a greater or lesser degree a genuine measure of Orthodoxy. All these facts must be taken into account: one cannot simply say that all non-Orthodox are outside the Church, and leave it at that; one cannot treat other Christians as if they stood on the same level as unbelievers.

1. *The Church is One*, section 2 (italics not in the original).

Such is the view of the more moderate party. But there also exists in the Orthodox Church a more rigorous group, who hold that since Orthodoxy is the Church, anyone who is not Orthodox cannot be a member of the Church. Thus Metropolitan Antony, head of the Russian Church in Exile and one of the most distinguished of modern Russian theologians, wrote in his *Catechism*:

QUESTION: Is it possible to admit that a split within the Church or among the Churches could ever take place?

ANSWER: Never. Heretics and schismatics have from time to time fallen away from the one indivisible Church, and, by so doing, *they ceased to be members of the Church*, but the Church itself can never lose its unity according to Christ's promise.[1]

Of course (so this stricter group add) divine grace is certainly active among many non-Orthodox, and if they are sincere in their love of God, then we may be sure that God will have mercy upon them; but they cannot, in their present state, be termed members of the Church. Workers for Christian unity who do not often encounter this rigorist school should not forget that such opinions are held by many Orthodox of great learning and holiness.

Because they believe their Church to be the true Church, Orthodox can have but one ultimate desire: the conversion or reconciliation of all Christians to Orthodoxy. Yet it must not be thought that Orthodox demand the submission of other Christians to a particular centre of power and jurisdiction.[2] The Orthodox Church is a family of sister Churches, decentralized in structure, which means that separated communities can be integrated into Orthodoxy without forfeiting their autonomy: Orthodoxy desires their reconciliation, not their absorption.[3] In all reunion discussions Orthodox are

1. Italics not in the original.
2. 'Orthodoxy does not desire the submission of any person or group; it wishes to make each one understand' (S. Bulgakov, *The Orthodox Church*, p. 214).
3. Compare the title of a famous paper written by Dom Lambert Beauduin and read by Cardinal Mercier at the Malines Conversations, 'The Anglican Church united, not absorbed'.

guided (or at any rate ought to be guided) by the principle of unity in diversity. They do not seek to turn western Christians into Byzantines or 'Orientals', nor do they desire to impose a rigid uniformity on all alike: for there is room in Orthodoxy for many different cultural patterns, for many different ways of worship, and even for many different systems of outward organization.

Yet there is one field in which diversity cannot be permitted. Orthodoxy insists upon unity in matters of the faith. *Before there can be reunion among Christians, there must first be full agreement in faith*: this is a basic principle for Orthodox in all their ecumenical relations. It is unity in the faith that matters, not organizational unity; and to secure unity of organization at the price of a compromise in dogma is like throwing away the kernel of a nut and keeping the shell. Orthodox are not willing to take part in a 'minimal' reunion scheme, which secures agreement on a few points and leaves everything else to private opinion. There can be only one basis for union – the *fullness* of the faith; for Orthodoxy looks on the faith as a united and organic whole. Speaking of the Anglo-Russian Theological Conference at Moscow in 1956, the present Archbishop of Canterbury, Dr Michael Ramsey, expressed the Orthodox viewpoint exactly:

The Orthodox said in effect: ' . . . The Tradition is a concrete fact. Here it is, in its totality. Do you Anglicans accept it, or do you reject it?' The Tradition is for the Orthodox one indivisible whole: the entire life of the Church in its fullness of belief and custom down the ages, including Mariology and the veneration of icons. Faced with this challenge, the typically Anglican reply is: 'We would not regard veneration of icons or Mariology as inadmissible, provided that in determining what is necessary to salvation, we confine ourselves to Holy Scripture.' But this reply only throws into relief the contrast between the Anglican appeal to what is deemed necessary to salvation and the Orthodox appeal to the one indivisible organism of Tradition, to tamper with any part of which is to spoil the whole, in the sort of way that a single splodge on a picture can mar its beauty.[1]

1. 'The Moscow Conference in Retrospect', in *Sobornost*, series 3, no. 23, 1958, pp. 562–3.

In the words of another Anglican writer: 'It has been said that the Faith is like a network rather than an assemblage of discrete dogmas; cut one strand and the whole pattern loses its meaning.'[1] Orthodox, then, ask of other Christians that they accept Tradition *as a whole*; but it must be remembered that there is a difference between Tradition and traditions.[2] Many beliefs held by Orthodox are not a part of the one Tradition, but are simply *theologoumena*, theological opinions; and there can be no question of imposing mere matters of opinion on other Christians. Men can possess full unity in the faith, and yet hold divergent theological opinions in certain fields.

This basic principle – no reunion without unity in the faith – has an important corollary: *until unity in the faith has been achieved, there can be no communion in the sacraments*. Communion at the Lord's Table (most Orthodox believe) cannot be used to secure unity in the faith, but must come as the consequence and crown of a unity already attained. Orthodoxy rejects the whole concept of '*inter*communion' between separated Christian bodies, and admits no form of sacramental fellowship short of full communion. Either Churches are in communion with one another, or they are not: there can be no half-way house.[3] (One slight qualification must be added. Occasionally non-Orthodox Christians, if entirely cut off from the ministrations of their own Church, are allowed *with special permission* to receive communion from an Orthodox priest. But the reverse does not hold true, for Orthodox are forbidden to receive communion from any but a priest of their own Church.) It is sometimes said that the Anglican or the Old Catholic Church is 'in communion' with the Orthodox, but this is not in fact the case. The two are not in communion, nor can they be, until Anglicans and Orthodox are agreed in matters of faith.

1. T. M. Parker, 'Devotion to the Mother of God', in *The Mother of God*, edited by E. L. Mascall, p. 74.
2. See p. 205.
3. Such is the standard Orthodox position. But there are individual Orthodox theologians who believe that some degree of intercommunion is possible, even before the attainment of full dogmatic agreement.

ORTHODOX RELATIONS WITH OTHER COMMUNIONS: OPPORTUNITIES AND PROBLEMS

The 'Separated' Eastern Churches. When they think of reunion, the Orthodox look not only to the west, but to their neighbours in the east, the Nestorians and Monophysites. In many ways Orthodoxy stands closer to the 'Separated' Eastern Churches than to any western confession.

The Nestorians are today very few in number – perhaps 50,000 – and almost entirely lacking in theologians, so that it is difficult to enter into official negotiations with them. But a partial union between Orthodox and Nestorian Christians has already occurred. In 1898 an Assyrian Nestorian, Mar Ivanios, bishop of Urumia in Persia, together with his flock, was received into communion by the Russian Church. The initiative came primarily from the Nestorian side, and there was no pressure – political or otherwise – on the part of the Russians. In 1905 this ex-Nestorian diocese was said to number 80 parishes and some 70,000 faithful; but between 1915 and 1918 the Assyrian Orthodox were slaughtered by the Turks in a series of unprovoked massacres, from which a few thousand alone escaped. Even though its life was so tragically cut short, the reconciliation of this ancient Christian community forms an encouraging precedent: why should not the Orthodox Church today come to a similar understanding with the rest of the Nestorian communion?[1]

The Monophysites, from the practical point of view, stand in a very different position from the Nestorians, for they are still comparatively numerous – more than ten million – and possess theologians capable of presenting and interpreting their traditional doctrinal position. A number of western and Ortho-

1. When visiting a Russian convent near New York in 1960, I had the pleasure of meeting an Assyrian Orthodox bishop, originally from the Urumia diocese, likewise called Mar Ivanios (successor to the original Mar Ivanios). A married priest, he had become a bishop after the death of his wife. When I asked the nuns how old he was, I was told: 'He says he's 102, but his children say he must be *much* older than that.'

dox scholars now believe that the Monophysite teaching about the person of Christ has in the past been seriously misunderstood, and that the difference between those who accept and those who reject the decrees of Chalcedon is largely if not entirely verbal. When visiting the Coptic Monophysite Church of Egypt in 1959, the Patriarch of Constantinople spoke with great optimism: 'In truth we are all one, we are all Orthodox Christians. . . . We have the same sacraments, the same history, the same traditions. The divergence is on the level of phraseology.'[1] Of all the 'ecumenical' contacts of Orthodoxy, the friendship with the Monophysites seems the most hopeful and the most likely to lead to concrete results in the near future. The question of reunion with the Monophysites was much in the air at the Pan-Orthodox Conferences of Rhodes, and it will certainly figure prominently on the agenda of future Pan-Orthodox Councils. During August 1964 an extremely friendly 'Unofficial Consultation' took place at Aarhus in Denmark between Orthodox and Monophysite theologians. 'All of us have learned from each other', the delegates from the two sides declared in the 'agreed statement' issued at the end of the meeting. 'Our inherited misunderstandings have begun to clear up. We recognize in each other the one orthodox faith of the Church. Fifteen centuries of alienation have not led us astray from the faith of our Fathers.' Further consultations met at Bristol (1967), Geneva (1970), and Addis Ababa (1971).

The Roman Catholic Church. Among western Christians, it is the Anglicans with whom Orthodoxy has at present the most cordial relations, but it is the Roman Catholics with whom Orthodoxy has by far the most in common. Certainly between Orthodoxy and Rome there are many difficulties. The usual psychological barriers exist. Among Orthodox – and doubtless among Roman Catholics as well – there are a multitude of inherited prejudices which cannot quickly be overcome; and Orthodox do not find it easy to forget the unhappy experiences

1. Speech before the Institute of Higher Coptic Studies, Cairo, 10 December 1959.

of the past – such things as the Crusades, the 'Union' of Brest-Litovsk, the schism at Antioch in the eighteenth century, or the persecution of the Orthodox Church in Poland by a Roman Catholic government between the two World Wars. Roman Catholics do not usually realize how deep a sense of misgiving and apprehension many devout Orthodox – educated as well as simple – still feel when they think of the Church of Rome. More serious than these psychological barriers are the differences in doctrine between the two sides – above all the *filioque* and the Papal claims. Once again many Roman Catholics fail to appreciate how serious the theological difficulties are, and how great an importance Orthodox attach to these two issues. Yet when all has been said about dogmatic divergences, about differences in spirituality and in general approach, it still remains true that there are many things which the two sides share: in their experience of the sacraments, for example, and in their devotion to the Mother of God and the saints – to mention but two instances out of many – Orthodox and Roman Catholics are for the most part very close indeed.

Since the two sides have so much in common, is there perhaps some hope of a reconciliation? At first sight one is tempted to despair, particularly when one considers the question of the Papal claims. Orthodox find themselves unable to accept the definitions of the Vatican Council of 1870 concerning the supreme ordinary jurisdiction and the infallibility of the Pope; but the Roman Catholic Church reckons the Vatican Council as ecumenical and so is bound to regard its definitions as irrevocable. Yet matters are not completely at an *impasse*. How far, we may ask, have Orthodox controversialists understood the Vatican decrees aright? Perhaps the meaning attached to the definitions by most western theologians in the past ninety years is not in fact the only possible interpretation. Furthermore it is now widely admitted by Roman Catholics that the Vatican decrees are incomplete and one-sided: they speak only of the Pope and his prerogatives, but say nothing about the bishops. But now that the second Vatican Council has issued a dogmatic statement on the powers of the episcopate, the Roman

Catholic doctrine of the Papal claims has begun to appear to the Orthodox world in a somewhat different light.

And if Rome in the past has perhaps said too little about the position of bishops in the Church, Orthodox in their turn need to take the idea of Primacy more seriously. Orthodox agree that the Pope is first among bishops: have they asked themselves carefully and searchingly what this really means? If the primatial see of Rome were restored once more to the Orthodox communion, what precisely would its status be? Orthodox are not willing to ascribe to the Pope a universal supremacy of 'ordinary' jurisdiction; but may it not be possible for them to ascribe to him, as President and Primate in the college of bishops, a universal *responsibility*, an all-embracing pastoral care extending over the whole Church? Recently the Orthodox Youth Movement in the Patriarchate of Antioch suggested two formulae. 'The Pope, among the bishops, is the elder brother, the father being absent.' 'The Pope is the mouth of the Church and of the episcopate.' Obviously these formulae fall far short of the Vatican statements on Papal jurisdiction and infallibility, but they can serve at any rate as a basis for constructive discussion. Hitherto Orthodox theologians, in the heat of controversy, have too often been content simply to attack the Roman doctrine of the Papacy (as they understand it), without attempting to go deeper and to state in *positive* language what the true nature of Papal primacy is from the Orthodox viewpoint. If Orthodox were to think and speak more in constructive and less in negative and polemical terms, then the divergence between the two sides might no longer appear so absolute.

After long postponement the Orthodox and Roman Catholic Churches set up a mixed international commission for theological discussions in 1980. Much is also being done informally through personal contacts. Invaluable work has been done by the Roman Catholic 'Monastery of Union' at Chevetogne in Belgium, originally founded at Amay-sur-Meuse in 1926. This is a 'double rite' monastery in which the monks worship according to both the Roman and the Byzantine rites. The Chevetogne periodical, *Irénikon*, contains an accurate and most sympathetic chronicle of current affairs in the Orthodox Church, as well as numerous scholarly articles, often contributed by Orthodox.

Certainly one must be sober and realistic: reunion between Orthodoxy and Rome, if it ever comes to pass, will prove a task of extraordinary difficulty. But signs of a rapprochement are increasing year by year. Pope Paul VI and Patriarch Athenagoras of Constantinople met three times (Jerusalem, 1964; Constantinople and Rome, 1967); on 7 December 1965 the anathemas of 1054 were simultaneously withdrawn by the Vatican Council in Rome and the Holy Synod in Constantinople; in 1979 Pope John Paul II visited Patriarch Dimitrios. Through such symbolic gestures mutual trust is being created.

The Old Catholics. It was only natural that the Old Catholics who separated from Rome after the Vatican Council of 1870 should have entered into negotiations with the Orthodox. The Old Catholics desired to recover the true faith of the ancient 'undivided Church' using as their basis the Fathers and the seven Ecumenical Councils: the Orthodox claimed that this faith was not merely a thing of the past, to be reconstructed by antiquarian research, but a present reality, which by God's grace they themselves had never ceased to possess. The two sides have met in a number of conferences, in particular at Bonn in 1874 and 1875, at Rotterdam in 1894, at Bonn again in 1931, and at Rheinfelden in 1957. A large measure of doctrinal agreement was reached at these gatherings, but they have not led to any practical results; although relations between Old Catholics and Orthodox continue to be very friendly, no union has been effected. In 1975 a full-scale theological dialogue was resumed between the two Churches, and an important series of doctrinal statements has been issued, showing once more how much the two sides share in common.

The Anglican Communion. As in the past, so today there are many Anglicans who regard the Reformation Settlement in sixteenth-century England as no more than an interim arrange-

ment, and who appeal, like the Old Catholics, to the General
Councils, the Fathers, and the Tradition of the 'undivided
Church'. One thinks of Bishop Pearson in the seventeenth
century, with his plea: 'Search how it was in the beginning;
go to the fountain head; look to antiquity.' Or of Bishop Ken,
the Non-Juror, who said: 'I die in the faith of the Catholic
Church, before the disunion of east and west.' This appeal to
antiquity has led many Anglicans to look with sympathy and
interest at the Orthodox Church, and equally it has led many
Orthodox to look with interest and sympathy at Anglicanism.
As a result of pioneer work by Anglicans such as William
Palmer (1811–79),[1] J. M. Neale (1818–66), and W. J. Birkbeck
(1859–1916), Anglo-Orthodox relations during the past hundred years have developed and flourished in a most animated
way.

There have been several official conferences between Anglican and Orthodox theologians. In 1930 an Orthodox delegation
representing ten autocephalous Churches (Constantinople,
Alexandria, Antioch, Jerusalem, Greece, Cyprus, Serbia, Bulgaria, Romania, Poland) was sent to England at the time of the
Lambeth Conference, and held discussions with a committee
of Anglicans; and in the following year a Joint Anglican–
Orthodox Commission met in London, with representatives
from the same Churches as in 1930 (except the Bulgarian).
Both in 1930 and in 1931 an honest attempt was made to face
points of doctrinal disagreement. Questions raised included the
relation of Scripture and Tradition, the Procession of the Holy
Spirit, the doctrine of the sacraments, and the Anglican idea of
authority in the Church. A similar Joint Conference was held
in 1935 at Bucharest, with Anglican and Romanian delegates.
This gathering concluded its deliberations by stating: 'A solid
basis has been prepared whereby full dogmatic agreement may
be affirmed between the Orthodox and the Anglican communions.'

In retrospect these words appear over-optimistic. During the
thirties the two sides seemed to be making great progress to-

1. Received into the Roman Catholic Church in 1855.

wards full doctrinal agreement, and many – particularly on the Anglican side – began to think that the time would soon come when the Anglican and Orthodox Churches could enter into communion. Since 1945, however, it has become apparent that such hopes were premature: full dogmatic agreement and communion in the sacraments are still a long way off. The one major theological conference between Anglicans and Orthodox held since the war, at Moscow in 1956, was much more cautious than its predecessors in the thirties. At first sight its findings seem comparatively meagre and disappointing, but actually they constitute an important advance, for they are marked by far greater realism. In the conferences between the wars there was a tendency to select specific points of disagreement and to consider them in isolation. In 1956 a genuine effort was made to carry the whole question to a deeper level: not just particular issues but the *whole faith* of the two Churches was discussed, so that specific points could be seen in context against a wider background.

An official theological dialogue, involving all the Orthodox Churches and the whole Anglican communion, was started in 1973. A crisis in the talks occurred in 1977–8, because of the ordination of women priests in several Anglican Churches. The conversations continue, but progress is slow.

In the past forty years a number of Orthodox Churches have produced statements concerning the validity of Anglican Orders. At a first glance these statements seem to contradict one another in a curious and extraordinary way:

(i) Six Churches have made declarations which seem to recognize Anglican ordinations as valid: Constantinople (1922), Jerusalem and Sinai (1923), Cyprus (1923), Alexandria (1930), Romania (1936).

(ii) The Russian Church in Exile, at the Karlovtzy Synod of 1935, declared that Anglican clergy who become Orthodox must be reordained. In 1948, at a large conference held in Moscow, the Moscow Patriarchate promulgated a decree to the same effect, which was also signed by official delegates (present at the conference) from the Churches of Alexandria, Antioch, Serbia, Bulgaria, Romania, Georgia, and Albania.

To interpret these statements aright, it would be necessary to discuss in detail the Orthodox view of the validity of sacraments, which is not the same as that usually held by western theologians, and also the Orthodox concept of 'ecclesiastical economy'; and these matters are so intricate and obscure that they cannot here be pursued at length. But certain points must be made. First, the Churches which declared in favour of Anglican Orders have not apparently carried this decision into effect. In recent years, when Anglican clergy have approached the Patriarchate of Constantinople with a view to entering the Orthodox Church, it has been made clear to them that they would be received as laymen, not as priests. Secondly, the favourable statements put out by group (i) are in most cases carefully qualified and must be regarded as provisional in character. The Ecumenical Patriarch, for example, when communicating the 1922 decision to the Archbishop of Canterbury, said in his covering note: 'It is plain that there is as yet no matter here of a decree by the whole Orthodox Church. For it is necessary that the rest of the Orthodox Churches should be found to be of the same opinion as the most holy Church of Constantinople.' In the third place, Orthodoxy is extremely reluctant to pass judgement upon the status of sacraments performed by non-Orthodox. Most Anglicans understood the statements made by group (i) to constitute a 'recognition' of Anglican Orders *at the present moment*. But in reality the Orthodox were not trying to answer the question 'Are Anglican Orders valid in themselves, here and now?' They had in mind the rather different question 'Supposing the Anglican communion were to reach full agreement in faith with the Orthodox, would it *then* be necessary to reordain Anglican clergy?'

This helps to explain why Constantinople in 1922 could declare favourably upon Anglican Orders, and yet in practice treat them as invalid: this favourable declaration could not come properly into effect so long as the Anglican Church was not fully Orthodox in the faith. When matters are seen in this light, the Moscow decree of 1948 no longer appears entirely inconsistent with the declarations of the pre-war period. Moscow based its decision on the present discrepancy between Anglican and Orthodox belief: 'The Orthodox Church cannot agree to recognize the rightness of Anglican teaching on the sacraments in general, and on the sacrament of Holy Order in particular; and so it cannot recognize Anglican ordinations as valid.' (Note that Orthodox theology declines to treat the question of valid orders in isolation, but considers at the same time the faith of the Church concerned.) But, so the Moscow decree continues, if in the future the Anglican Church were to become fully Orthodox in faith, then it might be possible to reconsider the question. While returning a negative answer at the present moment, Moscow extended a hope for the future.

Such is the situation so far as official pronouncements are concerned. Anglican clergy who join the Orthodox Church are reordained; but if Anglicanism and Orthodoxy were to reach full unity in the faith, perhaps such reordination *might* not be found necessary. It should be added, however, that a number of individual Orthodox theologians hold that under no circumstances would it be possible to recognize the validity of Anglican Orders.

Besides official negotiations between Anglican and Orthodox leaders, there have been many constructive encounters on the more personal and informal level. Two societies in England are specially devoted to the cause of Anglo-Orthodox reunion: the *Anglican and Eastern Churches Association* (whose parent organization, the *Eastern Church Association*, was started in 1863, mainly on the initiative of Neale) and the *Fellowship of Saint Alban and Saint Sergius* (founded in 1928), which arranges an annual conference and has a permanent centre in London, Saint Basil's House (52 Ladbroke Grove, W11). The Fellowship issues a valuable periodical entitled *Sobornost*, which appears twice a year; in the past the Anglican and Eastern Churches Association also published a magazine, *The Christian East*, now replaced by a Newsletter.

What is the chief obstacle to reunion between Anglicans and Orthodox? From the Orthodox point of view there is one great difficulty: the comprehensiveness of Anglicanism, the extreme ambiguity of Anglican doctrinal formularies, the wide variety of interpretations which these formularies permit. There are individual Anglicans who stand very close to Orthodoxy, as can be seen by anyone who reads two remarkable pamphlets: *Orthodoxy and the Conversion of England*, by Derwas Chitty; and *Anglicanism and Orthodoxy*, by H. A. Hodges. 'The ecumenical problem,' Professor Hodges concludes, is to be seen 'as the problem of bringing back the West . . . to a sound mind and a healthy life, and that means to Orthodoxy . . . The Orthodox Faith, that Faith to which the Orthodox Fathers bear witness and of which the Orthodox Church is the abiding custodian, is the Christian Faith in its true and essential form.'[1] Yet there are many other Anglicans who dissent sharply from this judgement, and who regard Orthodoxy as corrupt in doctrine and heretical. The Orthodox Church, however deep its longing for reunion, cannot enter into closer relations with the Anglican communion until Anglicans themselves are clearer about their own beliefs. The words of General Kireev are as true today as they were fifty years ago: 'We Orientals sincerely desire to come to an understanding with the great Anglican Church; but this happy result cannot be attained . . . unless the Anglican Church itself becomes homogeneous and the doctrines of its different constitutive parts become identical.'[2]

Other Protestants. Orthodox have many contacts with Protestants on the Continent, above all in Germany and (to a lesser degree) in Sweden. The Tübingen discussions of the sixteenth century have been reopened in the twentieth, with more positive results.

The World Council of Churches. In the Orthodox Church today there exist two different attitudes towards the World

1. *Anglicanism and Orthodoxy*, pp. 46–7.
2. *Le Général Alexandre Kiréeff et l'ancien-catholicisme*, edited by Olga Novikoff, Berne, 1911, p. 224.

Council of Churches and the 'Ecumenical Movement'. One party holds that Orthodox should take no part in the World Council (or at the most send observers to the meetings, but not full delegates); full participation in the Ecumenical Movement compromises the claim of the Orthodox Church to be the one true Church of Christ, and suggests that all 'churches' are alike. Typical of this viewpoint is the statement made in 1938 by the Synod of the Russian Church in Exile:

Orthodox Christians must regard the Holy Orthodox Catholic Church as the true Church of Christ, one and unique. For this reason, the Russian Orthodox Church in Exile has forbidden its children to take part in the Ecumenical Movement, which rests on the principle of the equality of all religions and Christian confessions.

But – so the second party would object – this is completely to misunderstand the nature of the World Council of Churches. Orthodox, by participating, do not thereby imply that they regard all Christian confessions as equal, nor do they compromise the Orthodox claim to be the true Church. As the *Toronto Declaration* of 1950 (adopted by the Central Committee of the World Council) carefully pointed out: 'Membership in the World Council does not imply the acceptance of a specific doctrine concerning the nature of Church unity. . . . Membership does not imply that each Church must regard the other member Churches as Churches in the true and full sense of the word.' In view of this explicit statement (so the second party argues), Orthodox can take part in the Ecumenical Movement without endangering their Orthodoxy. And if Orthodox *can* take part, then they *must* do so: for since they believe the Orthodox faith to be true, it is their duty to bear witness to that faith as widely as possible.

The existence of these two conflicting viewpoints accounts for the somewhat confused and inconsistent policy which the Orthodox Church has followed in the past. Some Churches have regularly sent delegations to the major conferences of the Ecumenical Movement, others have done so spasmodically or scarcely at all. Here is a brief analysis of Orthodox representation during 1927–68 :

Lausanne, 1927 (Faith and Order): Constantinople, Alexandria, Jerusalem, Greece, Cyprus, Serbia, Bulgaria, Romania, Poland.

Edinburgh, 1937 (Faith and Order): Constantinople, Alexandria, Antioch, Jerusalem, Greece, Cyprus, Bulgaria, Poland, Albania.

Amsterdam, 1948 (World Council of Churches): Constantinople, Greece, Romanian Church in America.

Lund, 1952 (Faith and Order): Constantinople, Antioch, Cyprus, North American Jurisdiction of Russians.

Evanston, 1954 (World Council of Churches): Constantinople, Antioch, Greece, Cyprus, North American Jurisdiction of Russians, Romanian Church in America.

New Delhi, 1961 (World Council of Churches): Constantinople, Alexandria, Antioch, Jerusalem, Greece, Cyprus, Russia, Bulgaria, Romania, Poland, North American Jurisdiction of Russians, Romanian Church in America

Uppsala, 1968 (World Council of Churches): Constantinople, Alexandria, Antioch, Jerusalem, Cyprus, Russia, Bulgaria, Romania, Serbia, Georgia, Poland, North American Jurisdiction of Russians, Romanian Church in America.

As can be seen from this summary, the Patriarchate of Constantinople has always been represented at the conferences. From the start it has firmly supported a policy of full participation in the Ecumenical Movement. In January 1920 the Patriarchate issued a famous letter addressed 'To all the Churches of Christ, wheresoever they be', urging closer cooperation between separated Christian bodies, and suggesting an alliance of Churches, parallel to the newly founded League of Nations; many of the ideas in this letter anticipate later developments in the Ecumenical Movement. But while Constantinople has adhered unwaveringly to the principles of 1920, other Churches have been more reserved. The Church of Greece, for example, at one point declared that it would only send laymen as delegates to the World Council, though this decision was revoked in 1961. Some Orthodox Churches have gone even further than this: at the Moscow Conference in 1948, a resolution was passed condemning all participation in the World Council. This resolution stated bluntly: 'The aims of the Ecumenical Movement . . . in its present state correspond neither to the ideals of Christianity nor to the task of the Church of Christ, as understood by the Orthodox Church.' This explains why at Amsterdam, Lund, and Evanston the Orthodox Churches behind the Iron Curtain were not represented at all. In 1961, however, the Moscow Patriarchate applied for membership of the World Council and was accepted; and this has opened the way for other Orthodox Churches in the communist world to become members as well. Henceforward, so far as one can judge, Orthodox will play a far fuller and more effective part in the Ecumenical Movement than they have done hitherto. But it must not be forgotten that there are still many Orthodox – including a number of eminent bishops and theologians – who are anxious to see their Church withdraw from the Movement.

Orthodox participation is a factor of cardinal importance for the Ecumenical Movement: it is mainly the presence of Orthodox which prevents the World Council of Churches from appearing to be simply a Pan-Protestant alliance and nothing more. But the Ecumenical Movement in turn is important for Orthodoxy: it has helped to force the various Orthodox Churches out of their comparative isolation, making them meet one another and enter into a living contact with non-Orthodox Christians.

LEARNING FROM ONE ANOTHER

Khomiakov, seeking to describe the Orthodox attitude to other Christians, in one of his letters makes use of a parable. A master departed, leaving his teaching to his three disciples. The eldest faithfully repeated what his master had taught him, changing nothing. Of the two younger, one added to the teaching, the other took away from it. At his return the master, without being angry with anyone, said to the younger: 'Thank your elder brother; without him you would not have preserved the truth which I handed over to you.' Then he said to the elder: 'Thank your younger brothers; without them you would not have understood the truth which I entrusted to you.'

Orthodox in all humility see themselves as in the position of the elder brother. They believe that by God's grace they have been enabled to preserve the true faith unimpaired, 'neither adding any thing, nor taking any thing away'. They claim a living continuity with the ancient Church, with the Tradition of the Apostles and the Fathers, and they believe that in a divided and bewildered Christendom it is their duty to bear witness to this primitive and unchanging Tradition. Today in the west there are many, both on the Catholic and on the Protestant side, who are trying to shake themselves free of the 'crystallizations and fossilizations of the sixteenth century', and who desire to 'get behind the Reformation and the Middle Ages'. It is precisely here that the Orthodox can help. Orthodoxy stands outside the circle of ideas in which western Christians have moved for the past eight centuries; it has undergone no Scholastic revolution, no Reformation and Counter-Reformation, but lives still in that older Tradition of the Fathers which so many in the west now desire to recover. This, then, is the ecumenical role of Orthodoxy: to question the accepted formulae of the Latin west, of the Middle Ages and the Reformation.

And yet, if Orthodox are to fulfil this role properly, they must understand their own Tradition better than they have done in the past; and it is the west in its turn which can help them to do this. Orthodox must thank their younger brothers, for through contact with Christians of the west – Roman Catholic, Anglican, Lutheran, Calvinist, Quaker – they are being enabled to acquire a new vision of Orthodoxy.

The two sides are only just beginning to discover one another, and each has much that it can learn. Just as in the past the separation of east and west has proved a great tragedy for both parties and a cause of grievous mutual impoverishment, so today the renewal of contact between east and west is already proving for both a source of mutual enrichment. The west, with its critical standards, with its Biblical and Patristic scholarship, can enable Orthodox to understand the historical background of Scripture in new ways and to read the Fathers with increased accuracy and discrimination. The Orthodox in turn can bring western Christians to a renewed awareness of the inner meaning of Tradition, assisting them to look on the Fathers as a living reality. (The Romanian edition of the *Philokalia* shows how profitably western critical standards and traditional Orthodox spirituality can be combined.) As Orthodox strive to recover frequent communion, the example of western Christians acts as an encouragement to them; many western Christians in turn have found their own prayer and worship incomparably deepened by an acquaintance with such things as the art of the Orthodox icon, the Jesus Prayer, and the Byzantine Liturgy. When the Orthodox Church behind the Iron Curtain is able to function more freely, perhaps western experience and experiments will help it as it tackles the problems of Christian witness within a secularized and industrial society. Meanwhile the persecuted Orthodox Church serves as a reminder to the west of the importance of martyrdom, and constitutes a living testimony to the value of suffering in the Christian life.

Further Reading

BYZANTIUM

General Works

A. Schmemann, *The Historical Road of Eastern Orthodoxy*, New York, 1963 (deals also with more recent Orthodox history).

J. M. Hussey, *The Byzantine World*, London, 1957.

J. M. Hussey (ed.), *The Cambridge Medieval History*, vol. IV, parts 1 and 2, *The Byzantine Empire*, Cambridge, 1966–7.

G. Ostrogorsky, *History of the Byzantine State*, Oxford, 1968.

D. Obolensky, *The Byzantine Commonwealth: Eastern Europe, 500–1453*, London, 1971.

G. Every, *The Byzantine Patriarchate*, 2nd ed., London, 1962.

J. Meyendorff, *Byzantine Theology: Historical Trends and Doctrinal Themes*, New York, 1974 (also gives a general survey of Orthodox doctrine).

J. Pelikan, *The Christian Tradition*, vol. II, *The Spirit of Eastern Christendom* (*600–1700*), Chicago/London, 1974.

The Schism between East and West

Y. M.-J. Congar, *After Nine Hundred Years*, New York, 1959.

S. Runciman, *The Eastern Schism*, Oxford, 1955.

R. W. Southern, *Western Society and the Church in the Middle Ages*, Pelican History of the Church, vol. II, 1970 (see pp. 53–90).

G. Every, *Misunderstandings between East and West*, London, 1965.

F. Dvornik, *The Photian Schism: History and Legend*, Cambridge, 1948.

J. Gill, *The Council of Florence*, Cambridge, 1959.

P. Sherrard, *The Greek East and the Latin West*, London, 1959. *Church, Papacy, and Schism*, London, 1978.

Hesychasm

Saint Symeon the New Theologian, *The Discourses*, trans. C. J. deCatanzaro, New York, 1980.

Archbishop Basil Krivocheine, *Dans la lumière du Christ*, Chevetogne, 1980 (on St Symeon).

J. Meyendorff, *A Study of Gregory Palamas*, London, 1964. *St Gregory Palamas and Orthodox Spirituality*, New York, 1974.

THE TURKISH PERIOD

The Acts and Decrees of the Synod of Jerusalem, trans. J. N. W. B. Robertson, London, 1899 (contains the *Confessions* of Cyril Lukaris and Dositheus).

S. Runciman, *The Great Church in Captivity: A Study of the Patriarchate of Constantinople from the Eve of the Turkish Conquest to the Greek War of Independence*, Cambridge, 1968.

G. Williams, *The Orthodox Church of the East in the Eighteenth Century, being the Correspondence between the Eastern Patriarchs and the Nonjuring Bishops*, London, 1868.

T. Ware, *Eustratios Argenti: A Study of the Greek Church under Turkish Rule*, Oxford, 1964.

RUSSIA

N. Zernov, *The Russians and their Church*, London, 1945.
Moscow the Third Rome, London, 1937.

W. H. Frere, *Some Links in the Chain of Russian Church History*, London, 1918.

G. P. Fedotov, *A Treasury of Russian Spirituality*, London, 1950.
The Russian Religious Mind, 2 vols, Cambridge, Mass., 1946–66.

P. Kovalevsky, *St Sergius and Russian Spirituality*, New York, 1976.

N. Arseniev, *Russian Piety*, London, 1964.

S. Bolshakoff, *Russian Mystics*, Kalamazoo/London, 1977.

P. Pascal, *Avvakum et les débuts du Raskol*, Paris, 1938.

N. Gorodetzky, *The Humiliated Christ in Modern Russian Thought*, London, 1938.
Saint Tikhon Zadonsky, London, 1951.

I. de Beausobre, *Flame in the Snow*, London, 1945 (on Saint Seraphim).

V. Zander, *St Seraphim of Sarov*, London, 1975.

The Way of a Pilgrim, trans. R. M. French, London, 1954.

Macarius of Optino, *Russian Letters of Direction 1834–1860*, ed. I. de Beausobre, London, 1944.

J. B. Dunlop, *Staretz Amvrosy*, Belmont, Mass., 1972.

P. D. Garrett, *St Innocent Apostle to America*, New York, 1979.

Spiritual Counsels of Father John of Kronstadt, ed. W. J. Grisbrooke, London, 1967.

FURTHER READING

Bishop Alexander (Semenoff-Tian-Chansky), *Father John Kronstadt: A Life*, London (?1978).

A. Schmemann, *Ultimate Questions: An Anthology of Modern Russian Religious Thought*, New York, 1965.

N. Zernov, *The Russian Religious Renaissance of the Twentieth Century*, London, 1963.

J. Pain and N. Zernov, *A Bulgakov Anthology*, London, 1976.

A. Elchaninov, *The Diary of a Russian Priest*, London, 1967.

S. Hackel, *Pearl of Great Price: The Life of Mother Maria Skobtsova*, London, 1981.

ORTHODOXY TODAY

Orthodoxy 1964: A Pan-Orthodox Symposium, edited by the Zoe Brotherhood, Athens, 1964.

P. Hammond, *The Waters of Marah*, London, 1956 (on the Greek Church).

M. Rinvolucri, *Anatomy of a Church. Greek Orthodoxy Today*, London, 1966.

W. Kolarz, *Religion in the Soviet Union*, London, 1961.

N. Struve, *Christians in Contemporary Russia*, London, 1967.

M. Bourdeaux, *Patriarch and Prophets. Persecution of the Russian Orthodox Church Today*, London, 1969.

C. Lane, *Christian Religion in the Soviet Union. A Sociological Study*, London, 1978.

S. Alexander, *Church and State in Yugoslavia since 1945*, Cambridge, 1979.

Orthodox Missionary Work

E. Smirnoff, *Russian Orthodox Missions*, London, 1903.

S. Bolshakoff, *The Foreign Missions of the Russian Orthodox Church*, London, 1943.

ORTHODOX THEOLOGY

General Studies

V. Lossky, *The Mystical Theology of the Eastern Church*, London, 1957 (extremely important).
   The Vision of God, London, 1963.
   In the Image and Likeness of God, New York, 1974.
   Orthodox Theology: An Introduction, New York, 1978.

G. Florovsky, *The Collected Works*, Belmont, Mass., 1972 onwards (in progress; vol. V appeared in 1979; important).

FURTHER READING

P. Evdokimov, *L'Orthodoxie*, Paris, 1959 (excellent).
A. Khomiakov, 'The Church is One', in W. J. Birbeck, *Russia and the English Church* (short but most valuable).
S. Bulgakov, *The Orthodox Church*, London, 1935.
F. Gavin, *Some Aspects of Contemporary Greek Orthodox Thought*, Milwaukee, 1923 (tends to see Orthodox theology through Latin spectacles).
P. N. Trembelas, *Dogmatique de l'Église Orthodoxe Catholique*, 3 vols, Chevetogne, 1966–8.
D. Staniloae, *Theology and the Church*, New York, 1980.
Archbishop Paul of Finland, *The Faith We Hold*, New York, 1980.
Kallistos (Timothy) Ware, *The Orthodox Way*, London, 1979.

Biblical Theology

G. Barrois, *The Face of Christ in the Old Testament*, New York, 1974.
Scripture Readings in Orthodox Worship, New York, 1977.
V. Kesich, *The Gospel Image of Christ: The Church and Modern Criticism*, New York, 1972.

Human Nature, the Church, the Holy Virgin

O. Clément, *Questions sur l'homme*, Paris, 1972.
P. Sherrard, *Christianity and Eros*, London, 1976.
E. L. Mascall (ed.), *The Church of God: An Anglo-Russian Symposium*, London, 1934.
The Mother of God: A Symposium, London, 1949.

Sacramental Theology

A. Schmemann, *Introduction to Liturgical Theology*, London, 1966.
For the Life of the World: Sacraments and Orthodoxy, New York, 1973.
Of Water and the Spirit, New York, 1974.
A Monk of the Eastern Church, *Orthodox Spirituality*, 2nd ed., London, 1978.
Nicholas Cabasilas, *The Life in Christ*, trans. C. J. deCatanzaro, New York, 1974.
P. Evdokimov, *Sacrement de l'amour*, Paris, 1962 (on marriage).
J. Meyendorff, *Marriage: An Orthodox Perspective*, New York, 1970.

ORTHODOX WORSHIP

There are many translations of the Liturgy. Among the most convenient are an edition issued by the Fellowship of St Alban and St Sergius, *The Orthodox Liturgy*, London, 1939; and an edition with Greek and English on opposite pages published by the Faith Press, *The Divine Liturgy of Saint John Chrysostom*, London (no date).

A great deal of material is to be found in *Service Book of the Holy Orthodox-Catholic Apostolic Church*, ed. I. F. Hapgood, 2nd ed., New York, 1922. Full texts for Christmas, Epiphany, and seven of the other great feasts are contained in *The Festal Menaion*, trans. Mother Mary and Archimandrite Kallistos (T. Ware), London, 1969. For Lenten services, see *The Lenten Triodion*, London, 1978, by the same translators; also A. Schmemann, *Great Lent*, New York, 1969. Consult also *La prière des Églises de rite byzantin*, ed. E. Mercenier, F. Paris, and G. Bainbridge, 3 vols, Chevetogne, 1947–53; new ed. of vols I and III, Chevetogne, 1972–5.

For the classic Byzantine commentary on the Liturgy, see:

Nicholas Cabasilas, *A Commentary on the Divine Liturgy*, trans. J. M. Hussey and P. A. NcNulty, London, 1960.

For the daily prayers used by an Orthodox Christian, see:

A Manual of Eastern Orthodox Prayers, London, 1945 (issued by the Fellowship of St Alban and St Sergius).
Prayer Book, Jordanville, N.Y., 1960.

On the Orthodox doctrine of prayer, see:

Igumen Chariton, *The Art of Prayer: An Orthodox Anthology*, trans. E. Kadloubovsky and E. M. Palmer, London, 1966. A Monk of the Eastern Church, *The Prayer of Jesus*, New York, 1967. *The Philokalia*, trans. G. E. H. Palmer, P. Sherrard, K. Ware, London, 1979 onwards (to be completed in 5 vols). See also the earlier translation of parts of *The Philokalia* (Russian text) by E. Kadloubovsky and G. E. H. Palmer: *Writings from the Philokalia on Prayer of the Heart*, London, 1951; *Early Fathers from the Philokalia*, London, 1954. For a modern writer in the 'Philokalic' tradition, see T. Colliander, *The Way of the Ascetics*, London, 1960.

FURTHER READING

ORTHODOX MONASTICISM

D. J. Chitty, *The Desert a City*, Oxford, 1966.

N. F. Robinson, *Monasticism in the Orthodox Churches*, London, 1916.

Sister Benedicta Ward (trans.), *The Sayings of the Desert Fathers. The Alphabetical Collection*, London, 1975.

Saint John Climacus, *The Ladder of Divine Ascent*, intr. K. Ware, New York, 1982.

Mount Athos

R. M. Dawkins, *The Monks of Athos*, London, 1936.

C. Cavarnos, *Anchored in God*, Athens, 1959.

P. Sherrard, *Athos The Holy Mountain*, London, 1982.

E. Amand de Mendieta, *Mount Athos: The Garden of the Panaghia*, Berlin, 1972.

ICONS

L. Ouspensky and V. Lossky, *The Meaning of Icons*, Olten, 1952.

L. Ouspensky, *Theology of the Icon*, New York, 1978.

G. Mathew, *Byzantine Aesthetics*, London, 1963.

C. Mango, *The Art of the Byzantine Empire*, New Jersey, 1972.

S. Runciman, *Byzantine Style and Civilization*, London, 1975.

REUNION

N. Afanassieff and others, *The Primacy of Peter*, London, 1963.

J. Meyendorff, *Orthodoxy and Catholicity*, New York, 1966.

Archbishop Methodios Fouyas, *Orthodoxy, Roman Catholicism, and Anglicanism*, London, 1972.

W. Palmer, *Notes of a Visit to the Russian Church in the Years 1840, 1841*, ed. Cardinal Newman, London, 1882.

W. J. Birkbeck, *Russia and the English Church*, London, 1895.

J. A. Douglas, *The Relations of the Anglican Churches with the Eastern-Orthodox*, London, 1921.

H. A. Hodges, *Anglicanism and Orthodoxy*, London, 1955.

H. M. Waddams (ed.), *Anglo-Russian Theological Conference, Moscow, July 1956*, London, 1958.

V. T. Istavridis, *Orthodoxy and Anglicanism*, London, 1966.

K. Ware and C. Davey (ed.), *Anglican-Orthodox Dialogue: The Moscow Statement*, London, 1977.

R. Rouse and S. C. Neill, *A History of the Ecumenical Movement*, 2nd ed., London, 1967.

Index

INDEX